Ökofeminismus und Theologie
Ecofeminism and Theology
Écoféminisme et Théologie

Elizabeth Green and Mary Grey (eds.)

Kok Pharos Publishing House - Kampen
Matthias-Grünewald-Verlag - Mainz

Jahrbuch der Europäischen Gesellschaft
für die theologische Forschung von Frauen

Yearbook of the European Society of Women
in Theological Research

Annuaire de l'Association Européenne des
femmes pour la recherche théologique

Volume 2

CIP-GEGEVENS KONINKLIJKE BIBLIOTHEEK, DEN HAAG

Cover Design By Margret Omlin-Küchler/adapted by Rob Lucas
ISBN 90 390 0204 5 (Kok Pharos)
ISBN 3-7867-1784-2 (Matthias-Grünewald-Verl.)

This Volume of the Jahrbuch is dedicated to the memory of Fokkelien van Dijk-Hemmes, a founder member of ESWTR, respected scholar, dear friend and esteemed colleague.

INHALT– CONTENTS – TABLE DES MATIÈRES

Editorial

The process of editing Volume II of this Yearbook has been a considerable learning experience for its two Editors as to the awareness of Ecofeminist Theology as a discipline throughout Europe. It is true that the ecological degradation is not so far advanced in Europe, as, for example, the increasing desertification in the southern hemisphere: – yet Europe itself is no stranger to ecological disaster through, for example, the Chernobyl and Seveso disasters, the oil tanker spillages in the North Sea, acid rain in North Europe, the deaths from leukemia linked with nuclear establishments and illegal nuclear waste deposits in several European countries. Since the collapse of the communist regimes in Eastern Europe in 1989 the full extent of ecological degradation and consequent suffering – human and non-human – has been slowly breaking into public awareness. But the theological reflection among Feminist Theologians in Europe as a whole has not kept pace with the extent of environmental disaster, and, for many reasons, seems confined to certain areas; a fact which is borne out by the provenance of the theme articles.

This does not mean, however, that European Feminist Theology is restricted in scope. For example, Anne Primavesi, in her article "A Tide in the Affairs of Women? Women and the Environment of Knowledge" makes a special plea for the construction of an ecological theology which fully respects and listens to the voices from the southern hemisphere in any response to the ecological crisis. A concrete example of this listening is reflected in Caroline Mackenzie's article "Cosmic Awareness and Sacred Space: the Integration of Feminine Symbolism in Indian Christian Art". The next two articles enter into dialogue with other thinkers in the area: Ina Praetorius in her article "Feministische Ethik und die Oekologiefrage" makes a critique of Hans Kung's Global Ethical Project on the grounds that this ignores the specificity of womens' experience, while Elizabeth Green offers a critique and appraisal of current ecofeminist theologies.

The key-note article in Forum, by the Italian scientist Elisabetta Donini, opens the debate on ecofeminist spirituality as a response to the ecological crisis. Celia Deane – Drummond responds from the perspective of Christian theology, Lene Sjørup from the perspective of women and mysticism and Aruna Gnanadason reacts as an Indian theologian from her experience of the ecological crisis. In "From the Countries" Dagny Kaul describes the situation within the nordic countries of environmental studies, ecofeminist theory and ecofeminism and theology as an academic discipline.

In our section "Womens' Traditions in Europe" there is an account of the first woman Rabbi in Europe, Regina Jonas, by Katharina Von Kellenbach, while Harriet Blankers comments on a text of creation by the Spanish mystic, Teresa of Avila. "The Book Market" section concentrates on material germane to 'Ecofeminism and Theology': thus it features reviews of important ecofeminist theological and philosophical books and includes a Bibliography of essential writings on ecofeminism and theology. Reviews of two Doctoral Theses of members of the Society have been included, as the content contributed to the theme of this Volume. We also reprint in full a review by Professor Kari Børresen, apologising that sections were omitted in the Year Book Volume 1.

"Only connect" is a slogan which has inspired ecofeminism: so, in conclusion, we would like to thank all members of the Society who have cooperated in bringing this Volume together, as well as Tony Norris of the Computing Department of La Sainte Union College, Southampton who typeset the text, and the many colleagues who assisted with translation; we hope that this issue of the Year Book could itself be a catalyst in stimulating other ecofeminist ecological connections, especially in those parts of the world which have not yet been heard into speech.

Elizabeth Green, Gravina, Italy and Mary Grey, Southampton, England, April 1994.

Anne Primavesi

A Tide in the Affairs of Women?

Introduction

Recently a passage from Shakespeare's *Julius Caesar* surfaced in my mind again after many years:

> *There is a tide in the affairs of men*
> *Which, taken at the flood, leads on to fortune;*
> *Omitted, all the voyage of their life*
> *Is bound in shallows and in miseries.*
> *On such a full sea are we now afloat;*
> *And we must take the current when it serves,*
> *Or lose our ventures*[1].

It came to mind during my reading of documents from the United Nations Conference on Environment and Development (UNCED). I found there a stated commitment to the inclusion of women in environmental decision-making, planning, technical and scientific advisory services and management[2]. There is also a commitment to the promotion of women's literacy, education, training, nutrition and health, as well as to the dissemination of gender-relevant knowledge to both women and men.

This tide in the affairs of women, if taken at the flood, is intended to lead to their inclusion in the decision-making processes necessary to preserve the human habitat on this planet. Omitted, not only women's lives will stay bound in shallows and in miseries. Their absence from environmental planning is seen by many to be, as indeed it is, a matter of justice. Worldwide, but especially in the South, women are in double jeopardy: they and their children are the most vulnerable physically to the effects of environmental degradation while they are the most powerless politically to do anything about them. Current political, social and economic structures deprive women of the power to implement the changes necessary for them to have a life worth living. The most obvious examples of this are the relative amounts spent by governments on arms (killpower) compared with those allocated to health, education and environmental research programmes (lifepower)[3].

---

1 *Julius Caesar*, Act IV, Scene iii.

2 See, for example, Chapter 24 of Agenda 21.

3 See the statistics in, for example, **World Military and Social Expenditures**, 1991, ed. Ruth Sivard, *World Priorities*, Washington DC, 1991, which has a special section on the enviroment. Compare the amounts spent on arms and education, taking note of the ratios of male/female literacy in those countries of Africa devastated by war and famine.

The hope and thirst for justice for women enshrined in the UNCED documents is shared by all those who contributed to them. What have women in particular learned from their participation in the UNCED process? It was described by one participant at the preparatory World Women's Congress for a Healthy Planet as 'seesawing constantly between small, homey examples of women's environmental activism and the awesomely daunting spectre of the global power wielded by men'[4]. The women at the Congress saw this tension between the personal and the political as a blueprint for incorporating the women's dimension into local, national and international decision-making from now on into the next century.

What is this dimension and what difference do they intend it to make? In this article I want to reflect on some of the developments in women's scientific, philosophical and theological education which may effect a difference not only in local, national and international environmental decision-making, but in academic and ecclesiastical institutions as well. The following developments in particular will be traced: the concepts of constructivism in science education and of contextualism in theology, together with ecological and feminist philosophies based on a relational, non-violent world-view. Their interweaving as the article progresses will be a conscious attempt to 'take the current when it serves'.

A Constructivist Model

The constructivist model of science education rests on the premise that the ways in which we build up our knowledge of our experiential world can be explored, and that an awareness of these ways can help us to explore it differently, and, perhaps, better[5].

Since opportunities for learning and discovery are culture-bound and time specific, knowledge-building can then be seen as a fabric woven by choice out of necessity. The choice usually applies to the present and the future; necessity, interior as well as exterior, often derives from the past, whether it be our personal, social, political or religious inheritance[6].

There is a sense, however, in which environmental decision-making today is driven by the necessity to arbitrate between the claims of present necessities and those derived from the future. The tension between the two claims is evident in the perceived need for development through use of finite resources (especially in societies where the quality of life is so bad as to make it impossible for people to reach their full potential otherwise) and the need to conserve those resources

[4] See *Official Report of World Women's Congress for a Healthy Planet*, WEDO, New York, 1991.

[5] I rely here on the many insights gained from the fruitful discussion with Carol Boulter, a friend who lectures in science education in Reading University. Sources for our discussion included: **Personal Experience and the Construction of Knowledge in Science**, Pope, M. and Gilbert J., in *Science Education* 62, pp. 193-203, 1983. Constructivist approaches in Educational Research, A. Jon Magoon, *Review of Educational Research* Fall 1977, Vol47, No 4, pp.651-693. *The Invented Reality*, ed. Watzlawick P.,W&W Norton, NY, 1984.

[6] See *Knowledge and the Future of Man*, ed. Ong. W., Holt, Rinehart and Winston, NY, 1968, p.22f.

for a sustainable future. However the problems present themselves, whether as demographic trends, illiteracy, bonded labour, militarism or climate change, we have to make decisions now which will determine necessities of life on the planet for coming generations. A constructivist approach helps us to be aware of the scope and limitations of our decisions: to distinguish between 'information' and knowledge; to acknowledge the personal worldview/environment within which we utilise and/or interpret facts and figures presented to us. By understanding how we shape the future we can take responsibility for doing so.

This differs from traditional approaches to knowledge-building, in which the activity of 'knowing' centres on the knowing subject conceived of as a 'pure' entity in the sense that it is essentially unimpeded by biological or environmental conditions, that is, by personal context. In company with feminist theory, constructivism quite deliberately breaks that conventional framework and, by taking biological/psychological factors into consideration, commits what professional philosophers and theologians, more or less disparagingly, dismiss as 'psychologism'. A further expansion of context is brought about through an ecological perspective which takes environmental factors into consideration as well.

The traditional disregard of physiological/contextual factors in knowledge-building ignores the fact, central to a constructivist model, that significant learning is likely to occur only if the 'facts' to be learned are construed by the learner as having personal relevance: if they are in some way bound to personal experience and evaluated against personal criteria. Personal knowledge is built up and expanded through transactions between a person and the environment.

A corollary to this, bearing directly on decision-making, is the fact that any programme of knowledge-building is not, cannot and should not be sealed off from everyday life, from its institutional or environmental setting or from its future effects. How a programme is conceived or carried on, who we do it for, what we think about its possible effects and what we choose to see as important in it can never be insulated from the environment of that programme. The boundaries of that environment become even more fluid once the results of the programme are communicated. Whether through environmental laws, papal encyclicals, mathematical symbols, metaphors or clichés, they call forth other issues, make connections with and have impacts on other environments unknown to those who conceived the original programme.

Therefore responsible programmes of knowledge-building include such questions as: how far into the future must the enquirer consider consequences of decisions made on the basis of his or her conclusions? A scientific example of this in our time is the decision to develop a mathematical equation into atomic power, leaving us and future generations with the problem of disposing of nuclear waste in its many manifestations after Hiroshima, Chernobyl, and the continuing production of weapons-grade plutonium. A religious example would be teachings about the human body which have reduced sexual power to its reproductive function. Through this write-off of sexuality our lives continue to be contaminated by negative sexual energy. And what influence does this have on the kind of decisions being taken now about genetic engineering and reproductive technologies?

The empowering character of the constructivist model lies in its forcing us to see and to take responsibility for the power we have to make decisions whose full effects cannot be either computed or controlled by us. It also presupposes the possibility of changing present social, religious and ideological constructs and therefore of creating different kinds of communities, flawed though they may be: of arriving at different perceptions of truth, incomplete though they may be.

A Contextual Model

On the broader sea, I find the difference between constructivist and traditional approaches exemplified in the tensions between contextual theologians in the South and ecclesiastical centres of power in the North[7]. Theological programmes in the North have, until recently, been conceived and carried through without acknowledgement either of the determining factor of their own context or of the differences between it and the context in which they are received. Within both contexts, a further exclusion, that of women, meant that the theological programmes, their methodologies and conclusions were dismissive of, if not hostile to women's experience. Their effects continue to be felt by women within the unjust/sexist infrastructures of the theological academy and of the churches, North and South.

In the North, these tensions appeared overtly in the rejection by some Northern theologians of Professor Hyun-Kyung Chung's presentation at the World Council of Churches Assembly in Canberra, 1991. They surface continually in debates about the ordination of women. From the Southern context, Leonardo Boff has rejected the Vatican's new 'universal' Catechism as a 'Big Mac' hamburger, the same the world over, with the same sins decried and the same virtues advocated at the North Pole, in the Amazon tropics, in Rome, in Bangkok and in Tahiti[8]. His metaphor is chosen deliberately. In common with many of the non-governmental organizations (NGOs) involved in the UNCED process, he links Northern economic hegemony, typified by Macdonald's, with the destruction of indigenous cultures. A Southern theologian, he links this hegemony to that of

[7] In the UNCED documents, the term 'North' designates 'those rich industrialised nations who, through disregard for and even manipulation of environmental concerns, enhance their financial, technological, industrial, commercial and political domination over the poorer developing countries of the world'. (See Statement of the participants in the hearing on **Environment North/South**, *10th Assembly of the Conference of European Churches*, 1-11 September, 1992). The term is also applied here to ecclesiastical centres in Europe and North America.

[8] Reported in, for example, *The Catholic Herald*, 3 September 1993.

Northern ecclesiastical power systems.

These are but a few of the tensions between constructivist and traditional theological knowledge-building programmes exemplified in Northern suspicion of contextual theologies and Southern reactions to Northern universalist claims. The Swedish theologian Per Frostin, after working in Africa, analysed this tension as differences in methodology. Northern theologies deal with ideas: of God, of salvation, of sin; contextual theologies deal with the social, economic and political impact of ideas on people: on their lives, on their bodies, on their possibilities for survival and growth, on their habitat[9]. This is another way of describing the tension between the 'pure' knowledge of traditional philosophy and theology and what is dismissed as 'psychologism'.

A Feminist Model

Tensions also surface whenever women claim primacy for their experience. This latter claim resonates with the constructivist assumption that the knower, through her inherent activity and organisation, actively participates in the construction of known reality. The radical element in constructivism puts in question any cognitive theory which sees the relationship between knowledge and reality in terms of correspondence. Such correspondence is assumed, however, in scientific, philosophical or theological discourse which uses terms such as 'seen', 'discovered,' or 'revealed' for the outcome of cognitive process. Knowledge then becomes a reflection or a picture of a world that is already there, that is, which exists before any consciousness sees it or experiences it in any other way than the one which has been presented by men as definitive.

So the philosopher of science Helen Longino points out that just as the task of Plato's philosophers was to discover the fixed relations among forms and the task of Galileo's scientists was to discover the laws of geometry written in the language of the grand book of nature, so the scientist's task in this tradition remains the discovery of fixed relations, however conceived[10]. Analogous to this, in my view, has been the assumption that the task of Christian theologians is to discover the fixed relations between the world, humankind and God written in the languages and canonical texts of the Christian Bible.

This assumption ignores other ways in which those relations have been conceived in the rest of the world, and especially in the South, in, for example, mythic narratives or ritual. This dismissal of indigenous religious perspectives is now commonly treated as an environmental issue. It needs to be taken seriously as an ecotheological one, since the wisdom of native peoples, bound inextricably to their religious traditions, has much to teach us about the unwisdom of our own

[9] See Per Frostin's analysis in *Liberation Theology in Tanzania and South Africa,* Lund University Press, Lund 1988, pp. 6-26.

[10] See her article, **Can there be a Feminist Science?** in *Women, Knowledge and Reality,* eds. Garry A. and Pearsall M., Unwin, Winchester Mass, 1989, pp.203-216.

devaluing and destruction of natural resources. Acknowledgment of our limited perspective is a necessary act of ecological humility. It is also vital to the kind of global decision-making called for by the UNCED documents. How, for instance, are the relations between God and world conceived in the other cultures in the Asian-Pacific region where Christians make up only 3% of the population, and specifically in the world's fastest growing economy, China?

The Chinese Context

The attempt to answer that question serves as a further example of Northern theological hegemony. The Chinese theologian Kwok Pui-Lan, in her book, *Chinese Women and Christianity: 1860-1927*, discusses what is known in China as 'the term question': the unsettling debate about how to render the word 'God' into the Chinese language. William Milne, one of the early Protestant missionaries, noted that 'the Chinese language possesses no single appellation expressive of the ideas which Christians connect with the words *elohim*, God, deity, etc'. (He made no mention of the fact that the word *elohim* would express a very different 'idea' for the Jews who coined it.) In the seventeenth century the Jesuit missionaries proposed to use *tian* (heaven) or *shangdi* (supreme ruler). But the Dominicans and Franciscans insisted on using *tianzhu*, (Master of Heaven). When the Protestant missionaries arrived in the early nineteenth century they wished to use another term for God to distinguish their religion from Roman Catholicism. They used *shen* and *shangdi*, with the British favouring *shangdi* and the Americans preferring *shen*. This is translated sometimes as God, sometimes as Spirit[11].

Even today, Chinese Roman Catholics use *tianzhu*, mainline Protestants use *shangdi* and evangelical Christians prefer the term *shen*. Kwok comments:

> *But the difference in language only reflects the deeper divergence in mental categories and thought processes. The missionaries believed there is a supreme being, who creates and rules the universe, and God is the name for this 'self-existent, eternal, almighty Being, the Creator of heaven and earth'. In contrast, the Chinese conceive of cosmogony as a dynamic, continuous and organismic process in which there is no creator who stands outside the universe. 'The analogy behind their thinking is not a man making a pot,' as A. C. Graham vividly describes it, 'but rather a tree growing from its hidden root and branching out* [12].

This reminds us in the North how much our speech betrays us. The content of our word 'God', understood from another context, describes a being who rules and masters the universe, is defined by and on behalf of sectarianism, nationalism and sexism. (Feminist theology, done within the context of exclusion from Northern ecclesiastical power, also experiences the force of that understanding and struggles to replace it with non-violent, inclusive content). Seen from within Europe by our Jewish brothers and sisters, our God rules through the terror of

[11] In conversation with Kwok, she underlines the deliberate ambiguity of *shen*

[12] Kwok Pui Lan, *Chinese Women and Christianity: 1860 -1927*, Scholars Press, Atlanta, 1992, p. 31f.

the pogrom and the horror of Auschwitz. From the Chinese perspective, he is a God who creates while standing outside the universe, that is, objectively, and as such is, in Kwok's words, 'totally unintelligible.'

The Model of Objectivity

This dominating, 'objective' God is a hallmark of western Christian models of divine relationship with the world. It is also, as criticisms from many quarters have forced Christians to acknowledge, a hallmark of European colonizing relationships with the rest of the world. It has been characteristic too of 'ideal' relationships between citizen and government, between husband and wife, between the scientist and whatever is being researched. Such claims to dominating objectivity, whether attributed to our relations with each other or with God, to knowledge and its communication or to anything else, need to have their conceptual and practical content rigorously examined. Speaking of the 'ideal of objectivity' within the legal system, the barrister Helena Kennedy describes it as a masculine value which has come to be taken as a universal one. Often when the law fails people, she says, it is because 'judicial objectivity' has meant a denial of the female or black or working class experience[13].

Evelyn Fox-Keller, writing on subject/object relations as a component of scientific objectivity, argues that not only in the denial of interaction between subject and other but also in the access of domination to the goals of scientific knowledge, one finds the intrusion of a self we begin to recognize as partaking in the cultural construct of masculinity[14].

The conjunction between the impulse toward domination and effective domination both of the female and of Nature as female is well documented[15].

The emphasis here is on the concept of objectivity in our relations with each other and in conceiving God's relationship with the world, and on how this functions as a controlling factor in making decisions. Speaking of claims by scientists to have no 'emotional attachment', no bias or wish-fulfilment in their work, Mary Midgley describes such claims as a triumph of hope over experience, since it is a claim that the subject-matter of the physical sciences is remote from human concerns (and, by extension, divine concerns) and can be handled with impartiality[16].

Having said that, however, there is a need for an objectivity that allows the object of our attention to be what it is, to retain its identity in our regard. How

13 Helena Kennedy, *Eve was Framed: Women and British Justice*, Chatto and Windus, London, 1992, p.266.

14 See Evelyn Fox-Keller's article, **Feminism and Science**, in *Women, Knowledge and Reality*, op. cit., above, pp.175- 186.

15 See, for example, Rosemary Ruether, *Gaia and God*, Harper, San Francisco, 1992, Chapter 7. See also Chapters 2 and 3 and the sources quoted in my book *From Apocalpyse to Genesis: Ecology, Feminism and Christianity*, Tunbridge Wells, Burns and Oates, Minneapolis, Fortress, 1991, or in the German edition, *Wir sind nicht de Herren der Schöpfung: ein Ökologisches Denkmodell*, Frankfurt, Knecht, 1993.

16 Mary Midgley, *Science as Salvation*, London, Routledge, 1992, p.23

do we achieve such an 'inclusive' objectivity in our knowledge-building? For we cannot develop fully on the basis of subjective experience alone but need and must create 'objective' concepts to filter, shape and share experience with others.

Empowering Models

Nelle Morton empowered women in this enterprise, describing it as the dynamic between the personal and the political.

> *We know solidarity with other women and all women simultaneously as most exquisitely personal and powerfully political. Often our first utterance was a cry or agonising gesture, but in that movement we knew that we had been heard and understood even before the cry was uttered. Our tongues were loosened and we experienced ourselves speaking a new speech - boldly, perhaps, or haltingly, but authentically for the first time in our lives. We experienced a speech that follows hearing, as opposed to the going logic that demands precise speech for more accurate hearing to take place. Hearing, for us, became a personally transitive verb that evoked speech*[17].

This passage presents 'hearing into speech' as a hearing engaged in by the whole body, a process that, she says, resists analysis and explanation[18]. It is the process experienced and recorded by the women who took part in the Women's Congress at Miami. 1500 women over four days heard into speech dramatic testimonies which on the fifth day were presented to Maurice Strong as a women's political environmental agenda. The philosopher of language Gemma Fiumara advocates similar attempts to retrieve the functions of listening. These may, she says, allow for truer forms of dialogue than the dialectical dismantlings which tend to repropose what has been demolished[19]. Through emphasis on hearing/listening, respect for individual difference, for context, is safeguarded. Evelyn Fox-Keller, discussing the interaction between emotional and cognitive experience, defines dynamic objectivity as a form of knowledge that grants to the world around us its independent integrity but does so in a way that remains cognizant of, indeed relies on, our connectivity with that world. She quotes Piaget in support of a pursuit of knowledge that makes use of subjective experience in the interests of a more effective objectivity[20].

This form of knowledge-building enables us to weave rafts by choice out of necessity whose structural integrity is strong enough to take us out from the shallows and to set us afloat on the full sea. Traditionally the emphasis in theories of knowledge has been on the who and the what, the subject and object of knowledge. Environmental theory extends our horizon to encompass the nature of the knower (who), the process of knowing (how), the context within which the process takes place (where and with whom), as well as the thing known (what)[21]. In this communal environment, effective objectivity can be reconceived

---

17 Nelle Morton, *The Journey is Home*, Boston, Beacon, 1985, p.99.
18 Ibid., p.128.
19 Gemma Fiumara, *The Other Side of Language: A Philosophy of Listening*, Routledge, London, 1990, p.13.
20 Evelyn Fox-Keller, *Reflections on Gender and Science*, Yale University Press, New Haven, 1985, p.115.
21 This formulation was worked out in discussion with Carol Boulter.

as a function of the communal structure of knowledge-building rather than as an individual property[22].

This resonates with Nelle Morton's description of what she called Piaget's 'organic approach, refusing to separate the mind from the body and the individual from the world [environment]'[23]. Otherwise, she says, the intellect is without roots and nourishment, tantamount to the body cut off from the spirit and the mind. She tackles some of the false theological problems which come from setting boundaries between emotion and thinking. Responding to an essay by a prominent male professor of theology who declared that women cannot have it both ways, 'organic and transcendent', she points out that for women, organic does not mean 'staying with the gut, nor is it limited to the senses as nouns'. Transcendent, evoking static immobility, she replaces with transcending, which arises out of the organic in process of reshaping self and society. In a statement which sums up much of a women's environmental theological agenda, she says,

> *Thus spiritual is experienced profoundly as sisterhood in its loftiest and most universal sense and, we may add redundantly, political action of the most radical sort on behalf of and ultimately including all humanity - women, children, and men* [24].

I would want to add, and all living beings.

It is possible now to see how a constructivist/environmental approach to knowledge-building, with its emphasis on personal experience and its refusal to separate that experience from construction of the world, shares a common agenda with the kind of knowledge-building women can and must bring to decision-making processes. The call for the inclusion of women in those processes by various groups responsible for pre- and post-Rio documents appears not only as a timely act of justice but as positively significant. In the context of an ecological philosophy which holds that the human person is compounded of interactions between elements of which we partake, it is a call to conscious awareness of those interactions and the necessity for sustaining them in a non-violent way. By crossing the boundaries between emotion and what is conventionally classed as thinking, the cognitive act becomes a non-violent act of understanding love between us, between us and all living being, between us and God[25].

Empowering Theology

In the theological context, it is possible now to see how 'the term question' about God forces us to question not only our use of the word 'God' but its content, the doctrines it depends on and supports. In particular we need to question its

---

22 This supports Longino's view of objectivity. See her article, op. cit., p.208.

23 Nelle Morton, op. cit., p.24.

24 ibid., p.98.

25 Arne Naess,*Ecology, Community and Life-Style*, Cambridge and New York, Cambridge University Press, 1989, p.63.

assumptions about the nature of the relationship between God and world. The ecological philosopher Arne Naess defines an environmental relationship as an intrinsic relation between two things A and B such that the relation belongs to the basic definitions of A and B. Without the relation, A and B are no longer the same things[26].

If the relation between us and the environment is such that we cannot define ourselves or the environment without it, is the same true for the relation between it and God, between God and ourselves, as the Chinese think? If so, then the 'where' and 'with whom' we know God has to be considered.

The cognitive jolt which comes from doing so and thus realising the limitations of one's theological presuppositions is well illustrated by Diana Eck's experiences in India. Growing up in the United States, she shared a common Christian perception of mountains - Sinai, Tabor, Zion - as 'where' God 'spoke'. She was astonished to find that in India the mythic cosmic mountain, said to anchor the universe at its very centre, has a greater circumference at the top than at the bottom. Who had ever imagined such a mountain? Inverting our usual image of a mountain peak, it spread out at the top, making room for the cities of a whole host of gods.

For her, schooled in the religious imagination of the west, the archetypal mountain peak of Sinai had room only for one God. This conforms with our notion that anything truly important should be unique, singular, not part of a set of seven or twelve. Musing on this, she discovered and confronted her own distinctively western habit of thought, grounded in the western monotheistic tradition: the expectation of singularity and uniqueness, and the valuing of such singularity and uniqueness. The singular is accepted as the proper number for Truth, for God, for Son of God, for Church. This is a myth, she says, in the sense that it is the powerful story we tell about reality, so powerful we do not recognize it as our story. The question of how many gods is not really a question of numbers, but of viewpoint. The singular is not the world-shaping myth of religious people alone, but is a particular way of seeing and evaluating in the West that has shaped the world-views of Marxists, scientists, humanists and atheists. It affects our way of thinking about authority and about truth questions[27].

It also affects our thinking about ourselves, about our behaviour as the norm, or as a departure from it. Anne Hunt Overzee expresses this succinctly when she says that it has been through her experience of a non-Christian spiritual tradition that she has come to understand her own spiritual growth and wholeness - indeed, 'salvation' in terms of embodiment[28]. We tend to think of our self as sin-

---

26 ibid., p.36.

27 Diana Eck, *Encountering God*, Boston, Beacon, 1993, p.59f.

28 See her article, **I Am My Relationships: a Personal Reflection on Creating Theology in a Multi-Faith Context**, in *Feminist Theology in a European Context: Yearbook of the European Society in Theological Research*, eds. Annette Esser and Luise Schottroff,Mainz, Grünewald, Kampen, Kok Pharos, 1993, pp,129-137.

gular, not as intrinsically relational. We tend then to make decisions on the basis of our singular perspective rather than allowing for a diversity of perspectives.

A conscious attempt to counteract this tendency is beginning to be accepted as fundamental to a global religious ethic. In particular, it seems to me, it calls for Christian theologians to extend their horizons beyond interchurch dialogue to interfaith pilgrimage. Lois Wilson called for this emendation at the Re-Imagining Conference, the mid-Decade event of the Ecumenical Decade of Churches in Solidarity with Women, Minneapolis, November 1993. Her attendance at the Parliament of the World's Religions in Chicago in August 1993 convinced her that all faiths are in pilgrimage and this must be acknowledged. Churches' failure to do so signals a lack of respect for diversity and the loss of their prophetic voice. They have to address the question posed to religious leaders at the Parliament:

> *What are the traditional teachings within your faith tradition concerning a proper relationship with those who differ in race or gender (conditions one cannot change), or culture, politics, or faith?* [29].

The Power of Difference

If we do try to have a proper relationship with those who differ from us in these ways, we find that respect for and encounter with contexts different from our own serve both as a clue to new modes of connectedness between us, and as an invitation to engagement with others. We also deepen our awareness of the suffering of the other. Our pain has different forms, but there is a very real need for Christians especially to perceive the injustice experienced by their Muslim, Jewish or Hindu neighbour[30]. This mode of knowledge-building constitutes a principle for ordering the world radically, theologically, in an all-encompassing compassion and respect, content with multiplicity[31].

This kind of knowledge invigorates and bears us on to new ventures, to a fusion of horizons where, recognising diverse contexts and respecting differences, we are invited to a form of engagement with the future, with the yet-to-be-experienced. Difference empowers, offering potential for innovation, for new structures, concepts, and combinations[32]. Something which does not fit or appear to fit with one's own experience challenges us (as Diana Eck and Anne Hunt-Overzee found in India, and as I found in conversation with Kwok Pui-Lan), not only to create a larger multidimensional pattern into which it might fit but also to see possibilities not available to us within our own context. Differences then offer understanding of ourselves and of others while allowing for the preservation of the individual. Transcending them, in Nelle Morton's sense of organic process

29 *Report of the Parliament of the World Religions,* August 28th-September 5th, 1993, in *Earthkeeping News: A Newsletter of the North American Conference on Christianity and Ecology,* Vol. III, No.2, St Paul, MN.

30 Hunt-Overzee, op. cit., p.133.

31 Fox-Keller, *Gender and Science,* op. cit., p.163.

32 Michael Polanyi, *Personal Knowledge,* London, Routledge, Kegan and Paul, 1958, p.259.

which reshapes self and society, we find that richness and diversity of life forms are indispensable to the flourishing of human and non-human life on earth. Life itself, as a process over evolutionary time, implies the potential for increase of diversity and richness[33]. 'What seems important for sustenance is not so much biodiversity as such, but potential biodiversity, the capacity of a healthy system to respond through diversification when the need arises', (p.390). This is ground for hope, a theological virtue which responds to the needs of an environmentally depleted world.

Writing of the scientist Barbara McClintock, Evelyn Fox-Keller remarks that in the relationship she describes with plants, as in human relations, respect for difference constitutes a claim not only on our interest but on our capacity for empathy - in short, on the highest form of love: love that allows for intimacy without the annihilation of difference. The crucial point for her was that she could risk the suspension of boundaries between subject and object through this kind of love, precisely because scientific knowledge, for her, was not premised on that division.

> *Self and other, mind and nature survive not in mutual alienation, or in symbiotic fusion, but in structural integrity. This is a mode of access, honoured by time and human experience, to reliable knowledge*[34].

For me, this structural integrity in knowledge-building enables us to venture our rafts onto the flood tide in affairs, and, we hope, to take them on to fortune.

(A version of this article appears in *Ecotheology: Voices from North and South*, ed David Hallman, World Council of Churches, Geneva, 1994.

[33] See James Lovelock, *A Numerical Model for Biodiversity*, in Phil. Trans. R. Soc., B, 338, 1992, pp.383-391.
[34] Evelyn Fox-Keller, op. cit., p.165.

Zusammenfassung

Dieser Artikel untersucht einige Konzepte des Konstruktivismus in der naturwissenschaftlichen Bildung und des Kontextualismus in der Theologie im Rahmen der Erklarungen der Vereinten Nationen zur Aufname von Frauen in Prozessen der Entscheidungsfindung als Teil einer globalen umweltbezogenen Strategie. Ein konstruktivistisches/feministisches Modell geht davon aus, dass wir die Art und Weise erkunden konnen, in der wir unsere Erfahrungswelt zusammensetzen, und dass, weil wir uns dieser Tatsache bewusst sind, unsere Welt auf andere Weise zu erkunden und aufzubauen. Ein kontextuelles Modell betont die Bedeutung der persönlichen, lokalen und globalen Dimensionen des Zusammenhanges in Strategiën der Wissenserwerbung die es uns ermöglichen, einen anderen Glauben zu respektieren, für einen Dialog offen zu sein und daraus zu lernen.

Sommaire

Cet article examine certains concepts du constructivisme dans l'enseignement scientifique, et de la théologie contextualiste, dans le cadre de déclaration faites par l'ONU (comme partie intégrante de sa stratégie écologique globale) concernant l'inclusion des femmes dans les processus exécutifs. Un modèle constructiviste/feministe présuppose que nous puissions explorer les manières dont nous construisons notre monde experientiel, et qu'une conscience de cela nous permette de le construire différement. Un modèle contextualiste met l'accent sur l'importance des dimensions personnelles, locales et globales du contexte dans ces stratégies épistémologiques qui nous permettent, non seulement de respecter et d'accueillir les dialogues inter-réligieux, mais aussi d'en bénéficier.

Biography

Anne Primavesi is an Irish research theologian living in England, with a Ph.D from London University in systematic theology. She co-authored 'Our God Has No Favourites: A Liberation Theology of the Eucharist', Burns & Oates, 1989 and published, in 1991, 'From Apocalypse To Genesis: Ecology, Feminism and Christianity', Burns & Oates, Tunbridge Wells, Fortress, Minneapolis. German edition: 'Wir Sind Nicht die Herren der Schöpfung', Frankfurt, 1993. She spoke on'Overcoming Militarism' at the WCC Conference in Rio at the time of the United Nations Earth Summit. She is a member of the Ecology and Bioethics Commission of the European Ecumenical Women's Forum and of the Environment and Development project group of the Joint European Bishops' Conferences.

Caroline Mackenzie

Cosmic Awareness and Sacred Space: The Integration of Feminine Symbolism in Indian Christian Art and Architecture

Introduction

Western feminist theologians have reflected much on inclusive language; but much less has been done on inclusive symbolism. Post enlightenment western Christianity has largely lost touch with imagination, emotion and the body. It has also lost touch with nature in a meaningful way. Sacred space or the environment in which we worship, meditate and pray is in many ways an extension of the body and the cosmos. In a sense it is where we meet with God. Sacred space might mean a grove of trees. More usually for us it means a room or a building where we worship God, or meditate or pray. The space is given a particular orientation through its shape and by the use of light. Visual symbols such as paintings and sculptures will help to focus the spiritual practice which we do in the space. It will make a lot of difference if the area is either very light or very dark. It will matter if the lines of the building/room are all straight or all curved, or a mixture. A round or square space with a central focus will say something different from a rectangular one with the focus against one wall.

As a result of our disconnection from the environment our sensitivity to sacred space is often dulled. Our western society has depended on a separation between human beings and nature. Our life becomes almost unbearable when we begin to realise what our life - style does to the environment. Studies such as 'The Death of Nature', by Caroline Merchant (San Francisco, Harper and Row, 1980) show how the desacralisation of nature paved the way for its ruthless exploitation. Not only was nature desacralised, but also women, who were conceived to be especially close to nature. The problems we are faced with now are so huge it is easy to give up. I suggest that one way that we could work with this situation is through the creation of Christian sacred spaces which clearly help us to realise and celebrate the sacredness of women, men and the earth. I propose to look at how sacred space is conceived in some of the inculturated Indian Christian churches, chapels and prayer halls. These places incorporate cosmic and feminine symbolism in a simple and refreshing way.

The Process of Inculturating Christianity in India

Ever since missionaries such as Robert de Nobili SJ came to India in the seventeenth century, there have been a few western Christians who showed an appreciation for Indian culture, and made some attempt to relate it to Christianity. However, on the whole, Christianity came to India clothed in Greek, Latin and perhaps a very little Celtic culture. Indians saw it as a foreign religion. Towards the end of the nineteenth century this was being questioned, a questioning which gathered momentum. With Independence and then the second Vatican Council the search for an authentic Indian Christianity was well under way and had official recognition. While the Churches of North and South India[1] have their own ways of 'inculturation', this interest in sacred space and symbolism connected with liturgy, is a predominantly Catholic phenomenon.

In 1991-92, I was in India for six months. I had previously lived there, working as an artist, for fourteen years. During this visit I was commissioned by the National Biblical Catechetical and Liturgical Centre (NBCLC), Bangalore, to photograph some of the inculturated churches and chapels[2]. This proved to be a fascinating experience, particularly as I participated in liturgical celebrations or meditated in these places. The overwhelming feeling that I had was of being included and at home, much more than in similar situations in the West. As in the West, the leaders were still men. However, because of the powerful non verbal symbolism, this did not matter so much. I found that on account of the way in which these places were arranged, as a woman I felt definitely made in the image of God. In spite of the Biblical passage that both men and women are made in the image of God (Genesis 1:27) in the western situation I often have the greatest difficulty in believing it. Besides this, the second most forcible impression was the way in which I became aware of the presence of God in nature. Nature was not just a peaceful background, but a major way of divine revelation. The Cosmic Christ felt very real. I felt connected with nature.

Characteristics of Indian Culture which have Influenced the Symbolism of the New Churches and Chapels

Whilst there is a strong sense of the transcendence of God in traditional Hindu belief systems, there is an equally strong experience of the divine immanence. Even in modern India which is becoming more and more influenced by western secular and consumer values, a visitor can get a feeling of the way in which the sacred is experienced as near or immanent. In the smallest, most dilapidated sweet shop an image of a deity will be pinned to the wall, and the shop owner will offer a prayer and wave incense before it each morning. Depending on one's

1 The Churches of North and South India are a union of several reformed and protestant denominations.

2 These photographs are on permanent display at NBCLC, Bangalore, India. The author has her own set mounted, which form a portable exhibition. A Book on 50 Indian churches (including Churches of South and North India) is now in preparation and due to be published in 1995.

perspective, this will seem like blind superstition or as a means of honouring a reality which is beyond, yet it does give meaning to our limited human life by means of a symbol. At a much more impressive level, the great temples, adorned with a glorious variety of sculptures stand as monuments to the meeting point between the seen and the unseen worlds. The images on these temples include every aspect of life. The division into sacred and profane with which we are familiar in the West is not relevant here. All aspects of reality discover meaning through their relationship to a sacred centre. It is more a matter of levels of consciousness. What in the West we would call profane, in Hindu thought would be seen as that which is relatively less conscious of the relationship to the divine.

All aspects of life are celebrated as being capable of revealing God's glory. This celebratory tendency is tempered by many checks and balances which require a certain renunciation and detachment from what is limited and mortal. This sense of celebration and immanence enters into the Christian sacred spaces. At Anjali Ashram in Mysore, the church, which there is called a mandir, is made in the form of the Cosmic Egg. This is a symbol which affirms life giving and birth. The curved shapes make one think more of a feminine, than a masculine body. This shape contrasts strongly with the pointed gothic spires of much western Christian architecture. The round building is set into a sort of 'moat' with water. The overall effect is that it is emerging out of the earth or the cosmic ocean. So there are two images of birth giving, the egg being born out of the earth/water, and the egg itself as a birth giving image. Inside in the centre of the mandir is the 'samadhi' or grave of the founder, Fr Amalor Pavadass. Birth is inseparably connected with death.

This circular space can be used either with a central focus, or with a congregation of people facing the celebrant for Mass. For devotional practices like bhajan singing (repetitive chants slightly similar to Taizé chants) a lamp can be put in the centre, and all the people sit round in a circle. This arrangement emphasises God at the centre, the immanence of God, God at the core of each person. When the space is arranged more as a rectangle, with the priest and people facing each other, then there is more focus on the relationship between God and human beings and more stress on otherness, or transcendent relationship.

At Sambalpur in Orissa, there is a Regional Theologate where many of the seminarians are from tribal backgrounds. With this in mind and as a source of inspiration, the church is based on the theme of 'The Cosmic Covenant'. The idea has been to incorporate the exuberant, celebratory nature of the tribal culture into the Christian context. The central image is not a crucifix but a mosaic depicting Christ as a story teller. Around him are images from nature such as the seed, sheep, trees and so forth, that he used in his story telling. He sits cross-legged on the earth and a stream of water flows out from his heart. He seems to be speaking on behalf of the creation because he himself is part of it.

Much of the symbolism in the church is based on dancing and the tribal drum. One is aware of the rhythms of nature and the way that through drumming and dancing human beings come to feel part of these natural rhythms. One of the window grills depicts 'the earth mother' with her arms outstretched, standing beside an ant hill. A wall mosaic shows on the left, the woman who washed Jesus' feet with her tears and anointed them with costly ointment, while on the right, Christ washes Simon Peter's feet. It is quite typical of Indian culture to incorporate the masculine and feminine dimensions of any situation or story. When I first went to India I was astounded by the multitude of images of the divine feminine. These goddesses are clearly and unquestionably goddesses, unlike the endless ambiguities built up around the Virgin Mary. It is not that the Judaic Christian world view does not acknowledge the divine feminine, but that it emphasises the God as a father, thus losing the wholeness of the image of God.

In very many of the Christian sacred spaces that I visited one receives the sense of the masculine and feminine symbolism within the godhead. This is not conveyed through a direct translation of god and goddess figures. Rather the vision comes through a response to the holistic background which gave rise to the images. A few examples will clarify how this is done. At Ashirvad, a Jesuit centre for further education in Bangalore, the chapel is based on the Yin Yang symbol. It is by the artist Jyoti Sahi who also designed Sambalpur. As you enter, the central focus of the chapel is the crucifix and tabernacle which are set into a yin yang shape. The crucifix represents the masculine symbol and the tabernacle, the feminine one (see illustration p.30). The crucifix is sharp and angular, with the male figure of Christ. It is placed on the 'yin' (feminine) part of the setting. The tabernacle is based on the symbol of the giving hands, with the water of life flowing out. It is a curved, gentle and profoundly female image. It is set in the white 'yang' (masculine) part of the setting. The simple rectangular room is divided into two levels, one slightly raised above the other by means of a double curve. The introduction of this curved line really gives a 'feminine' dimension to the otherwise severely straight lines of the space.

Another example of masculine and feminine symbolism at the centre of sacred space is to be found at Maitri Sagar. This is a social work centre dedicated to helping ex-bonded labourers. The vision behind this place comes from Sr Celestine, an Indian Joseph of Tarbes sister. In this example the 'masculine' element is provided by the pillar of fire. This is symbolised as a stone pillar, with a flame on top and seven oil lamps each side. In the centre is the tabernacle. On the door there is an annunciation scene, where Mary accepts the message of the fiery angel (see illustration p.30). The idea is to focus on God's involvement in the process of liberation. Thus the pillar of fire is a symbol to guide the Israelites and the angel shows Mary her destiny in the process of liberation. Both the pillar and the angel are accepted in faith.

The Ground of Being: the Importance of What Emerges from Below

In the Maitri Sagar sanctuary the tabernacle is set into the pillar so that it is at eye level for someone squatting on the floor. Meditation practices such as the Adoration of the Blessed Sacrament can be done in this setting in a meaningful way. Because it is the custom to sit on the ground, one is very much aware of the earth. The western tradition has stressed the notion of the divine descending from above, entering from outside. In the east there is more of an equal focus on above and below. Just as the pillar rises out of the earth, so the lotus flower grows up out of the muddy water. This is an obvious symbol for the integration of below and above or dark and light. In order to grow it has to emerge from the mud and reach up towards the sunlight; its flower blossoms a few inches above the water. This is understood as a symbol of the soul rising above its gross nature, while still being inseparably connected with it and as much dependent on it as on the sunlight.

The symbol of the lotus is often used in a Christian context. At Anjali Ashram, near Mysore, the tabernacle setting is fixed to the floor. It is in the form of a large lotus (see illustration p.31). The box containing the host is in the bud of the flower. A setting such as this not only emphasises the earth as well as the sky, but it also enables the worshipper's imagination to open up to the Cosmic Christ. Thinking about the presence of Christ in the Blessed Sacrament, which is visually simply a white circle, helps to get away from the over emphasis on the historical male who was Jesus. It seems to me that for women who find the specific maleness of Jesus difficult, this form of contemplation can be helpful.

Another very original tabernacle is to be found at Sameeksha, Centre for Indian Spirituality, Kerala. This tabernacle would be quite a triumph for a western art student, as it is made from 'found objects'! During some storms several coconut trees were blown down in the compound. Br Mampilly SJ noticed this and was impressed by the shape of the root. Along with Fr Sebastian Painadath SJ (the director), he saw how this root could be made into a tabernacle. They called the local carpenter who 'shaved off' the root tendrils and hollowed out the middle. This was then set in teak wood roots. It is like a huge heart, or womb or pot. The roots are like the veins of the heart. In the centre a door was made in the form of an eye; it is the eye of consciousness. Inside here the sacrament is kept. This evokes the idea of Christ as the supreme consciousness, hidden in the human heart and in the whole of nature. Developing the heart symbolism, they decided to add a guava tree trunk (also blown down in the storms) 'growing' out of the top of the coconut root. At the top there is a cross and crown of thorns (see illustration p.31). The hackneyed symbol of the sacred heart here becomes a powerful image linking the macrocosm, God in nature, with the microcosm, God in the human heart.

Interiority and Darkness

Darkness is a quality which has often been associated with feminine symbolism. The womb is a dark place. The earth is dark. Indian Christian spirituality tends to experience darkness as something positive and helpful. Darkness facilitates the search within by creating a safe hidden place of growth which leads to birth or rebirth. The chapel at Sameeksha has a zero watt bulb so that after dark a dim atmosphere can be created. The sanctuary lamp which creates a very conducive atmosphere for contemplation is actually inside the 'eye' of the tabernacle. One can see the continuity here with the Hindu culture. At the centre of the temple there is the 'garbha griha' (see plan p.31) or womb house which is a small room without any windows. In a sense the worshipper is 'reborn' from this sacred centre.

At Shantivanam, the ashram where the late Fr Bede Griffiths lived for much of his life, the sanctuary is very much like a garbha griha. The tabernacle and altar are rather high compared with later ones. This is because they were made before the Second Vatican Council, and there was a statutory height prescribed. The sanctuary area can be closed up with doors, thus creating a real womb like space. There is a little window in the door, through which one can see the sanctuary lamp, which is a traditional oil one. On top of this sanctuary area, the 'vimana' or tower is built. This symbolises transcendence. The idea is that through going deeper and deeper inside, the gateway to the transcendent is found. In symbolic terms this inner journey employs a 'feminine' symbol, the womb, while the transcending movement uses a 'masculine' symbol, the mountain.

Natural Symbols Integral to the Spiritual Journey

Theologians such as Matthew Fox help us to realise that the Western religion lacks a cosmology. The Indian world view is primarily a cosmic one and humanity is experienced as part of nature rather than as separated and over against it. Both the anthropocentric and cosmic world views have their own contributions to make. The human-centred world view tends to give more importance to prophecy and social justice whilst the cosmic one stresses mysticism and the interconnectedness of the whole world. Since in the West we are strong on the anthropocentric model, it is helpful to see how we could become more open to the cosmic vision.

At Sameeksha, besides the chapel, with the coconut root tabernacle described above, there is another sacred space. This is an inter-faith meditation hall (see illustration p.31). It is a good example of how natural symbolism can be integrated into a spiritual search. The hall is square, with a roof sloping up equally from the four sides to the pinnacle over the centre of the space. This design, by a traditional Hindu architect, is especially helpful for meditation. On top of the roof, where the four sides meet there is a lotus bud symbolically awaiting the touch of the sun to come into blossom. Inside the hall, the central focus is a constantly burning oil lamp which is set into a lotus shaped holder. Around this, in the four directions, are placed symbols of the elements: a coconut for earth, a bowl of water, flowers for air and incense for ether. In Indian thought there are five elements. Between the elements, resting on the floor on stands made from roots, there are four holy books - The Koran, The Upanishads, The Dhammapada and The Bible. Each tradition is 'rooted' in the earth or ground of being through its particular scripture, and in the shared context of the elements, relates to the light.

In order to emphasise this shared elemental reality, outside again in the four directions there are larger symbols. For earth, there is a sacred tulasi bush, for water, there is a lotus pond, for fire a Kerala style stone oil lamp, measuring about eight feet in height. This is lit on festival days only. Air and ether are represented by nothing. The whole arrangement is a mandala, ie a symmetrical pattern used for integrating the microcosm and the macrocosm, or the individual and the universal.

Although we are not focusing here specifically on inter- faith issues, it is perhaps interesting to note that several Indian Christian places have two sacred spaces. One will be for exclusive Christian devotions, and usually has a tabernacle, a cross, or image of Christ and the other emphasises what is common and shared between religions. At Sameeksha it is the elemental symbols which provide this shared environment, and there is nothing oppressively Christian or Catholic in the symbols. Each religion is equally represented.

Prophetic Symbolism

The purpose of the meditation hall at Sameeksha is to create a contemplative atmosphere. At Maitri Sagar (mentioned above in connection with the tabernacle), the prophetic dimension is more evident. On account of her work with bonded labourers, Sr Celestine is particularly inspired by the Exodus story. In the church/temple at Maitri Sagar the journey from captivity to freedom has been depicted through natural symbols. There are pillars around a central pond and the devotee can circumambulate the area, passing the symbols carved on the pillars which 'tell' the Exodus story. These images include, the seed, tree, egg and so on (see illustration p31). One gets the idea of the whole of nature being bonded and God intervening and leading 'her' towards freedom. Lest we should fear too much our involvement in this work, the story of the reluctant prophet Jonah is depicted on the doorway.

It seems to me that daily worship in the context of this cosmic liberation story could significantly affect our relationship to the ecological crisis. As Matthew Fox rightly says, unless we name our oppression no prophets can be born. Because of the process of inculturation, the symbols of the Exodus story have been rediscovered from the angle of the cosmic Indian world view. This seems to be a particularly happy collision of cultures. While Indian and really Hindu culture is very strong on the contemplative and cosmic elements, it has not been so good on the prophetic dimensions. Equally, the Jewish and Christian traditions have tended to focus on prophetic action. As a Christian place it is not surprising that the primary concern of Maitri Sagar is human beings as bonded labourers. And yet now this human struggle becomes through such symbolic interpretation, the struggle of the whole of nature. On account of the seriousness of our present crisis, contemplation alone is not sufficient and radical action needs to be undertaken. If this is seen in the context of the Exodus story, then the elements of faith and hope, clearly linked to our tradition, are incorporated into this action, in the same way that much social work has been in the past.

Imagination and Liberation

The Exodus story gains its cosmic dimension at Maitri Sagar through the use of imagination. One could say that it has been used as a 'myth of liberation'. Indian thinking in religious matters has been predominantly mythic and symbolic. In Hinduism many of the key scriptures cannot be fixed in history. They are 'true' myths which become meaningful in the life situation, or one might say, in the historical reality of the person who believes in and lives out the myth. It is not that Indian Christians do not value the historical foundation of the Bible stories. However, they do not feel the need to reduce everything to that. This is particularly liberating with regard to women: if a story is about a man, it can equally be applied to a man or a woman. In fact this has always been the case; all Christians, men or women are trying to become Christ like, yet because of our literal way of depicting things, this normally does not show in iconography.

At the centre of the Maitri Sagar church/temple on the sanctuary doors, the 'Anger of Moses' is depicted. On the right, the image is male and on the left, it is female. Along with Jyoti Sahi another artist, I was involved in designing this temple and created this particular design. It was inspired by talking to Sr Celestine. I could feel how strongly she identified with the anger of Moses. Like Moses she felt angry at the oppression of 'her people', which in her case meant the bonded labourers. In the course of this discussion, I realised that I felt equally angry at the oppression of women and nature in my society. Situating this feeling of anger in the context of the Exodus story was one of the most liberating experiences of my life. It took the feeling beyond the purely personal and situated it in the context of a 'true' story where God intervenes and shows Moses, who feels so inadequate, what to do. As far as I know no one has objected to this 'non-biblical' female Moses.

Conclusion

The places mentioned here represent only a small proportion of the inculturated sacred spaces. In relation to the whole church in India they are, however, only a very small minority. This sort of inculturation still tends to be something quite specialised. There are plenty of Indian Christians who are perfectly content with western style Christianity. In fact the westerness might even be part of the attraction. The places discussed here are in the context of ashrams[3] or religious houses founded and run by monks or nuns. They are, without exception, the fruit of a certain person's vision, often working in association with artists or craftspeople. On the whole there is not a conflict between the inculturating Christians and those who are content with the status quo, but eventually, perhaps, the innovative places will influence the others.

Indian Christians who are involved with inculturation show a striking awareness of the connection between their priesthood, spirituality and world view and the environment for liturgy. They are sensitive to the continuity between images and their own priesthood. If women are to lead liturgy, one has to consider what symbolism they bring with them. Some types of feminism have rebelled against the identification of women and nature; others have incurred the birth-giving symbolism in a positive way. A woman can symbolise and therefore speak on behalf of nature in a special way and the environment in which she does this will make this symbolic identification a source of oppression or liberation.

Many women in the West feel profoundly alienated from their local parish churches; they meet together for creative liturgies, and many create their own sacred spaces in their homes where they pray or meditate each day. Particularly when we speak of eco-feminism it seems to me that it is really important to consider the environment in which we attempt to give concentrated attention to God. Nature does not speak in words, but through sounds, sights, smells, touch and taste. The microcosm of our sacred space can act as a bridge between this non verbal world and the world of scripture and so on. It is the place we can move from pantheism to panentheism. The developments in India show how this can be done in surprisingly simple ways. These examples may inspire us to create our own sacred spaces which celebrate the sacredness of the earth, of women and men and may even help to inspire us towards prophetic ecological action.

[3] Ashram - a place of spiritual search, often with a group of disciples/seekers gathered round a 'guru' or spiritual master. This person can be a man or a woman, the qualification being his/her spiritual experience, wisdom etc.

Zusammenfassung

Die Natur bringt sich selbst nicht in worten zum Ausdruck; wir sind der Natur eher durch unsere Sinne verbunden. Unsere westliche Kultur neigt dazu, sehr Sprachorientiert zu sein. Es ist bislang viel über geslechtsunspezifische Sprache und wenig über die geslechtsunspezifische Symbolik gesagt worden. Die Autorin zeigt durch die Betrachtung Indiens neuer, in die Kultur integrierten katholischen Kirchen und Kapellen auf, wie Natur und feminine Symbolik in christliche, heilige Orte aufgenommen werden können. So ist es möglich, dass sie zum einem Teil der Ausübung geistlichen Handelns werden können. Diese symbolen können auf einer unterbewussten Ebene dazu dienen, unser uns innewohnendes Gefühl, mit der Schöpfung verbunden zu sein, wiederzuwecken, und möglicherweise inspiriert es uns zu prophetischem Verhalten, im Interesse der frauen, Männer und der Natur.

Sommaire

La nature ne s'exprime pas au moyen de la parole; nous nous lions à la nature à travers nos sens. Notre culture occidentale s'oriente de façon caractéristique vers la parole. On a beaucoup discuté du langage inclusif; par contre, très peu a été dit sur le symbolisme inclusif. De par son étude des églises et chapelles catholiques nouvellement 'naturalisées' en Inde, l'auteur démontre de quelle manière la nature et le symbolisme féminin pourraient s'incorporer à l'espace sacré chrétien de sorte qu'ils s'intègrent également à la pratique spirituelle. Les symboles peuvent agir au niveau de l'inconscient: ils savent restaurer notre sens inhérent d'appartenance à la création, tout en nous inspirant une action prophétique de la part des femmes, des hommes, et de la nature.

Caroline Mackenzie is an artist theologian, now living in Wales. She trained at St Martin's School of Art, London, and lived in India for 14 years. She has undertaken public commissions for the Church, both in India and the west, as well as holding her own exhibitions.

ASHIRVAD
TABERNACLE

MAITRI SAGAR TABERNACLE-
ANNUNCIATION

ASHIRVAD
CRUCIFIX AND TABERNACLE
SET INTO YIN YANG DESIGN

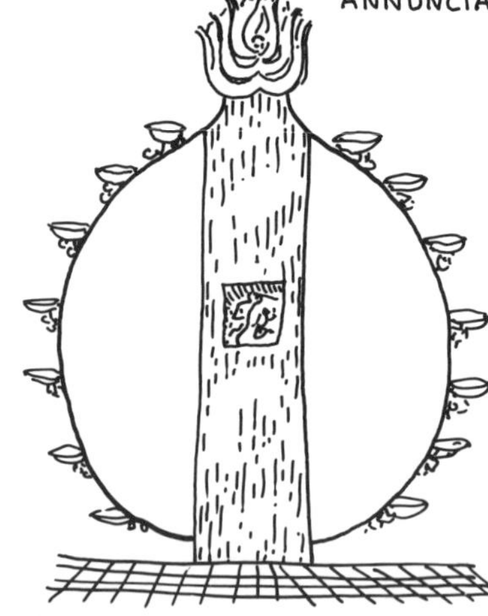

MAITRI SAGAR
PILLAR OF FIRE WITH
TABERNACLE

ANJALI ASHRAM
LOTUS TABERNACLE

Caroline Mackenzie '93

SAMEEKSHA - TABERNACLE

MAITRI SAGAR
SANCTUARY DOOR
" THE ANGER OF MOSES "

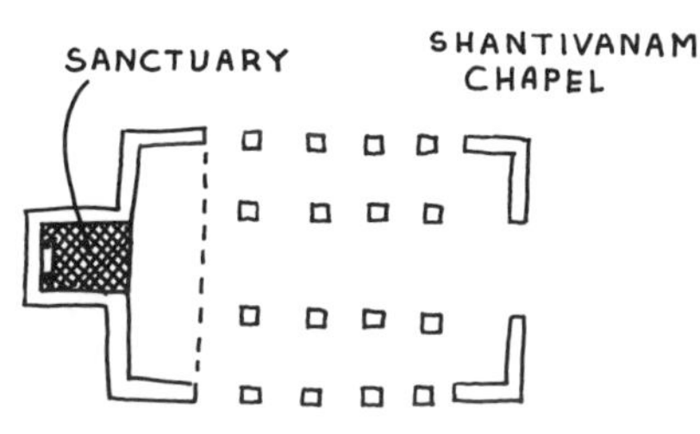

SHANTIVANAM CHAPEL

SAMEEKSHA
- LATER - FAITH
MEDITATION HALL

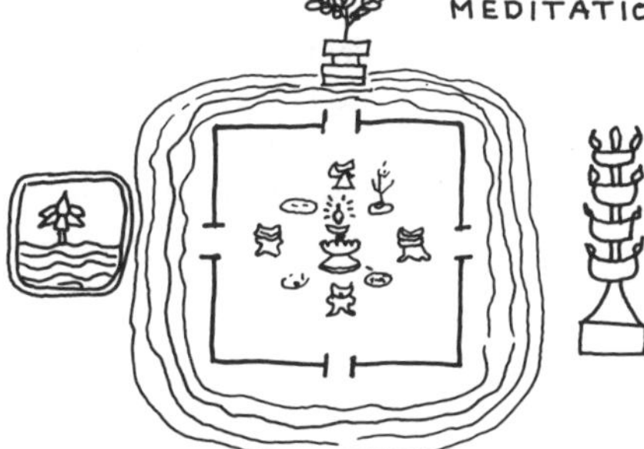

SEAD

TREE

COSMIC EGG

TREE WITH ROOTS IN HEAVEN EMERGING FROM EGG

MAITRI SAGAR
PILLAR DESIGNS EXODUS JOURNEY

Ina Praetorius

Feministische Ethik und die Oekologiefrage

Einleitung

Die Ökologiefrage' bedeutet alltägliche Verzweiflung für diejenigen, die ihrer Offenheit für Schreckensnachrichten nicht bewußt Grenzen setzen. Weiter leben zu wollen heißt ständig Wissen zu unterdrücken. Für viele heißt es bereits heute: die Sinne abstumpfen lassen. LehrerInnen fragen sich, ob sie ihren SchülerInnen die Wahrheit zumuten sollen. Sie fürchten die depressive Verstimmung des 'No Future'. ('Man muß den Jugendlichen doch Hoffnung machen.') Wer genug Geld hat, verdrängt vorzugsweise durch Teilhabe am reichhaltigen Konsumangebot, was – in wachen Momenten – die Verzweiflung steigert, da Mitkonsumieren zumeist Mitzerstören heißt. Wer wenig Geld hat, braucht Zeit für den Existenzkampf. 'Die Ökologiefrage' wird dann entweder zum Problem zweiter Ordnung oder sie verschlimmert das Elend: wozu um die eigene Existenz kämpfen in einer zugrundegehenden Welt?

Die voralpinen Wiesen, die ich von meinem Schreibtisch aus überblicke, passen sich dem Tanz meines Bewußtseins an: gestern noch ekelte mich ihr überdüngtes *Giftgrün*, heute entscheide ich mich voller Trotz für die *saftiggrüne* Idylle. Wäre die in Tracht gekleidete Bauernfamilie gestern mit ihren kürzlich im Embryonalstadium aus den USA importierten glockenbehängten Swiss Brown im Sonnenschein unter archaischem Jodeln auf die Alp gezogen, ich hätte die Vorhänge zugezogen. Heute winke ich ihr zu: Switzerland life, widerständig aufrechterhaltenes Brauchtum in ozongesättigter Luft unter verdorrenden Fichten, Pseudokrupp unter Trachtenblusen. Das Absurde, so steht es derzeit in Trendblättern zu lesen, hat seinen Reiz: Genuß jetzt.

Über 'die Ökologiefrage' *schreiben* heißt, einen 'rationalen' Umgang mit dem Absurden wählen: Sich an den Schreibtisch setzen, die Schublade ziehen, in der die akademische Gemeinschaft das Thema 'Ökologie' aufbewahrt, eine sinnvolle Gliederung entwerfen, Argumente in eine nachvollziehbare Ordnung bringen, dem einen zustimmen, dem anderen widersprechen, publizieren wollen, vieles vergessen.

Ich habe vor, in diesem Aufsatz schwerpunktmäßig zwei Aspekte des Themas zu diskutieren: zum einen werde ich einige charakteristische Passagen aus der derzeit sehr populären androzentrischen Umweltethik einer Kritik unterziehen. Im Kontrast zu solcher androzentrischer 'Öko-Ethik' werde ich feministische Basiserkenntnisse zur Ökologieproblematik darstellen. Ich werde zunächst den

Konsens aufsuchen, den feministisch sensibilisierte Denkerinnen sich erarbeitet haben. Danach werde ich einige Dissenspunkte markieren, an denen sich kritische Frauen auf dem Weg zu einer feministisch-ökologischen Ethik abarbeiten.

Androzentrismus und oekologische Ethik

Die Oekologieproblematik hat wesentlich dazu beigetragen, daß die lange vernachlässigte Disziplin Ethik in der etablierten Philosophie und Theologie einen beachtlichen Aufschwung erlebt hat. Hans Jonas hat mit seinem 'Prinzip Verantwortung'[1] im Jahr 1979 einen Anfang gesetzt: Ausgehend von der Einsicht, daß "die Verheißung der modernen Technik in Drohung umgeschlagen ist"[2] fordert er "entgegen dem positivistisch-analytischen Verzicht der zeitgenössischen Philosophie" eine radikale ethische Neubesinnung. Die Diskussion über seine These, Philosophie solle angesichts globaler Bedrohung wieder "in die Metaphysik reichen"[3] und eine absolute Begründung für den Imperativ menschlichen Überlebens setzen, ist seither nicht abgebrochen. Viele haben sich Hans Jonas angeschlossen.

Die Theologen, die den Kontakt zur Metaphysik über die Jahrhunderte bewahrt haben, beeilen sich, einer angesichts der Überlebenskrise ratlosen Philosophie zu Hilfe zu kommen. Dabei ist die Genugtuung darüber, daß 'der Mensch', wenn es hart auf hart geht, eben doch nicht auf Religion verzichten kann, unüberhörbar.

Theologen bieten der im "Vakuum des heutigen Wertrelativismus"[4] orientierungslos gewordenen Gesellschaft ein geläutertes christlich Bekenntnis bzw. Religion überhaupt als Orientierungshilfe an: "Das Kategorische des ethischen Anspruchs... läßt sich nicht... vom vielfach bedingten Menschen her, sondern nur von einem *Unbedingten* her begründen: von einem Absoluten her, das einen übergreifenden Sinn zu vermitteln vermag.... Das kann nur die letzte höchste Wirklichkeit selbst sein, die zwar nicht rational bewiesen, aber in einem *vernünftigen Vertrauen* angenommen werden kann."[5]. Hans Küng setzt 1990 mit seinem 'Projekt Weltethos' einen neuen Akzent: Er fordert den an der globalen Überlebensfrage statt an Glaubensinhalten orientierten, weltweiten interreligiösen Dialog: "Diese eine Welt braucht das eine Grundethos; diese eine Weltgesellschaft braucht gewiß keine Einheitsreligion oder Einheitsideologie, wohl aber einige verbindende und verbindliche Normen, Werte, Ideale und Ziele"[6]. Innerkirchlich ist die Bewegung hin zu einem christlich-ökologischen Bekenntnis längst im Gange: die 'Ökumenische Bewegung für Gerechtigkeit, Frieden und Bewahrung

1 Hans Jonas, Das Prinzip Verantwortung, Frankfurt a.M. 4.Aufl. 1983.
2 Ebd. S 7.
3 Ebd.S.8.
4 Ebd. S.7.
5 Hans Küng, Projekt Weltethos, 4.Aufl.1992, S.77, (Hervorhebungen von Hans Küng).
6 Ebd. S. 14.

der Schöpfung' sucht seit ihrer Gründung Mitte der achtziger Jahre und auch nach ihrem offiziellen Abschluß 1990 in Seoul nach einem christlich-ökologischen Konsens.

Wenn ich im folgenden drei exemplarische Texte aus diesem ökologisch motivierten ethischen Diskurs einer Kritik unterziehe, bediene ich mich der in der feministischen Wissenschaft inzwischen eingebürgerten "Hermeneutik des Verdachts"[7]. Das heißt: ich halte es angesichts einer inzwischen großen Anzahl feministischer Untersuchungen zum Androzentrismus der gesamten westlichen Wissenschaftskultur[8] für wahrscheinlich, daß auch diese Texte eine androzentrische Weltsicht spiegeln, und frage: Welches Bild vom 'Menschen' liegt den Texten zugrunde? Wo und wie kommen Frauen vor? Wie verhalten sich die Konzepte von 'Mensch' und 'Frau' zu den im feministischen Diskurs erarbeiteten Einsichten über Menschen und Frauen.

Hans Jonas, Das Prinzip Verantwortung

Jonas beginnt seine Reflexion über die durch moderne Technologie grundlegend veränderte Qualität 'menschlichen' Handelns mit dem bekannten Chorlied aus Sophokles' Antigone. In diesem antiken Preislied auf 'den Menschen' gelten als dessen prägende Eigenschaften: Jagd- und Eroberungseifer, Erfindungsreichtum, Verwegenheit, die Tendenz, im Bemühen um die eigene Sicherheit Natur zu vergewaltigen:

Ungeheuer ist viel, und nichts
ungeheurer als der Mensch.
Der nämlich, über das graue Meer
im stürmenden Süd fährt er dahin,
andringend unter rings
umrauschenden Wogen. Die Erde auch,
der Göttlichen höchste, die nimmer vergeht
und nimmer ermüdet, schöpfet er aus
und wühlt, die Pflugschar pressend, Jahr
um Jahr mit Rössern und Mäulern.

Leichtaufmerkender Vögel Schar
umgarnt er und fängt, und des wilden Getiers
Stämme und des Meeres salzige Brut
mit reichgewundenem Netzgespinst -
er, der überaus kundige Mann.
Und wird mit Künsten Herr des Wildes,
des freien schweifenden auf den Höhen,
und zwingt den Nacken unter das Joch,
den dichtbemähnten des Pferdes, und
den immer rüstigen Bergstier...[9]

---

[7] Vgl. Elisabeth Schüssler-Fiorenza, Brot statt Steine, Die Herausforderung einer feministischen Interpretation der Bibel, Freiburg/Schweiz 1988, S. 49-58.

[8] Vgl. Anm 12.

[9] Hans Jonas a.a.O.S.17.

Die offensichtliche Androzentrik dieser antiken Anthropologie ist für Jonas kein Thema. Der moderne 'Mensch', der heute angesichts der selbstgeschaffenen Möglichkeit globaler Selbstzerstörung die Furcht vor seinen eigenen Erzeugnissen lernen muß und dem daher die Pflicht der Verantwortung für die Zukunft aufgegeben ist, hat sich nach Jonas "in einer endlosen Laufbahn der Eroberung"[10] kontinuierlich aus dem 'kundigen Mann' der Antike entwickelt. Jonas' scheinbar bahnbrechendes 'Prinzip Verantwortung' richtet sich – wie der überwiegende Teil androzentrischer Ethik – an einen einzigen Adressatentypus: an den 'Menschen', der selbst durch aktive Teilnahme an einer Kultur ungebremster Naturbeherrschung im Laufe der Jahrhunderte die Mittel für die Zerstörung der Natur, und damit seiner selbst, bereitgestellt hat.

Feministinnen haben in zahlreichen Detailuntersuchungen offengelegt, daß sich im "universalen Neutrum Mann/Mensch"[11] der weiße Mann westlicher Prägung ein Denkmal gesetzt hat[12]. Die vermeintliche Allgemeingültigkeit herkömmlicher Ethik verbirgt, daß es sich in Wahrheit um einen Diskurs handelt, an dem nur ein kleiner Teil der 'Menschen' faktisch teilnimmt bzw. teilnahmeberechtigt ist. Androzentrische Ethik ist "die Form der Humanen unter den Herrschenden, den Inhumanen (unter den Herrschenden) etwas beizubringen"[13].

Jonas' Ideal des *moralischen* Menschen ist, wie in den meisten herkömmlichen ethischen Entwürfen, dem androzentrischen Konzept von 'Weiblichkeit' verwandt. Das ist logisch, denn innerhalb der androzentrischen Ordnung bildet 'Weiblichkeit' den gleichzeitig idealisierten und zur 'minderen Menschlichkeit' abgewerteten Widerpart des Männlich-Menschlichen. Wenn Jonas 'dem Menschen' Ehrfurcht vor dem Heiligen, Furcht, Bescheidenheit, Sorge, Empfindlichkeit des Gefühls, Demut, Frugalität[14] etc. als Tugenden der Zukunft anempfiehlt, grenzt er sich denn auch vorsorglich gegen die minderen weiblichen Varianten dieser Tugenden ab: "Wir unsererseits fürchten nicht den Vorwurf der Kleinmütigkeit..., wenn wir derart Furcht zur Pflicht erklären...: begründete Furcht, nicht Zaghaftigkeit; vielleicht gar Angst, doch nicht Ängstlichkeit; und in keinem Falle Furcht oder Angst um sich selbst"[15]. Auch im philosophischen Kernstück des 'Prinzips Verantwortung', wo die elterliche Verantwortung

10 Ebd.S.19

11 Adriana Caverero. Ansätze zu einer Theorie der Geschlechterdifferenz, in Diotima Philosophinnengruppe aus Verona, Der Mensch ist zwei. Das Denken der Geschlechterdifferenz, Wien, 1989, S.65-102, S.67.

12 Vgl. hierzu u.a.: Silvia Bovenschen, Die imaginierte Weiblichkeit, Exemplarische Untersuchungen zu Kulturgeschichtlichen und Literarischen Präsentationsformen des Weiblichen, Frankfurt a.M, 1979; Diotima Philosophinnengruppe a.a.O; Evelyn Fox Keller, Liebe, Macht und Erkenntnis: Männliche oder Weibliche Wissenschaft? München Wien,1986; Sandra Harding, Feministische Wissenschaftstheorie: Zum Verhältnis von Wissenschaft und sozialem Geschlecht, Hamburg, 1990; Ina Praetorius, Anthropologie und Frauenbild, in der deutschsprachigen protestantischen Ethik seit 1949, Gütersloh, 1993.

13 Ruth Egloff, in: Projektgruppe Ethik im Feminismus, Vom Tun und vom Lassen, Feministisches Nachdenken über Ethik und Moral, Münster, 1992, S.22.

14 Hans Jonas a.a.O., S.388-393. Vgl. auch, Hans Jonas., Auf der Schwelle der Zukunft: Werte von gestern und Werte für morgen, in : Ders., Technik, Medizin und Ethik: Praxis des Prinzips Verantwortung, Frankfurt a M. 1985, S.392.

15 Hans Jonas, Das Prinzip Verantwortung, S.392.

gegenüber dem Neugeborenen zum "zeitlosen Urbild aller Verantwortung"[16] erhoben wird, unterscheidet Jonas, getreu der androzentrischen Trennung männlich besetzter Freiheit von weiblich besetzter Naturwüchsigkeit, zwischen der *instinktgeleiteten* Fürsorge, die er hier ausdrücklich den Müttern zuschreibt[17], und der *reflektierten moralischen* Entscheidung, sich von der Bedürftigkeit des Säuglings zum Handeln bewegen zu lassen.

Feministisch gelesen ist Jonas' Aufbruch in eine ökologiebewußte ethische Philosophie wohl als eine sinnvolle Selbstkorrektur *innerhalb des androzentrischen Diskurses* zu werten. Das 'Prinzip Verantwortung' ist aber sicher keine allgemeingültige Formulierung der "neu erschienene(n) Pflicht des Menschen jenseits des Wertsubjektivismus"[18]. Denn – abgesehen vom kategorischen Imperativ des Überlebens als solchem – enthält es keine brauchbaren Verhaltensmaximen für Menschen, denen es bis heute nicht gestattet ist, sich als Nachfahren des Prometheus zu verstehen.

Hans Küng, Projekt Weltethos

Hans Küng operiert nicht nur in der anthropologischen Grundlegung seines 'Projekts Weltethos' mit dem unrevidierten Konzept 'Mensch'. Er erhebt zusätzlich ausgerechnet das Prinzip 'Menschlichkeit' zum übergreifenden Kriterium des interreligiösen Dialogs, an dem im übrigen seiner Meinung nach in erster Linie die "religiösen Führer"[19] beteiligt sein sollen: "Sollte es nicht möglich sein, mit Berufung auf die gemeinsame Menschlichkeit aller Menschen ein allgemein-ethisches, ein wahrhaft oekumenisches Grundkriterium zu formulieren, das auf dem Humanum, dem wahrhaft Menschlichen, konkret auf der Menschenwürde und den ihr zugeordneten Grundwerten, beruht?"[20]. Feministische Kritik bestreitet diese Möglichkeit, zumindest solange die androzentrische Parteilichkeit im Begriffsfeld 'Mensch' nicht aufgearbeitet ist. Ich meine, daß ein Theologe, der die "implizite Parteilichkeit"[21] des Konzeptes in der eigenen Kultur nicht reflektiert, schwerlich in der Lage ist, mit Angehörigen anderer Kulturen über Menschlichkeit zu kommunizieren, ohne dabei unbewußt Herrschaft auszuüben.

Im Gegensatz zu Jonas kommt Küng mehrfach – im Jahre 1990 nicht erstaunlich – auf die innovative Rolle der Frauenbewegung zu sprechen[22]: Die Frauenbewegung, die stets innerhalb von Aufzählungen neben anderen 'Alter-

16 Ebd.S. 234.

17 Vgl.ebd.S.235: Jonas verweist auf der Neugeborene, desses "blosses Atmen unwidersprechlich ein Soll an die Umwelt richtet, nämlich: sich seiner auzunehmen", nimmt den Anspruch absoluter Unwidersprechlichkeit jedoch gleich wieder mit dem Hinweis auf kulturelle Praktiken wie das Erstgeburtsopfer oder die Kindesaussetzung zurück. Bezeichnenderweise schreibt er jedoch, dass die Weigerung, sich dem Sägling instinktiv fürsorglich zuzuwenden "mindestens im Falle der Muttern... als Entartung angesehen wird".

18 Ebd. S.8.

19 Hans Küng, a.a.O, S.102 und passim.

20 Ebd. S.119.

21 Silvia Bovenschen a.a.O. S.20.

22 Küng erwähnt die Frauenbewegung mindestens fünfmal (S.22, 41,87,94,117) und zwar immer positiv.

nativ' – Bewegungen (Friedensbewegung, oekumenische Bewegung...) erscheint, macht für ihn einen wichtigen Teil des Paradigmenwechsels hin zu einer gewaltloseren Gesamtkonstellation aus. Der gute Wille, das sogenannte 'Frauenproblem' in die Analyse zu integrieren, ist unverkennbar vorhanden und entspricht dem Stand der meisten 'fortschrittlichen' oekumenischen Dokumente seit den siebziger Jahren.

Küng erwähnt jedoch in seinem ausführlichen Anmerkungsapparat mit Ausnahme von Dorothee Sölle keine Frau[23]. Entsprechend ungenau sind die im Text geäußerten Vorstellungen darüber, was denn nun an der Frauenbewegung eigentlich so innovativ sein soll. Küng spricht ganz allgemein von der "Gleichheit aller Menschen"[24] und davon, daß die "Emanzipation der Frau" in allen Religionen zu einem zentralen Anliegen werde[25]. Er erwähnt außerdem die Notwendigkeit einer "partnerschaftliche(n) Weltordnung"[26] und hofft auf ein "postpatriarchales System"[27]. An einer Stelle erklärt er etwas ausführlicher, wie er sich die durch die Frauenbewegung ausgelösten Veränderungen vorstellt: "weg von den Trennungen zwischen Männern und Frauen in Kirche und Gesellschaft, – weg von der Abwertung und dem Unverständnis für die unverzichtbaren Aufgaben der Frauen, – weg von den ideologisch fixierten Rollen und Stereotypen für Männer und Frauen, – weg von der Weigerung, die den Frauen geschenkten Gaben für das Leben und für die Entscheidungsprozesse der Kirche anzuerkennen"[28].

Zwei Dinge fallen mir auf: Zum einen benutzt Küng mit 'Gleichheit', 'Emanzipation' und 'Partnerschaft' Begriffe, die im Feminismus selbst umstritten sind. Alle drei Begriffe entstammen bürgerlich-liberalem Denken und machen die Befreiung der Frauen in erster Linie an ihren sich verändernden Beziehungen *zum Mann* fest: Frauen sollen gleich werden *wie Männer*, sie sollen sich emanzipieren *von Männern*, und sie sollen in Partnerschaft leben *mit Männern*. Im Feminismus geht es aber je länger je weniger darum, wie Frauen ihr Verhältnis zu Männern verändern wollen, sondern darum, wie sie sich, nachdem ihr 'natürliches Wesen' jahrhundertelang auf die Mann-Bezogenheit reduziert worden ist, in ein Verhältnis zu anderen Frauen setzen wollen. Die These heißt: erst wenn wir die uns aufgedrängte Definition als mann-bezogene Wesen zurückweisen, ist Befreiung zu einer lebensfreundlicheren Ordnung möglich.

Zum zweiten scheint mir, daß Küng, wenn er die Wichtigkeit der Frauen-

23 Küng wirft Soelle hier vor, die habe in ihrem Buch 'Gott-denken' seine theologische Paradigmenanalyse abgeschrieben, "ohne sich freilich, wie es scheint, die notwendige wissenschaftstheoretische Grundliteratur selber angeeignet zu haben". Sie werde deshalb mit ihrem "historisch ungenauen und oberflächlich systematisierenden Schema..der komplexen postmodernen Situation kaum gerecht" (S.179).

24 Ebd. S.93.

25 Ebd. S.117

26 Ebd. S.94.

27 Ebd. S.41.

28 Ebd.S.94

bewegung für ein ökologiebewußtes Weltethos betont, im wesentlichen an Verhaltensänderungen von Männern denkt: er will "Abwertung und Unverständnis" abbauen, sich nicht länger weigern, "die den Frauen geschenkten Gaben... anzuerkennen". Im Feminismus geht es aber je länger je weniger darum, Veränderungen von einem neuartigen Verhalten der Männer zu erwarten als vielmehrdarum, Handlungsfähigkeit von Frauen allererst als solche zu thematisieren. Solange Frauen nämlich als mann-bezogene Wesen definiert sind, ist weibliche Handlungsfähigkeit ein Paradox. Eine wichtige feministisch-ökologische These heißt daher: die Welt verändert sich erst dann, wenn das zur Selbstverständlichkeit gewordene Vorurteil, nur erwachsene Männer seien im strengen Sinne moralfähige und freie Menschen, durchbrochen wird in Richtung auf eine Handlungsfähigkeit aller.

Auch Küng hat, obwohl er, anders als Jonas, die Frauenbewegung ausdrücklich in seine Überlegungen einbezieht, eine Handlungsanweisung für erwachsene Männer, konkret: für die 'Führer' der Weltreligionen, geschrieben. Die Struktur, die mir in seinem und in vielen anderen sogenannt 'fortschrittlichen', aber nicht feministischen Texten begegnet, könnte man als 'liberalistischen Fehlschluß ' bezeichnen: der Autor meint, durch die bloße lobende Erwähnung der Frauenbewegung sei deren Kritik bereits Genüge getan. Unter der fortschrittlich scheinenden Oberfläche lebt aber die alte Ordnung weiter, die die Menschheit in handlungsfähige, rationale und dialogbegabte männliche Wortführer und mann-bezogene Frauen einteilt.

Umweltbekenntnis der Schweizerischen Evangelischen Synode

Stellvertretend für eine große Anzahl ähnlich lautender moderner liturgischer Texte zitiere ich den ersten Artikel eines Bekenntnisses, das für eine Versammlung der 'Schweizerischen Evangelischen Synode' im Mai 1986 von zwei Theologinnen und sieben Theologen formuliert worden ist[29]:

Wir bekennen unsere Schuld.
Uns selbst haben wir zum Maß der Schöpfung gemacht
und Gottes Liebe zu allem, was er schuf, vergessen.
Das Leben der anderen Kreatur haben wir mißachtet,
Lebensräume zerstört
und letzte Grenzen überschritten.
Wir sind dabei, die ganze Erde zu vernichten.
Gott aber, der Schöpfer und Erhalter dieser Erde, zieht seine Hand nicht zurück.
Gegen alle Mächte, die zerstören, bleibt er der Herr über alle Kreatur.
Dafür danken wir.

Das kollektive 'Wir', das hier seine Schuld bekennt, ist offensichtlich die

[29] In Schlussdokumente der Schweizerischen Evangelischen Synode, Heft 6 'Bekennen',S.16/17. Die 'Schweizerische Evangelischen Synode' ist eine inzwischen offiziell abgeschlossene Basisbewegung im Vorfeld des 'GFS' Prozesses, die über mehrere Jahre hinweg immer wieder mit Tagungen, fortschrittlichen politischen Anstössen und Verlautbarungen an die Öffentlichkeit getreten ist.

Gemeinschaft der aktiven Umweltzerstörer. Daß dieses 'Wir' die in der Theologie noch immer übliche Vereinnahmung aus der Perspektive des männlichen Theologen impliziert, verdeutlicht eine Ersatzprobe, die all denjenigen, die das Bekenntnis sprechen sollen, ohne weiß und männlich zu sein, zu empfehlen ist:

> *Wir Kinder bekennen unsere Schuld. Uns selbst haben wir zum Maß der Schöpfung gemacht und Gottes Liebe zu allem, was er schuf, vergessen...etc.*
>
> *Wir Kleinbäuerinnen haben Lebensräume zerstört und letzte Grenzen überschritten. Wir Bäuerinnen sind dabei, die ganze Erde zu vernichten...etc.*
>
> *Wir Hausfrauen haben uns selbst zum Maß der Schöpfung gemacht. Wir haben Lebensräume zerstört und letzte Grenzen überschritten...etc.*

Was für das Selbstbewußtsein der VerfasserInnen zutreffen mag, gerät auf die schiefe Ebene, sobald sich andere Gruppen an die Stelle des 'Wir' setzen. Das Bekenntnis ist aber – wie die meisten herkömmlichen christlichen Bekenntnisse – ausdrücklich als ein *allgemeines* verfaßt, das von Sekretärinnen und Putzfrauen, von Jugendlichen, Alten, menschen mit Behinderungen ebenso gesprochen werden soll wie von erwachsenen, 'gesunden' Pfarrern, Professoren und Managern. 'Wir' sollen uns also laut diesem Schuldbekenntnis als die bösen Herren der Welt verstehen. Als diese Herren, die ihre Bosheit jetzt endlich erkennen, danken wir dem einen guten Herrn für seine gute Herrschaft:

> *Gott aber, der Schöpfer und Erhalter dieser Erde, zieht seine Hand nicht zurück. Gegen alle Mächte, die zerstören, bleibt er der Herr über alle Kreatur. Dafür danken wir.*

Die Anrufung des *einen* Herren gegen die Herren der Welt ist eine theologisch übliche Denkfigur, die hier und da ihren Sinn gehabt haben mag. Heute wird diese Denkfigur als ein androzentrisch-zeitgebundenes Konzept von immer breiteren Kreisen in Frage gestellt[30]. Dem Konzept des 'guten Herren' ist die Beibehaltung der starren Herr-Knecht- bzw. Subjekt-Objekt-Logik inhärent, die auch viele Theologen inzwischen als fatal erkannt haben, deren Existenz in den Texten der *eigenen* Tradition sie aber oft nicht wahrhaben wollen[31]. Wenn Theologie 'ökologisch' werden will, so wird es nicht beim Denken und Glauben solcher Herrscher-Untertan-Verhältnisse bleiben können, und seien sie noch so fürsorglich vorgestellt. Es scheint mir kein aussichtsreiches Unterfangen zu sein, ein von allen negativen Konnotationen - Herrschaft, Gewalt, Kontrolle etc. - befreites Verständnis von 'gutem' Herr-Sein dem entgegensetzen zu wollen, was Theologen als 'unsere' Schuld erkannt zu haben meinen.

---

30 Das sich diese Kritik auch schon in offiziellen oekumenischen Verlautbarungen niederschlägt, beweist z.B. das Schlussdokument der GFS-Weltsammlung von Seoul (5-12. März 1990). In diesem Dokument sind falsche Verallgemeinerungen wie diejenigen im SES-Bekenntnis sehr viel seltener, wenn auch nicht gänzlich verschwunden.

31 Häufig wird die Subjekt-Objekt-spaltung von Theologen als Sündenfall der europäischen Aufklärung betrachtet, dem das theologische Menschenbild dann als vorbildhaft und heilend entgegengesetzt werden kann.

Feministische Ethik und die Oekologiefrage

Die kritische Durchsicht einiger exemplarischer Texte aus dem Bereich herkömmlicher Umweltethik enthüllt einen ziemlich ungebrochenen Androzentrismus dieses Diskurses. Die nichtfeministische 'Oeko-Ethik' versucht, das Problem im Rahmen androzentrischer Denkgewohnheiten zu lösen: der Mensch bleibt der Mann. Und daran ändert auch die Tatsache nichts, daß dieser Mann-Mensch sich schuldbewußt an seine Brust schlägt und wieder einmal alles ganz anders machen will. Gott bleibt der ferne, souveräne, ganz andere gute Herr, der nach Gutdünken strafen oder lieben, schaffen oder zerstören kann.

Das Nachdenken über Ökologie und Ethik muß auf einer anderen, grundsätzlicheren Ebene ansetzen. Meine These, die ich im folgenden im feministisch-ethischen Diskurs verorten werde, lautet: Nur, wer den grundlegenden, alle Lebensäußerungen durchformenden Androzentrismus der christlich-abendländischen Kultur erkennt, hat die Chance, ihn zu überwinden. Und nur wer den Androzentrismus als Denk- und Lebensform hinter sich läßt, ist auf dem Weg zum guten Überleben aller Menschen. Denn wer – vorsätzlich oder naiv – der androzentrischen Ordnung verhaftet bleibt, wird weiterhin die Welt in Subjekt und Objekt, Souverän und Untertan, Kultur und Natur aufspalten. Nur eine Welt, in der der Gegensatz von wertvollem Geist und wertloser *Materie* aufgehoben ist, kann heil werden.

Ein feministischer Konsens

Feministinnen, die am Aufbau eines feministisch-ethischen Diskurses arbeiten, haben sich, so verschieden sie im einzelnen vorgehen mögen, auf einige Grundlagen für ihr Denken geeinigt[32]:

1. Feministische Ethik erkennt, daß ein großer Teil herkömmlicher Ethik androzentrisch ist. Sie setzt sich zum Ziel, androzentrische Strukturen im ethischen Diskurs aufzudecken, zu kritisieren und letztlich zu überwinden. (*Welche* Texte der herkömmlichen Ethik androzentrisch sind, wird anhand von detaillierten Textanalysen entschieden.)
2. Feministische Ethik lehnt die zwei Grundvoraussetzungen ab, auf die androzentrische Ethik baut: (a) Frauen sind, was ihre moralische Kompetenz und ihre Stellung in der Gesellschaft angeht, Männern untergeordnet. (b) Den Schwerpunkt der ethischen Reflexion bildet das Nachdenken über männliches moralisches Verhalten und über moralische Maximen für Männer (wobei die Parteilichkeit zugunsten der Männer sich zumeist hinter dem

---

[32] Alison M. Jaggar,Feminist Ethics: Projects, Problems,Prospects, in: Claudia Card ed. Feminist Ethics, Kansas: The University of Kansas Press 1991, S.78-104, vgl. bes.S.97-100. (Der Aufsatz ist auch erschienen in : Herta Nagl-Docekal, Herlinde Pauer-Studer Hgg, Denken der Geschlechterdifferenz. Neue Fragen und Perspektiven der Feministischen Philosophie, Wien, 1990). Meine Zusammenstellung feministisch-ethischer Konsenspunkte lehnt sich an Alison M. Jaggar an. Jagger schlägt vor, ethisches Denken, das sich ausserhalb dieser Annahmen bewegt, als nichtfeministisches Denken zu bezeichnen.

Konstrukt des zum 'Menschen' universalisierten männlichen Sozialcharakters verbirgt)[33]. Feministische Ethikerinnen setzen diesen androzentrischen Annahmen die Überzeugung entgegen, daß Frauen über eine gleichwertige (aber andersgeartete? hier beginnen die Differenzen) – moralische Kompetenz verfügen, und daß die moralische Erfahrung von Frauen prinzipiell ebenso sorgfältiger Reflexion bedarf wie diejenige der Männer. Feministische Ethik hebt die stillschweigende Voraussetzung, daß nur erwachsene weiße Männer vollgültige moralische Subjekte und mithin die primären Adres-saten moralischer Imperative sind, aus den Angeln. Sie erhebt prinzipiell alle Menschen – und in erster Linie die Unterdrückten – in den Stand des moralisch kompetenten Subjektes.

3. Aus diesen Voraussetzungen ergeben sich Themenbereiche feministischer Ethik: Moralische Praktiken, die Unterdrückung perpetuieren, werden kritisiert. Moralisch angemessene Verhaltensweisen zur Überwindung der Unterdrückung werden konzipiert. Gesellschaftliche Bedingungen, in denen keine Unterdrückung mehr existiert, werden entworfen.
4. Feministische Ethik erkennt nicht nur den konstruierten Gegensatz von Männlichkeit und Weiblichkeit, sondern alle hierarchischen Dualismen, auf denen die androzentrische Ordnung ruht (Geist/Körper, Öffentlich/Privat, Kultur/Natur etc.) und die auf das Mann/Frau-Gegenüberverhältnis abbildbar sind, als unangemessen und sucht sie zu überwinden. Daraus läßt sich ableiten, daß Feministische Ethik sich den Unterteilungen herkömmlicher Ethik in 'Frauenthemen' und 'allgemeine Themen', 'politische Ethik' und 'Sexualethik', 'Sozialethik' und 'Individualethik' etc. widersetzt.
5. Feministische Ethik versteht sich als historische Denkbewegung, nicht als Suche nach der 'ewigen Wahrheit'. Sie betrachtet auch diejenigen Diskurse, die sich selbst zeitenthobene Gültigkeit zuschreiben, als historisch und standortgebunden. Ihr Ziel ist nicht der eine kategorische Imperativ oder die eine wahre Letztbegründung für moralisches Handeln, sondern die konkrete Befreiung konkreter Individuen und Gruppen im Horizont des guten Überlebens in einer lebensfreundlichen Welt.

Feministisch-ethische Rekonstruktion der Oekologiefrage

Auch was die feministische Rekonstruktion des 'Ökologieproblems' angeht, lassen sich, anknüpfend an die allgemeinen Konsenspunkte, Gemeinsamkeiten herausarbeiten:

1. Die Kritik der androzentrischen symbolischen Ordnung und die alltägliche Erfahrung von Frauen mit Gewalt und Kontrolle führen zu dem Schluß, daß ein enger Zusammenhang zwischen verschiedenen Unterdrückungsformen,

[33] Vgl. S.36 dieses Aufsatzes.

hier speziell: zwischen Frauenunterdrückung und Ausbeutung der Natur besteht:[34] Daß Frauen 'der Natur näherstehen als Männer' ist ein Gemeinplatz androzentrischer Ideologie, der z.B. die symbolische und reale Fixierung der Frauen auf soziale Mutterschaft und ihren Ausschluß aus wissenschaftlichen Berufen legitimiert hat. Im Gegenüberverhältnis Mensch/Natur stehen Frauen nicht eindeutig auf der Seite des kontrollierenden und herrschenden menschlichen Subjektes; sie sind tendenziell – wenn auch selten vollkommen und unverstellt – in den Objektbereich hineindefiniert. Herrschaft über Frauen wird also mit ähnlichen Argumenten legitimiert wie Herrschaft über die Natur: beide gelten als unberechenbar, geschichtslos, vernunftlos, blind funktionierend. Das herrschende Denken konstruiert eine Pyramide, deren Spitze der mit dem erwachsenen weißen Mann identifizierte 'vollgültige Mensch' und deren Basis die 'Natur' bildet. Nicht allen Frauen wird in dieser Ordnung *derselbe* Platz zugewiesen, und auch vielen Männern wird das Recht, den Spitzenplatz einzunehmen, abgesprochen. Allerdings gilt für *alle* Frauen und nur für einen *Teil* der Männer, daß sie keinen Zugang zur Position des vollgültigen menschlichen Subjektes haben, das sein Selbstbewußtsein daraus bezieht, *nicht Natur* zu sein.

2. Feministische Ethikerinnen bestreiten nicht einfach die Position der Frauen zwischen 'Mensch' und 'Natur', sondern das dualistische Gegenüberverhältnis *als solches*. Als in den Objektbereich hineindefinierte Subjekte stellen sie jedoch historisch betrachtet und unabhängig davon, wie sie ihre Position neu bestimmen die Frage, wie es zur lebensbedrohlichen Ausbeutung der Natur kommen konnte, von einem anderen Standpunkt aus als Männer. Feministinnen fragen nicht (wie z.B. Hans Jonas oder Hans Küng) nach dem abstrakten Verhältnis 'des Menschen' zu 'der Natur', sondern analysieren das *Herrschaftsgefüge*, das *einigen* Menschen das zweifelhafte Privileg einräumt, die sogenannte Natur zu ihren Zwecken zu benutzen und sie schließlich zu zerstören.

3. Feministische Ethikerinnen haben den fernen, souveränen, beziehungslosen Gott ebenso ad acta gelegt wie die unbestechliche, zeitenthobene, 'objektive' Vernunft. Beide Konzepte, die für die herkömmliche theologisch- bzw. philosophisch-ethische Arbeit als zentral und unverzichtbar gelten, verharren in der androzentrischen Ordnung, indem sie – als dem Männlichen zugeordnete Konzepte – auf ihr 'weibliches', untergeordnetes Gegenüber angewiesen sind. Als intellektuelle Werkzeuge für die Bearbeitung der Ökologieproblematik sind Begriffe, die die androzentrische symbolische

[34] Als Beleg für diese These werden immer wieder dieselben Texte angeführt, die inzwischen eine Art feministisch – wissenschaftskritischen 'Kanon' bilden: Mary Daly, Gyn/Oekologie. Eine Meta-Ethik des Radikalen Feminismus, München, 1980, Francoise D'Eaubonne, Feminismus oder Tod. Thesen zur Ökologiedebatte, München 1975, Evelyn Fox Keller a.a.O, Susan Griffin, Frau und Natur, Frankfurt a. M, 1987, Sandra Harding a.a.O(u.a).

Ordnung bestätigen, statt sie zu dekonstruieren, ungeeignet. Feministische Ethikerinnen arbeiten am Abbau der androzentrischen Ordnung und bemühen sich um eine *andere*, nicht androzentrische Begrifflichkeit. Es gibt jedoch nicht die *eine, richtige* 'Methode' für die dekonstruierende "Arbeit an der symbolischen Ordnung", sondern eine Vielfalt von Überlegungen und diskursiven Praktiken, die sich in diese Richtung bewegen[35].

4. Feministische Ethikerinnen halten *alle* Frauen und Männer für fähig, wirksame Beiträge zur Beendigung der Zerstörung zu leisten. Allerdings erkennen sie die scheinbar allgemeingültigen Imperative androzentrischer 'Öko-Ethik', die ihrer Struktur nach allesamt 'Rücknahme hybrider Herrschafts- und Kontrollansprüche' meinen, als partial: diese Imperative richten sich an 'den Menschen', an erwachsene weiße Männer also. Was Frauen in ihren unterschiedlich gelagerten, von verschiedenen Unterdrückungsformen geprägten Lebensbedingungen tun sollen, legen Frauen aufgrund kontextbezogener herrschaftskritischer Analysen selbst fest.

Mütter und Amazonen

Die Frage, wie denn nun 'Frauen' oder 'die Frau' ökologisch handeln sollen, wird Feministischen Ethikerinnen zwar oft gestellt, sie läßt sich aber nicht beantworten, denn 'die Frau' existiert ebensowenig wie 'der Mensch'. Die Mehrzahl der Ethikerinnen ist inzwischen überzeugt, daß der Versuch, eine allgemeine 'weibliche' moralische Perspektive konstruieren zu wollen, als Reaktion auf androzentrische Ethik zwar verständlich, als Basis für eigenständige ethische Reflexion jedoch untauglich ist. Das moralische Bewußtsein und Handeln der Frauen ist vielfältig, es läßt sich nicht auf eine einzige Perspektive reduzieren[36]. Es ist bezeichnend, daß die zuerst von Carol Gilligan vertretene These, es gebe innerhalb der menschlichen Moral eine "andere Stimme"[37], die (vor allem) von Frauen zu Gehör gebracht und vom androzentrischen Ethik-Diskurs ignoriert werde, zu Diskussionen geführt hat, die letztl in die Erkenntnis der Vielfalt moralischer Stimmen münden. Denn Gilligan hat, indem sie ihre These entwickelte, gleichzeitig drei Dinge getan: sie hat den androzentrischen ethischen Diskurs kritisch herausgefordert, sie hat die Selbstwahrnehmung vieler (nicht aller) Frauen angemessen auf den Begriff gebracht und sie hat – tendenziell – eine bestimmte, privilegierte Lebensform mit *der* weiblichen Perspektive gleichgesetzt. Die zen-

[35] Die "Arbeit an der symbolischen Ordnung ist von der Diotima Philosophinnengruppe zum Programm erhoben worden. Bemühungen um einen schöpferischen Umgang mit der anstehenden dekonstruktiven Arbeit finden sich jedoch überall im feministischen Diskurs. Vgl.z.B. Joyce Treblicot, Ethics of Method. Greasing the Machine and Telling Stories, in : Claudia Card a.a.O., S 45-51. Ruth Ginzberg, Philosophy is not a Luxury, ebd. S.126-145.

[36] Vgl. hierzu Michele M.Moody-Adams, Gender and the Complexity of Moral voices, in Claudia Card, a.a.O., S.195-212.

[37] Carol Gilligan, In a Different Voice. Psychological Theory and Womens' Development, Cambridge, Mass., Harvard University Press 1982. (Deutsch: Die andere Stimme. Lebenskonflikte und Moral der Frau, München 1984).

trale, von Frauen immer wieder gestellte Frage in der Auseinandersetzung mit Gilligans These lautet: Soll ich, wenn ich auf andere, bewußtere Art und Weise handlungsfähig werden will, sogenannt weibliche Eigenschaften *kultivieren* oder soll ich sie *verweigern*? Befürworterinnen des 'Caring' -Ansatzes'[38] Carol Gilligan, Nel Noddings[39], Sara Ruddick[40] u.a., argumentieren, daß die lange in die Privatsphäre eingeschlossene, nicht als ethischer Standpunkt ernstgenommene Mütterlichkeit der Frauen weitreichende, politisch relevante Wirkungen entfaltet, sobald sie aus ihrem Gefängnis befreit und bewußt als ethische Perspektive gestaltet wird. Gegnerinnen, im deutschsprachigen Raum v.a. Christina Thürmer-Rohr[41] und Frigga Haug,[42] in den USA Frauen, die dem Leitbild der Mutter dasjenige der Amazone[43] vorziehen und sich der lesbischen Gemeinschaft mit ihren ethischen Ent-würfen[44] verbunden fühlen, setzen dem vor allem drei Argumente entgegen: (a) Die Ethik der mütterlichen Fürsorge idealisiert mit dem Konzept 'Mütterlichkeit' ein unter den Bedingungen patriarchaler Dominanz entstandenes Verhaltensrepertoire. 'Mütterlichkeit' ist keine eigenständige moralische Perspektive, sondern die abhängige Kehrseite der Männermoral. Die Kultivierung von Mütterlichkeit läuft deshalb Gefahr, repressive Verhaltensformen unreflektiert mitzutransportieren. (b) Mütterlichkeit, wie sie Gilligan, Noddings u.a. beschreiben, ist ein Verhalten, das typisch ist für westliche, weiße Mittelschichtsfrauen. Sie kann deshalb nicht zur 'weiblichen Perspektive schlechthin' stilisiert werden. (c) Wenn Frauen 'Mütter-lichkeit' öffentlich kultivieren, treten sie zwar aus dem Schatten der isolierten Kleinfamilie, sie stellen aber nicht die androzentrische Ordnung *als solche* in Frage, sondern stabilisieren sie noch, indem sie weiterhin das Gegenüberverhältnis Mann/Frau betonen.

Die Gefahr, den aus eigener Erfahrung gewonnenen Standpunkt zum Standpunkt an sich zu verabsolutieren, besteht auch für Frauen. Deshalb ist permanente Kritik innerhalb der feministischen Diskursgemeinschaft wichtig, gerade dann, wenn die traditionellen Lebensbedingungen *privilegierter* Frauen zum Maßstab für alle erhoben werden sollen. Einer Feministischen Ethik, die sich die Befreiung konkreter Individuen und Gruppen im Horizont des guten Überlebens in einer lebensfreundlichen Welt zum Ziel setzt, muß es darum gehen, aus den

38 'Care' oder 'Caring' (Fürsorglichkeit) hat sich zum Schüsselkonzept dieses feministischen- ethischen Teildiskurses entwickelt, der die herkömmliche Rolle der Frauen als Mutter und Forsorgerinnen zum Ausgangspunkt der Reflexion macht.

39 Nel Noddings, Caring. A Feminine Approach to Ethics and Moral Education, Berkeley, University of California Press, 1984.

40 Sara Ruddick, Maternal Thinking, towards a Politics of Peace, Boston, Beacon, 1989, (Deutsch: Mütterliches Denken. für eine Politik der Gewaltlosigkeit, Frankfurt/New York 1993).

41 Christina Thürmer-Rohr, Vagabundinnen. Feministische Essays, Berlin 1987.

42 Frigga Haug, die Moral ist zweigeschlechtlich wie der Mensch. Zur Theorie weiblicher Vergesellschaftung, in; Argument Studienhefte SH 61 'Frauen und Moral', Berlin 1984, S.6-27.

43 Bezeichnenderweise sind Frauen, die sich vom Ideal der Mütterlichkeit ebenso wie von der Lebensform Mutterschaft distanzieren, innerhalb der androzentrischen Ordnung gezwungen, sich der entwürdigenden Negativkategorie 'Nichtmutter' zuzuordnen.

44 Insbesondere die neue Texte von Mary Daly und: Sarah Lucia Hoagland, Lesbian Ethics. Toward New Value, Palo Alto 1988 (Deutsch: Die Revolution der Moral, Berlin 1991).

unterschiedlichen Bedingungen, unter denen Frauen leben, moralisch angemessene Verhaltensweisen zur Überwindung aller Formen von Unterdrückung und Zerstörung zu entwickeln. *Nicht alle* Frauen sollen und können mütterlich sein, *nicht alle* Frauen sollen und können sich am Leitbild der Amazone orientieren.

Ich meine, daß z.B. der Ansatz Sara Ruddicks, das "mütterliche Denken" als *eine*, von Frauen und Männern wählbare moralische Perspektive zu konzipieren, zukunftsweisend ist.[45]. Die Perspektive Mütterlichkeit wird hier nicht an ein Geschlecht, sondern an *eine bestimmte* Praxis, nämlich die alltägliche Verantwortungsübernahme für Kinder, gebunden. Sie läßt sich ausbauen zu *einer möglichen* friedens- und ökologiepolitischen Perspektive, die nicht beansprucht, *die weibliche* oder - im Sinne des Slogans 'Die Zukunft ist weiblich' – gar die einzig zukunftsweisende zu sein. Die bewußte Kultivierung mütterlicher Eigenschaften kann neben der amazonischen Lebensform – und vielen anderen – bestehen. Sie kann Elemente aus ihr übernehmen, wenn z.B. Mütterlichkeit bestimmten Zielgruppen (Ehemännern) gegenüber verweigert, anderen (z.B. jüngeren Frauen) gegenüber[46] kultiviert wird. Verschiedene moralische Perspektiven, die sich am guten Überleben in einer lebensfreundlichen Welt orientieren und als Denkweisen aus *begrenzten* Praxisformen hervorgehen, können in einen Dialog zueinander treten. Dieser Dialog hat begonnen, wo Frauen einander geduldig und verbunden durch das gemeinsame Engagement für eine lebensfreundliche Welt, ihre manchmal ähnlichen, manchmal sehr verschiedenen Geschichten erzählen:

> *Stories, even if 'about' only one person, have implications for others as well. A story that makes sense of part of a woman's life includes accounts – 'analyses' – of how she is connected to people and practices and institutions around her – and there are lots of general claims in that. So, one might say, feminism reconstructs the concept of theory as an account of reality that does not move either inductively or deductively between the general and the particular but, rather, sites the general in the particular. Someone trained in philosophy might say something like that*[47].

Noch immer fällt mein Blick, wenn er vom Bildschirm abschweift, auf gift- und saftgrüne voralpine Wiesen. Was hat es gebracht, den akademischen Zugang zur Ökologieproblematik zu wählen und einen Text zu schreiben? In der Zeit, in der ich diesen Aufsatz geschrieben habe, hätte ich meinen Biogarten pflegen, einen Solarkocher bauen oder an einer Greenpeace-Aktion gegen die Freisetzung gentechnologisch Nutzpflanzen teilnehmen können. Ich hätte auch schlafen oder Musik hören können. Ich habe aber einen Text geschrieben und dazu einen Computer benutzt, der viel Energie braucht und später, als Abfall, Erde, Wasser

---

[45] Sara Ruddick a.a.O. Mir scheint zwar, dass Ruddick stellenweise in eine ontologisierende Redeweise zurückfällt. Die Gesamtanlage ihres Textes läuft aber darauf hinaus, die Ineinssetzung von 'müttlicher' mit 'weiblicher' perspektive ausdrücklick zurückweisen.

[46] Dabei ist jedoch zu beachten, dass das Konzept 'Mütterlichkeit' haufig repressive Verhaltensformen in sich birgt. Vgl. dazu die Diskussion um das Konzept 'Affidamento' anschliessend an : Libreria delle donne di Milano, Wie weibliche Freiheit ensteht: Eine neue politische Praxis, Berlin, 1988. Vgl. auch : Sarah Lucia Hoagland, Some Thoughts about 'Caring', in Claudia Card a.a.O., S.246-263.

[47] Joyce Treblicot, Ethics of Method. Greasing the Machine and Telling Stories, in Claudia Card a.a.O., S. 45-51, S.49.

und Atemluft belasten wird. Wenn ich einen Aufsatz zur Feministischen Ethik schreibe, rette ich die Welt nicht. Wenn ich einen Biogarten pflege, auch nicht. Was bleibt, ist: dasjenige tun, das hier und jetzt meine Sache ist. Frauen neigen dazu, die ganze Welt retten zu wollen, und, wenn ihnen das nicht gelingt, sich in kultivierte Ohnmacht zurückzuziehen. Sich auf dasjenige zu beschränken, das jetzt meine Möglichkeit ist, ohne den Blick aufs Ganze loszulassen und ohne an ihm zu verzweifeln, das könnte ein 'Imperativ' Feministischer Ethik werden.

Summary

The "ecology-ethic", strenuously promoted for some years by male philosophers and theologians, is largely androcentric, as shown by the analysis of three key texts (Hans Jonas, Hans Küng and a modern confessional text). Feminist discourse offers clear alternatives: rather than as a search for "eternal truth", ethics are now to be seen as a historically relative, environmentally-conscious discourse, which addresses the variety of womens' everyday experience, and is to be seen as working to evaluate and deconstruct the androcentric order. A consensus is developing that "woman" cannot be the subject of feminist ethics. Rather, it is the *heterogeneousness* of women which makes specific contributions to the planetary survival and well-being of us all. In particular, this article recognizes work done by the group of women philosophers 'Diotima' and by the contemporary American discussion group (Card, Gilligan, Hoagland, Jaggar, inter alia) and relates them to each other.

Sommaire

L'éthique écologique, que des philosophes et théologiens de sexe masculin épousent avec ardeur depuis quelques années, est pour la plupart androcentrique, comme le montre l'analyse de trois textes-clé (Hans Jonas, Hans Küng, et un texte confessionnel moderne). Il y a dans la discours féministe des alternatives précises: l'éthique se présente maintenant, non comme la recherche d'une vérité "humaine" éternelle, mais comme un discours exprimant une conscience de l'environnement et ayant lieu dans l'histoire. Elle s'adresse à la variété de l'expérience quotidienne des femmes et vise à évaluer et à déconstruire l'ordre androcentrique. L'idée que la femme en tant qu'individu ne peut être le sujet d'une éthique féministe devient de plus en plus le point de vue répandu. C'est plutôt l'hétérogénéité des femmes qui fait des contributions spécifiques à la survie et au bien-être de tous nous. En particulier, cet article fait connaître des textes produits par le groupe de philosophes-femmes 'Diotima' et par le groupe de discussion de la culture américaine contemporaine (Card, Gilligan, Hoagland, Jaggar et autres), les rapprochant les uns des autres.

Ina Praetorius Dr.theol. Studium der Germanistik und ev. Theologie in Tübingen, Zürich und Heidelberg. 1983-1987 Assistentin am Institut fur Sozial-ethik der Universität Zürich, seit 1987 freischaffend als Autorin, Lehrbeauftragte, Erwachsenenbilderin, Hausfrau und Mutter. Wohnhaft in Krinau/Toggenburg, Schweiz.

Elizabeth E Green

The Transmutation of Theology: Ecofeminist Alchemy and the Christian Tradition

Introduction

Who has never succumbed to the fascination which the alchemist, buried within the collective unconscious, exerts upon us? Among her crucibles and alembics those early chemists melted, separated and distilled seeking to achieve the ultimate transmutation, gold. It seems that we are engaged in a task not unlike our foremothers' but, rather than trafficking in metals and chemical vapours we experiment with the symbols, metaphors and concepts that ecology, feminism and theology provide[1].

Yet whoever approaches this particular laboratory will be daunted, if not overcome, by the task at hand. For here hissing and bubbling are not three diverse yet simple elements: ecology, feminism and theology, but many compound substances: the various expressions of feminist theology, ecotheology and, on occasion, ecofeminist theology[2]. The latter unites a feminist theology's hermeneutic of suspicion with ecology's critique of Christianity[3]. Starting from the feminist analysis of binary oppositions, it constructs a holistic perspective of beings in relation[4]. The meeting of feminism, ecology and theology is a highly complex thought experiment calling for a broad competency and uncommon powers of transmutation of which this particular alchemist has, if at all, only a very modest share. It aims at no less than the transmutation of patriarchal theology into a theology which is at the same time Christian, feminist and ecological. By drawing on the work of Sallie McFague, Mary Grey, Anne Primavesi, Rosemary Ruether and Dorothy Soelle, I will show how ecofeminist theology endeavours to reshape the whole complex of relationships between God and the world, humanity and

---

1 On women alchemists see Margaret Alic, *Hypatia's Heritage: A History of Women in Science from Antiquity to the Late Nineteenth Century*, London: Women's Press (1986) 35-41, 59-61, 95-100.

2 In feminism I am thinking of liberal, socialist and romantic; in theology of orthodox, liberal and liberation; in ecology of shallow, deep and comunitarian. Cf. Rosemary Radford Ruether, *Sexism and God-Talk: Towards a Feminist Theology*, London: SCM 1983, 41-45; Dorothy Soelle, *Thinking about God: An Introduction to Theology*, London: SCM (1990); Rex Ambler, **Global Crisis,** *Theology in Green,* 3 (1992), 16-18

3 Anne Primavesi, *From Apocalypse to Genesis: Ecology, Feminism & Christianity*, Tunbridge Wells, Burns & Oates (1991) 17. For the ecological critique cf. Lynn White's original formulation **The Religious Roots of our Ecological Crisis,** *Science*, 155 (1967) 1203-1207.

4 Dorothy Soelle, *To Work and To Love: A Theology of Creation*, Philadelphia: Fortress (1984) 24; Primavesi, op. cit., 19-23 and Sallie McFague, Models of God: Theology for an Ecological Nuclear Age, London: SCM (1987) 6-13.

nature. After a survey of some emerging trends I shall locate and briefly discuss the theological issues at stake.

Emerging Trends in an Ecofeminist Theology of Creation, the Human and the End

The traditional view of a male sovereign "God, the Father, almighty" bringing creation into being by divine fiat is, for some feminist theologians, the quintessence of what is wrong with the God-world relationship[5]. The monarchical model of God has, according to McFague, "three major flaws": "God is distant from the world, relates only to the human world, and controls that world through domination and benevolence"[6]. He is, we might also add, male. Indeed, for Ruether such a concept of God is a projection of masculine desire for absolute autonomy, transcendence and infinity[7]. Convinced that the notion of divine freedom, aseity and self-sufficiency vis à vis the world do not reflect the love and vulnerability God showed the world in Jesus, ecofeminist theology conceives God as more immanent to the world's processes. Mutuality replaces dominance and submission in the God-world relationship, while female symbols and metaphors, as well as ones taken from the world of nature become vehicles of the divine. Process theology's idea of a di-polar God, in constant interaction with the dynamic evolutionary processes of the human and non-human world, who lures and persuades rather than commands and coerces, reflects the same holistic understanding of reality. Yet, while open to the insights which process thought offers, ecofeminist theologians have preferred the enfleshed language of metaphor to the abstract **logoi** of metaphysics[8].

One such metaphor describes God's relation to the world as analogous to a person's relation to her body: the world is God's body. This brings God right into the world without reducing her to it and enables us to see God relating "from within" to all forms of human and non human life. This model is understood as an expression of the Christian doctrines of creation, incarnation and resurrection[9]. McFague stresses that such a metaphor must be completed by the use of "personal agential metaphors" for God such as the trinitarian model of mother, lover and friend. In this model God the mother gives birth to her body, the world: "The universe is bodied forth from God. It is from the 'womb' of

5 Ruether, *Liberation Theology*, ch. 8; *Sexism and God-Talk*, 54f.; *Gaia and God: An Ecofeminist Theology of Earth Healing*, New York: Harper Collins (1992) 83; Primavesi, op. cit., 202.

6 McFague, op. cit., 65.

7 *Liberation Theology*, ch. 8

8 Ruether, *Gaia and God*, 246f. Soelle, op. cit., 25f.; Primavesi, op. cit.,109; Mary Grey, *Redeeming the Dream: Feminism, Redemption and Christian Tradition*, London: SPCK (1989) 34ff.

9 McFague, op. cit., 69-78. Grace Jantzen, *God's World, God's Body*, London: Darton, Longman & Todd (1984) provides the philosophical underpinnings for this metaphor which is also adopted by Catherine Halkes, *New Creation: Christian Feminism and the Renewal of the Earth*, London: SPCK (1991) 152ff. Unfortunately, McFague's most recent book: *The Body of God: An Ecological Theology*, London: SCM (1993), appeared too late to be included in this study.

God, formed through 'gestation'"[10]. Ruether's concept of God/ess as "Primal Matrix" and Grey's contention that "creation is first of all about God giving birth to myriad forms of mutuality" tend to move in the same direction[11].

Restoring sacrality to nature would act, according to ecotheology, as powerful barrier to its exploitation. Some feminist theologians claim that women are in a special position to recapture and give words to humans' closeness to nature (and to the divine). Carefully steering their way between a simple identification of women with static immanence (Nature) or masculine transcendence (Culture), Grey and Ruether argue that women are vulnerable and open "to admit and welcome the sacredness of the earth as humanity's true home"[12]. Nature becomes "the place of encounter with divine"[13]; the interconnectedness of all natural processes (ecology) reveals the relational nature of God. The American Indian tradition has helped shape this viewpoint, but so has Christian sacramental theology. The world as God's body becomes "the basis for a revived sacramentalism, that is, a perception of the divine as visible, as present, as palpably present in our world"[14]. Without recourse to the God's body metaphor, Ruether also sees the cosmos as "the mediating context of all theological definition and spiritual experience[15]. The natural organic and inorganic world is thus imbued with an intrinsic value of its own[16]. If the human no longer bears a privileged relation to God or to the rest of creation, how does ecofeminism envisage theological anthropology? The broad consensus achieved by ecofeminist theology tends to disappear in the area of anthropology. Ecofeminism is concerned to overcome the spirit/matter dualism that has plagued the Western view of man. According to a holistic paradigm, spirit and matter are on a continuum. Ruether, inspired by Teilhard's vision, writes:

> *When we proceed to the inward depths of consciousness or probe beneath the surface of visible things... the visible disappears. Matter itself dissolves into energy. Energy, organized in patterns and relationships, is the basis for what we experience as visible things* [17].

If ecofeminist theology stresses the "spiritual" element in all beings, it also emphasises the bodily nature or "dust factor" of human existence. In fact the metaphor "God's world, God's body" depends on the view that embodiment is intrinsic to personhood[18]. Whatever approach is taken, humanity's affinity with

---

10 McFague, op. cit., 110. Carter Heyward has given poetic expression to this thought in her **Blessing the Bread Litany**, cited in Grey, op. cit., 140.

11 Ibid., 138ff. Cf. also **Does Christianity Need the Goddess?"** *Theology in Green* 6 (1993) 8 ; Ruether, *Sexism and God-Talk*, 70, 257

12 Grey, *Redeeming the Dream*, 48, and **Does Christianity Need the Goddess?"** 9; Ruether, *Sexism and God-Talk*, 70; *Gaia and God*, 254

13 Primavesi, op. cit., 157. Cf. McFague, op. cit., 185.

14 McFague, op. cit., 77; Cf. Soelle, op. cit., 3, 17f

15 *Gaia and God*, 229.

16 Primavesi, op. cit., 152

17 *Sexism and God-Talk*, 86; cf. *Gaia and God*, 247s.

18 Ibid., 87; McFague, op. cit., 11; Soelle, 29; Jantzen, op. cit., 67ff.; Primavesi, op. cit., 205f

the rest of creation is underlined; human being is grounded in and supported by the whole ecological community[19].

The ecological critique of Christianity points to its anthropocentrism, which feminist theology correctly names androcentrism. Science, technology and Christian theology are for the most part products of the universal male subject. As ecofeminist theology calls that subject into question, diverse positions on the equivalence-difference issue emerge[20]. While all ecofeminist theologians agree in positing as their starting point a special relationship between women and nature, they disagree on the nature of that relationship. However, they all envisage a renewed male/female relationship in terms of reciprocity and mutuality which would have profound effects on the social order undermining the public/private split on which the present free market economy, is structured[21].

If ecofeminist theology seeks to maintain a continuity between all forms of life, how then does it conceive the imago Dei traditionally used to express the specificity of the human? Ruether situates the imago in human intelligence or self consciousness, a product of the evolutionary process which brings with it freedom: the choice we make for or against the well-being of creation. "We alone can sin" and invert the evolutionary process[22]. In Primavesi's reading of Genesis, human self awareness was gained from God through Eve's action. Once this is seen in a positive light, the whole Fall/Redemption schema - considered anthropocentric - breaks down. Sin now becomes "a choice made in favour of or in rejection of one's fellow earth creatures"[23]. Ruether concludes: "The biblical concept of humans as the 'image of God', into whose hands care of nature is given, assumes a more profoundly ethical meaning"[24].

For ecofeminist theology, human responsibility means actively participating in God's continuing creation by mending our broken relations to the earth, to each other and to God, that is, redemption through justice[25]. In fact, for Soelle: "The more a person develops her creativity, delves into the project of liberation and transcends her own limitations, the more God is God"[26]. The ecological paradigm would seem to suggest, however, that we need rather "a new culture of acceptance of finitude and limits"[27]. This apparent contradiction paradoxically

---

19 Ruether, Sexism and God-Talk, 87; Primavesi, op. cit., 232f

20 Ruether and Halkes maintain that psychological and social differentiation with their corresponding gender stereotypes are the results of culture and socialization. Primavesi agrees that the connection between women and Nature is provided by the concept of the Other, yet maintains that a biological link exists between them. Grey, on the other hand, recognizes that we "need to establish a range of human qualities exhibited by both men and women" and yet, because women and men have "vastly different experiences... these lead to disparate understandings of their own identity", op. cit., 23f

21 Primavesi, op. cit., 49-54; Ruether, *New Woman*, 204-210; *Gaia and God*, 258-268.

22 *Sexism and God-Talk*, 88. Cf. McFague, op. cit., 77.

23 Op. cit., 233, 235. Cf. Soelle, op. cit., 75ff.

24 Ruether, *Gaia and God*, 222. Cf. Mc Fague, op. cit., 76.

25 Grey, op. cit., 34f

26 Soelle, op. cit., 39f

27 Ruether, *To Change the World: Christology and Cultural Criticism*, London: SCM (1981) 66

disappears in ecofeminist theology's treatment of the end.

Ecofeminist theologians argue that, as spirit and matter are indissolubly conjoined, so are history and nature. In fact not only does nature, through evolution, have a history, but evolution itself is advanced through human history which is, if we accept the Gaia hypothesis, a part of nature anyway[28]! The Hebrew scriptures reveal that the natural world suffered because of Israel's infidelity to the covenant, but was to be renewed in the messianic reign. Christian theology, however, has privatized the message of biblical apocalyptic, by separating humankind from the earth and projecting future hope into another world. Christians have withdrawn from justice seeking instead of working for the reconciliation of humanity and nature[29]. To achieve this, the linear time of history must be reconciled with the cyclical time of nature. This does not just mean becoming more aware of our body rhythms and living in harmony with the cosmos. For Ruether, building on the biblical Jubilee tradition, it signifies interrupting the linear view of time with repeated "conversions to the centre": the Shalom of God[30]. There is thus no ultimate consummation of the reconciliation process:

> *This concept of social change as conversion back to the centre, rather than to a beginning or end point in history, seems to me a model of change that is more in keeping with temporal existence, rather than subjecting it to the tyranny of impossible expectations* [31].

It also means that humans must reconcile themselves to their own limits, that is, death. The desire for individual immortality is considered a male prerogative, part of that mindset which, in its pursuit of transcendence, is responsible for the destruction of the planet. Death is a part of nature and is to be accepted. "Death has its moment in the circuit of each life" writes Primavesi who, together with Ruether, severs the link between death and sin[32]. As Ruether explains:

> *Our existence as individuated ego/organism (...) dissolves back into the cosmic matrix of matter/energy, from which new centres of individuation arise. It is this matrix, rather than our individuated centres of being, that is "everlasting", that subsists beneath the coming to be and passing away of individuated beings and even planetary worlds. Acceptance of death, then, is the acceptance of the finitude of our individuated centres of being, but also our identification with the larger matrix as our total self that contains us all* [33].

Through our death, then, we actually bring others into existence and achieve the supreme form of relationality.

---

28 Ruether, *Sexism and God-Talk*, 86; Primavesi, *Gaia and God*", Ursula King (ed.), *Liberating Women: New Theological Directions*, University of Bristol (1991) 95.

29 Primavesi, *From Apocalypse to Genesis*, 68ff., 77; Ruether, **The Biblical Vision of the Ecological Crisis**, *Christian Century* 95 (1978) 1129-1132; Soelle, op. cit., 81, 163.

30 *To Change the World*, 69: "The return to harmony in the covenant of creation us not a matter of a cyclical return to the same, for each new achievement of workable balances is different, based on new environments and technologies. It is a historical project that has to be undertaken again and again in changing circumstances".

31 Ibid. The prior rejection of creatio ex nihilo and the positing of the world as God's body means that just as the world has no temporal beginning, neither will it have a telos. For a detailed discussion: Jantzen, op. cit., 130-145.

32 *From Apocalypse to Genesis*, 244; cf. Ruether, *Sexism and God-Talk*, 235s; *Gaia and God*, 128, 141.

33 *Sexism and God-Talk*, 257; *Gaia and God*, 253. Cf. Soelle, op. cit., 162.

Promises and Problems of Ecofeminist Theology

Like the authors I have been considering, I am committed to a theology which incorporates both a feminist and an ecological consciousness, yet I do not think that the Christian tradition is as ecologically bankrupt as some ecofeminist theologians implicitly assume[34].

I am, therefore, a little uneasy about some trends which are emerging in current ecofeminist theology. My critical comments aim to contribute to the ongoing task of the transmutation of theology so that it is feminist, ecological and also Christian. I shall thus point to those aspects of ecofeminist theology which, to my mind, are pregnant with promise while as well as those areas that appear more problematic.

My thesis is that ecofeminist theology presents two different (and so far incompatible) understandings of reality which can be termed, for sake of convenience, cosmocentrism (or perhaps biocentrism) and anthropocentrism. While its protology and eschatology reflect a cosmocentric world view thus overcoming humanocentrism, its anthropology remains (understandably enough) anthropocentric[35]. These two schemes, present in varying degrees in all the theologians I have surveyed, lead to some contradictory conclusions and, I suggest, reveal the weakness of their starting point.

Feminist, political and ecotheologies have pushed a renewed appreciation for a non-hierarchical vision of the Trinity to the forefront of current theological debate[36]. The trinitarian understanding of God is important for ecofeminist theology in that it posits a dynamic relationality right in the heart of the Godhead replacing the vertical relation of dominance and submission with one of circularity and mutuality. Yet if "the Trinitarian society is not just a critical tool for 'us' to use on 'them' but also a critical tool for us to use upon ourselves", then we should expect it to point up some weaknesses in ecofeminist theology[37]. One such weakness concerns the role of the Spirit. Ecofeminist theology often speaks of the Spirit's presence in the world but does not clarify her relationship to the biomorphic spirit which Ruether and Primavesi, for example, individuate in every form of existence[38]. Whereas Christianity has always been careful to distinguish between God and the world and thus safeguard their distinct ontological reality, it is not clear to me how some expressions of ecofeminism, their allegiance to panentheism notwithstanding, actually avoid pantheism, the iden-

34 Despite a difference in terminology, I am in fundamental agreement with Margaret Atkins, **Green Theology: Some Methodological Reflections**, *Theology in Green* 6 (1993) 26-32.

35 I first developed this thesis in relation to Ruether's work in **Hacia una escatología ecólogica y feminista**, Studium Ovetense 18 (1990) 150.

36 Jürgen Moltmann, *Gott in der Schöpfung: ` Oekolgische Schöpfungslehre*, Munich: Chr. Kaiser (1985); Mary Grey, **The Core of Our Desire: Re-imaging the Trinity**, *Theology* 93 (1990) 363-372.

37 Jane Williams, **The Doctrine of the Trinity: A Way Forward for Feminists**, Teresa Elwes, *Women's Voices: Essays in Contemporary Feminist Theology*, London: Marshall & Pickering (1992) 43.

38 *From Apocalypse to Genesis*, 259; Ruether, *Gaia and God*, 227.

tification of nature with God which ultimately deprives us of both God and the world[39]. The question I am raising concerns the status of nature in ecofeminist theology. For Ruether, nature and God actually meet[40]. Yet, by offering us a "revived sacramentalism", ecofeminist theology falls prey to a contradiction. To put it bluntly, sacramentalism "works" only when nature is not considered divine. As John Zizioulas notes:

> *In Christian Cosmology the world is contingent and contains in itself no guarantee of survival except in so far as it is in communion with what is not world by nature - not what is part of nature - namely God as understood in the bible*[41].

Drawing on his Orthodox tradition, Zizioulas suggests that liturgy effects this communion by opening nature up to transcendence. Christianity has traditionally maintained that God herself has established the distinction between divine reality and the world; the Spirit informs, transforms and finally transfigures creation[42].

The question of God's immanence and transcendence re-emerges in the creation-as-birth metaphors favoured by ecofeminist theology. It is not insignificant that the scriptural witness, tends to modify this metaphor[43]. Ecofeminist theology is aware of the problems it raises. McFague asks: "Is this creation, then God's child or God's body? The model of creation as birth of the universe from God wavers at this point"[44], and, Jantzen actually rejects the notion for implying a concept of God which is still far too transcendent[45]. This does not mean that there is no room for powerful birth symbolism in an ecofeminist theology but female symbolism for God (required theologically) does not necessarily lead us to speak of creation in terms of birth[46]. Creation by the word can be a source of empowerment to women in naming ourselves and our world as well as a symbol of female transcendence[47].

---

39 For the discussion: Karl Rahner, *Grundkurs des Glaubens*, Freiburg: Herder (1977) ch. 2 r 2; Jantzen, op. cit.,122-130, 144-154; John Polkinghorne, *Science and Creation: The Search for Understanding*, London: SPCK (1988) ch 4; Pierre Gisel, *La Création*, Geneva: Labor et Fides (1980), ch. 3.

40 *Gaia and God*, 249:'What we have traditionally called "God", the "mind" or rational patterns holding all things together, and what we have called "matter", the "ground" of physical objects, come together. The disintegration of the many infinitely small "bits", and the "One", or unifying whole that connect all things together, coincide'.

41 John Zizioulas, **Preserving God's Creation (1)**, *Theology in Green* 5 (1993) 21.

42 Moltmann, op. cit Ch. 1 §5: "The presence of the divine Spirit must be further differentiated theologically; for we have to distinguish between his cosmic, his reconciling and his redeeming indwelling". Cf. J. Auer, *El Mundo, Creación de Dios*, Barcelona: Herder (1979) 99, 108.

43 Claus Westermann, *Schöpfung*, Stuttgart: Kreuz Verlag (1971) ch. 2 §1 but see Leo Perdue, *Wisdom in Revolt: Metaphorical Theology and The Book of Job*, Sheffield: Almond (1991) 32-38

44 McFague, op. cit., 111.

45 Later she writes: "There is still all the difference between formation and generation, creation and begetting. The universe may be understood as God's body, but the Son must be understood as in some sense God's person" (op. cit., 141)

46 Thus Paul K. Jewett, *God, Creation and Revelation*, Grand Rapids: Eerdmans (1991) 444. Ruether issues an important warning about overdoing the maternal symbolic, asking "whether elements of male resentment are not built into the matricentric pattern", *Gaia and God*, 169. I am still unsure that she herself overcomes the problem, ibid, 254s.

47 For this proposal see my **Women's Words: Sexual Difference and Biblical Hermeneutics** forthcoming in *Feminist Theology*.

In ecofeminist theology, humans have an important part to play in creating and preserving ecological integrity. By placing ecological responsibilities within God's covenant with humanity[48] it allows us to name sexism, classism and ecological destruction sin, and makes a powerful call for us to assume our responsibility to the human and non human community in an ethics of partnership. This strength depends, however, on an emphasis on the human; it is in fact Primavesi's critique of Christianity's humanocentrism (and here she is more consistent than the other theologians we are considering) which leads her to underplay the category of sin. Ecofeminist theology finds itself in a somewhat peculiar position. Its commitment to the liberation of women means it stresses the notion of women as imago Dei, but its commitment to ecological integrity means it seeks to avoid that anthropocentrism which the imago dei has traditionally grounded. If women's freedom means transcending the structures of patriarchy, this might be construed as clashing with the limits ecological integrity imposes. Similarly, if ecological integrity means maintaining our niche in the immanent processes of nature, this could be understood as dashing women's hope for freedom. Part of the problem is that when ecofeminist theology addresses the relationship of women to nature it does so in precisely those terms used to describe the inter human relationship: mutuality. This unresolved tension comes to the fore in its eschatology. If ecofeminism wavers uneasily between cosmocentrism and anthropocentrism, in its eschatology the former definitely gains the upper hand. The many - humans, animals, plants - are absorbed into the one God-world which knows no end. This vision has, however, serious consequences for the entire enterprise[49]. Concerning individual eschatology, human beings are deprived of their grounding in the future of God. Bodiliness, an exceptionally important category for ecofeminist theology, actually has no future. The potentialities released by our death go into a sort of giant lucky dip from which the world now takes its pick. The same fate also awaits personhood. As ecofeminist theology has so well argued, the idea of a body-less person is absurd. Yet this is precisely the final vision we are offered: the selfhood women have strived to gain, and in which feminist theology has played a vital part, is actually renounced in favour of that "total self that contains us all"[50]. Finally, the community of liberated women and men living in relationships of mutuality is absorbed into the One. By cosmologizing the resurrection in this way, ecofeminist theology is inadequate to women's basic longings for a reconciled corporeity, true selfhood and a just community. I would like to

---

[48] Ruether has dedicated a chapter of *Gaia and God* to the covenantal tradition yet fails to integrate it sufficiently into the sacramental tradition thus reproducing the aporia I have detected in her previous thought. Cf. p. 24 n. 1

[49] For what follows see Elizabeth Green, **Hacia una escatología ecológica y feminista**, 132-150. For the essentially non-Christian nature of this thought see Laura Marchetti, **Apparizioni di Una Dea**, Laura Marchetti and Peter Zeller (eds.), *La Madre, il Gioco, la Terra*, Bari: Laterza (1992), 13-46

[50] Ruether, *Sexism and God-Talk*, 257. Unfortunately *Gaia and God* reproduces the same inner contradiction, cf. 251s.

suggest that an ecofeminist reading of the resurrection is called for[51]. Indeed, the Christian view of resurrection, far removed from the Greek idea of immortality, actually requires us to grant ultimate worth to bodily reality and the limits this imposes. By grounding the specificity or personhood of the individual, it enables and preserves true (eschatological) community. This seems better news for women than the prospect of merging with the whole, a characterization all too familiar within the patriarchal construct.

While ecofeminist theology seems to privilege the cosmos in detriment to the human, such privilege is actually illusory as the world's processes know no final consummation. Great weight is placed on the part humans play in the ongoing creative and redemptive task, but we have no assurance that God's redemptive purpose for all creation will be fulfilled. This means that the choices we are called to make concerning our fellow creatures do not ultimately count, and the human and non-human victims of ecological destruction never experience ultimate vindication. Political theology reminds us of the importance of apocalyptic's message for keeping alive the memory and guaranteeing the future of the victims[52]. Ecofeminist theology makes a vital contribution in including amongst those victims the whole ecological community. Yet it then seems to abandon the project half-way, for by indefinitely postponing the telos of the divine economy not only are ecological destruction and economic injustice (sin) never finally overcome, but a world view is proposed which sees the future as just more of the same. This is not the hopeful message ecofeminist theology purports to proclaim and may indeed be particularly conducive to the technoscientific development it so deplores[53].

Conclusion

It is time then to leave the workshop where we have witnessed, at times fascinated at times disturbed, the transmutation of theology. The experiment, far from complete, requires that we adjust a test tube here, an alembic there, and add more elements to our crucible. Ecofeminist theology starts from the association of women with nature, however that is interpreted. Nearly two decades ago Ruether wrote:

> *Since women in Western culture have been traditionally identified with nature, and nature in turn has been seen as an object of domination by man (males), it would seem almost a truism that the mentality that regarded the natural environment as an object of domination drew upon imagery and attitudes based on male domination of women*[54].

---

51 For a first step in this direction see my **Nato da Donna**, *SAE, Chi dite che io sia? Gesu Interpella a l'Ecumenismo e il Dialogo Interreligioso*, Roma Dehoniane (1992), 165-170

52 Johann Baptist Metz, *Glaube in Geschichte und Gesellschaft*, Magunz: Matthias Grünwald (1977) ch. 6; cf Nash, op. cit., 129-133; Atkins, op. cit.,31.

53 Metz, Op. cit., ch. 10

54 *New Woman*, 186

Yet by choosing the same starting point, ecofeminist theology inadvertently tends not only to reproduce the stereotyping of the patriarchal symbolic order, but also to distance itself from a specifically Christian position. In its rereading of the distorted dualisms ecofeminist theology has almost consistently privileged the "feminine" pole now - as locus of the divine - seen in an exclusively positive way[55].

I suggest that ecofeminist theology needs to theorize more adequately its starting point: the relationship between women and nature. Does femaleness unite women above and beyond class, racial and ethnic differences so that the connection of women to nature postulated by some is valid for all? And is that connection to nature experienced in the same way regardless of race and class? Further analysis may suggest not. An anthropology, however, which by conceptualizing "connection in difference" attempts to take difference seriously, can perhaps help us overcome those systems which can only guarantee identity through opposition (the distorted dualisms of patriarchy) or uniformity (the God-female-nature continuum of ecofeminism). In fact the time may well have come for us to abandon the analysis of dualisms which has served us well but seems unable to further our constructive task. In other words I am suggesting that we need to develop a way of holding equivalence, difference and differences together. A trinitarian theology, designed to think unity in diversity may be the answer ecofeminism needs if it is to overcome the aporia which an examination of its doctrine of creation, the human and the end has evidenced.

---

[55] Thus it is not surprising that male ecotheologians such a Moltmann, Boff, McDonagh and Carmody continue to reproduce those stereotypes that feminist theologians once denounced, and that feminist theologians such as Ruether and Grey come close to the Goddess spirituality of which they have, in some cases, been critical.

Zusammenfassung

Die öko-feministische Theologie ist karakterisiert mit zwei verschiedene Verständnissen der Realität: Cosmocentrisme und Antropocentrisme. Das bringt es zu verschiedenartigen Folgen die öffenbar sind in derer Eschatologie, die die Schwäche ihres Anfangs enthüllt: die Vereinigung der Frauen mit der Natur im Hinblicke auf den Widerstand der patriarcalische sinnbildliche Ordnung. Nach einem überblick der Behandlung von Gott vom Standpunkt der Öko-feministische Theologie, das menschliche und das Ende, ein neuer Ausgangspunkt für die öko-feministische Theologie, die die Gleichwertigkeit, Unterschiedlichkeit und Unterschiedenheit miteinand ererfassen wird verlangt.

Sommaire

La théologie écoféministe est caracterisée de deux appréhensions différentes de la réalité: celle du cosmocentrisme et celle de l'anthropocentrisme. Cela la pousse à tirer des conclusions contradictoires, qui sont évidentes dans l'eschatologie, où se révèle la faiblesse de son point de départ: c'est-à-dire, du point de vue des oppositions binaires de l'orde symbolique patriarcal, l'association des femmes à la nature. Après un aperçu de la façon de la théologie écoféministe traite du divin, de l'humain de la fin, la théologie écoféministe est appelée à repartir de nouveau, tout en assurant la cohésion de l'équivalence, de la différence et de différences.

Elizabeth Green studied theology in Rüschlikon, Switzerland and Salamanca, Spain, with a DTh on Ecology, Feminism and Theology. She works as a Baptist minister in Southern Italy and has taught courses in feminist theology in Rome and Ruschlikon. She publishes both in English and Italian and her first book *Dal Silenzio alla Parola* appeared in 1992.

Elisabetta Donini

Women and a Politics of Diversity: A Perspective of Radical Immanence

Introduction

Caution and care are required in any discussion concerning ecofeminism because of the ways each one of the women involved chooses, or not as the case may be, to be identified with an ecofeminist position. In fact, in current debates the term "ecofeminism" is often used either in too broad or too narrow a way. In the first case, ecofeminism is conflated so as to include feminism on the one hand, and each and every initiative undertaken by women on environmental and peace issues, on the other. In the second case, ecofeminism is put in a straitjacket so that only one of its many expressions - the 'spiritual' version of the West coast of the USA, or the socialist version of Europe and Australia, or that resembling "deep ecology", or, on the contrary, the radical eschewing of these fundamentalist leanings - is granted legitimacy (Salleh 1991).

Here I will take as my starting point some of those propositions that are considered the foundations of ecofeminism by its adherents. By dealing with actual texts and the meanings expressed therein, I am attempting to avoid abstractions and generalizations which would make my case easier. One thing, however, is certain: those who see in ecofeminism the promise of "healing the wounds" (Plant 1989) are by no means the only ones to be looking for domination-free relationships among human beings and with nature. Rather, many women the world over are building interdependent relations and opposing the degeneration of conflict into war, without necessarily defining themselves as ecofeminists. However effective "isms" may be in generating collective strength, they tend to segment subjects, lives and transformative processes into segments.

Where are the Roots? Ecofeminist Discourses Between Origin and Future

Irene Diamond, in her synthetic and incisive introduction to ecofeminism, is careful to present it as a "heterogeneous movement". However, while refusing to simplify its complex and problematic nature, she does claim that ecofeminism is pervaded by a unifying force: "The celebration of diversity and the interconnectedness of life, the search for common grounds is the promise of this new politics" (Diamond 1992, p.371). The core question is the "issue of spirituality":

> *Narratives which deny or ignore the spiritual threads of this loose constellation fail to acknowledge some of its most creative features ... To reclaim Goddess imagery and create new stories and narratives*

of humans and the cosmos in the 1970s form a vital component ofwhat we now label eco-feminism (ibid., p.372).

In an altogether different context (and without the tendency to write goddess with a capital "g" which I personally find worrying), Barbara Holland-Cunz has also underlined "this celebration of the goddess" as an important phenomenon whose causes and development are to be understood even by those who do not necessarily share the same vision:

The reference to the goddess and other feminist religious occupations are part of building an identity, whatever that is. I do not agree with building such an identity, but I guess this is why it is done and why it is referred to in popular culture. At the core of this religious identity-building is the building of symbols and rituals. Building symbols - new symbols - seems to be helpful as an orientation, and for group identification (Holland-Cunz in Kuletz 1992, p.74).

During the interview I am quoting, Holland-Cunz draws a detailed outline of the origins and development of ecofeminism as follows: those tensions present in some utopian literature have been interwoven with radical feminism, the libertarian components of various (and often contrasting) anarchist, marxian and marxist strands of thought and, most of all, with a variety of experiences originating in anti-nuclear, anti-militarist and environmental activity. Holland-Cunz is concerned with a project of "re-visioning" social relations in a threefold way through deconstructive critique, recovering those precedents in which we are rooted and gaining inspiration from a utopian vision (ivi, pp.76-77).

We can thus note quite a considerable convergence of thought between these two authors. For Diamond, "the reclamation of the Goddess imagery" means recovering the ancient connection to "the Earth as sacred" (Diamond 1992, p.376), which also becomes "the promise of ... new politics" (ibid., p.371). Similarly, for Holland-Cunz:

Rewriting history is one vital feminist task ... we need to explore and engage in a practice of rewriting Vorgeschichte - prehistory. In this way, we may search for non patriarchal forms of society and community. (Holland-Cunz in Kuletz, 1992, p.74)

Her attempt in this direction is as courageous as it is unusual. Concerning the essentialism which she sees as "the core problem of eco-feminism", she states:

I tend toward an historical materialist view regarding woman and nature but I would not discredit essentialism as such ... the danger of ess-entializing should be balanced by some kind of epistemological aware-ness (ibid., pp.71-72).

To achieve this, Holland-Cunz attempts to read in a historical perspective and in the light of concrete political involvement, what she considers "the heart of ecofeminist philosophy":

The idea of nature as subject ... vitality and productivity, as well as spirit and soul were granted to nature (again). There are very few ecofeminist philosophies who never address "her" as a living subjectivity, a sister living being. Ecofeminism could be interpreted as a philosophy of nature as sister subject (ibid., p.71).

Later I will mention those other positions in which the metaphor of nature as mother predominates. The point I am trying to make emerges quite clearly from the material I have quoted: the (re)sacralization of nature is not only practised but also theorized as the founding core of the ecofeminist vision. Such a (re)sacralization aims at a twofold liberation: of the past, by claiming a history which is not inscribed in the androcentric universe of patriarchal hierarchies; and of the present and future, by restoring to women their supreme connection to life in terms of sisterhood.

Both points of view maintain that the problem at issue is the new identity that ecofeminists are trying to build for themselves as individuals and for women as a gender. Holland-Cunz, quoted above, is clear about this: the building of new symbols and rituals will help to guide group identification processes. The need I detect, however, is of quite a different kind. In fact I am trying to discover intellectually, but most of all through lived experience, if it is possible to sketch a horizon in which the reinvention of "our" gender identity does not rest on symbols and rituals, but rather is rooted in the immediacy of relations among women, among women and men, among living beings in general, among these and the physical, historical and social environment and so on, along the inexhaustible chain of material and cultural interdependencies which make up the very stuff of dynamic processes.

Immanence and Transcendence - Can We Leave this Dichotomy Behind?

An almost obligatory step in most feminist (and not only ecofeminist) discussions of the difference between the relation of men and women to nature, continues to be Simone de Beauvoir's work (1949) which, often revisited via Sherry B. Ortner's key text (1974), has opened up new possibilities for rethinking the male/female polarizations in terms of the nature/culture duality. Here I shall only mention that part of de Beauvoir's thought which ecofeminist writings have built on while reversing its meaning:[1] men have treated women and nature as the Other to be dominated. Yet if for de Beauvoir, women's subjugation to the species is the prison of immanence from which women – if they are to gain fulfillment – need to escape, for ecofeminists[2], the affinity between women and nature is a value to celebrate and a resource to use "as the basis for an alternative culture, more peace-loving, less hierarchical and able to address issues in a wider social, personal and ecological context" (Mellor 1992, p.51).

1 Elsewhere I have analysed in more detail de Beauvoir's historical and anthropological presuppositions and how, thanks to a new perspective generated by the critical capacity of recent feminist investigation into origins, these have now changed. Cf. Donini 1990, pp.146-151, 204-206.

2 For an analysis of the meanings in this recovery and reversal as well as for a more general discussion on ecofeminism, cf. Battaglia 1990.

According to Ynestra King (1983, pp.122-123), ecofeminism is in fact able to provide a "third direction" for women once we accept, along with de Beauvoir and Ortner, that women's history has been shaped by their connection to nature. Women are faced with the following dilemma: either to cut themselves off from such a privileged connection and be integrated into the (male) world of culture, or to reinforce this tie entrusting themselves to a spontaneous concern for life as a means of ecological salvation. The third direction proposed by ecofeminism consists in transforming the purported connection between women and nature into a conscious decision:

> *(To create) a different kind of culture and politics that would integrate intuitive/spiritual and rational forms of knowledge, embracing both science and magic insofar as they enable us to transform the nature/culture distinction itself and to envision and create a free, ecological society (King 1983, p.123).*

We have thus reached an important juncture: while de Beauvoir-Ortner aspire to reconceptualize women as able to be "equally involved in projects of creativity and transcendence" (Ortner 1974, p.87), in ecofeminist writings the dilemma seems to be resolved in favour of a decision intended to exalt the immanence of women's connection to nature in the light of spirituality and the sacred no less than of rationality and science.

Why? Why has so much effort been invested in deconstructing those dichotomies, manifested in the body/mind, nature/culture, passion/reason dualities, which for millenia the androcentric tradition has used to express not only a series of oppositions but also of hierarchical subordinations, only to end up by reproposing transcendence or landing on the shores of a resacralized immanence? Is it really possible to existentially sustain this last suggestion, let alone prove it logically?

I shall not attempt to solve this dilemma here, but – while still leaving many questions open – I shall suggest a way ahead. In fact, I propose to approach the problem from a different direction: the transcendence/immanence duality expresses a different kind of tension if, instead of considering it a universal and metahistorical phenomenon, we look at it within its precise spatial and temporal limits. In fact, in the works I have cited as well as the cultural matrix from which they spring, this issue appears as an issue, profoundly internal to the intellectual tradition of the West and witnesses as much to its Jewish, Christian and Greco-Roman heritage as to its more recent reinvention by science and technology.

God-rooted Approach to Objectivity

The governing principle of philosophy, theology and religion as well as of those systems of knowledge of, and action on, the physical world which has, in different forms and often through turbulent events, established itself as the modern canon of rationality (especially as far as its claims to univocity and objectivity have legitimated the scientific enterprise) has been characterized by the law of separation of subject from object, of mind from nature, of God from the world, of the observer from the observed and so on. We may call this strictly a male canon because of the way that the gender identities of women and men[3] have been modelled, throughout history, in that geographical area known as the West[4].

I have argued elsewhere (Donini 1990, chapters VII & VIII) how and why the world view which emerged victorious out of the 1500-1600 revolution onwards (a revolution in notions of knowledge and thus "scientific", in social relations and thus "bourgeois", in means of production and thus "industrial") signified the triumph of an exclusively male dynamic which I shall call acting "from the outside". I am using this all too summary catch-phrase to refer not only to the objectifying system of the new born scientific method but also to the entrepreneurial dynamics of modern capitalism which emerged at the same time. In this context, transcendence assumes precise connotations as both the projects of knowing and acting upon nature in order to subject and manipulate it, were legitimated and guaranteed by reference to God the Father.

Thus, the Creator-Lawgiver provides the essential foundation of the gnoseological and ethical framework of the West. The story of the death of nature and the concomitant reduction of women and the feminine to passivity at both a social and a symbolic level, has been admirably told by recent feminist historians (Merchant 1979; cf. also Keller 1985, chapters II & III). It is important to realize, however, that this science, permeated by the patriarchal mode of relating to the things of the world as objects "from the outside", is still the dominant mediator between nature and culture.

In other words, I do not consider it wise to embark on a deconstruction of the nature/culture dichotomy if we are not prepared, at the same time, to undertake a detailed critique of the whole conceptual system of modern science (and not limit ourselves, as do some ecologists, to its use or possible application). In contrast to King, I do not think that bringing together "intuitive/spiritual and rational forms of knowledge ...science and magic" can constitute a "third direction". In my opinion these forms of knowledge are not divergent trends at all, but considered historically, are actually consubstantial with the same male dominated genetic line.

A radical alternative to the above option is offered, it seems to me, by those who attempt to undermine the basis of objectifying separation by calling on that

3 I cannot go into the reasons why the social, historical and cultural category of "gender" is effective than the biological one of "sex". It is noteworthy, however, that many ecofeminists are either unaware of the issue or choose to speak of "sex", a significant clue, I think, to those tendencies towards a deterministic ontologization which seem to characterize a hasty assimilation of women to nature.

4 In spite of the radically different solution which many Eastern cultures have given compared with the West – the transcendence/ immanence question, if one looks at women's social and symbolic inequality in those regions one can hardly delude oneself that there male domination has been milder. For some pertinent considerations on the way some "green spirituality" is rather simplistically attracted to the East, cf. Mellor 1992, pp.43-45.

core gender identity which many feminists today are reinventing as "locating oneselves as women". Referred to by some as "standpoint" (Hartsock 1983; Harding 1986 & 1991) and by others as "situated knowledge" (Haraway 1988 & 1991), I prefer to see it as the challenge to develop forms of "contextualized knowledge" in which subjectivity is nourished in that critical/self critical process provided by continually shifting perspectives. According to this view, the subject is not an isolated given entity but is constituted in time through those dynamic relations which connect her or him to the environment of which she or he is part.

Even though I am proceeding in a very schematic fashion, a clarification is necessary at this point. While the above is particularly relevant to the debate on science and notions of knowledge, those external conditions which have generated such an epistemological stance – in all its significance – are, however, of a strictly practical and political nature. The "awareness of partiality" to which I am referring has taken shape in the women's movement as women have gradually come to terms with their journeys into subjectivity or, to use the happy phrase of bell hooks (1990, p 15), with the endeavour of "becoming subjects".

In the case of Italy, our desire to build an autonomous horizon outside the so-called needs imposed by the logics of industrialism and technoscientific development, led us to elaborate some new keywords such as "conscience of limits" and an "ethic of responsibility" (Leonardi, 1986; Donini, 1990). These function as guidelines to carry us beyond the dictates of 'progress' with its tragic consequences of disaster from Bhopal to Chernobyl, as well as the increasing gap between the overdeveloped countries (Mies, 1986 pp.39-40) and those women and men crushed by war and hunger.

Recognizing our Diversity, Without the Mediation of Rites or Symbols

In the case of the United States, where the disparities of colour rapidly undermined white feminism's original and simplistic notion of an oppression common to all women, the significance of "situated knowledges" lies in their attempt to make room for diversity: "location" and "identity politics"[5] are important themes in postcolonial feminism. However, the question of the many differences between women which cannot just be silenced by appealing to that difference from men all women share, is becoming a pressing issue. Because of this, those encounters and exchanges aimed at building elements of coexistence and mutual acceptance among the women of peoples in conflict[6] knit together with the ever

[5] Without going into further detail it is worth noting that "identity politics" have been heavily criticized by those who have seen it as harbouring dangerously essentialist leanings. The form which I consider promising is the constructionist and contextualized version argued for, among others, by Alcoff 1988, Butler, 1990, Haraway 1991.

[6] Here I am referring, due to my personal involvement, to the relations created from 1987 between Palestinian, Israeli and Italian women. Cf Calciati 1989, Inchiesta, 1991. An equally radical and even more problematic attempt has been made to keep relations open among Serbian, Croatian and Bosnian women together with women from other countries so that, in the midst of violence, mourning and devastation, they are not crushed by the ethnic and religious hostilities in which they are caught.

more urgent need to deconstuct some of the basic categories of war which we have inherited from centuries of culture's science and politics. The categories of race, nation, religious and ethnic roots as well as fundamentalisms are in the process of being scrutinized with the help of a gender analysis[7]. Many women are using such terms as "hybridization", "nomadism" and "contamination" to sketch a prospect which is able to dynamically re-evaluate the bonds of solidarity, while at the same time opening them up to that transformation which will reblend the sedimentations of history and our ways of perceiving each other.

Against the backcloth of these new attitudes to diversity, I would like explain the opposition to rites and symbols I expressed previously, and to clarify the meaning of radical immanence or commitment to concrete relations between diverse women and men. Maria C. Lugones has recently underlined that "the theory and practice of white/Anglofeminism have not succeeded in including egalitarianism across differences ... sameness, not equality, has been stressed" (Lugones 1992, p.407). In fact, in the best of cases, the issue tends to be resolved by recognizing the diverse-other as similar to oneself, projecting onto her one's own powerful gaze, rather than thinking oneself in relation to the other. So, Lugones concludes, "white feminists are not theoretically or practically in a good position vis à vis women of colour to propose sisterhood as a model for our relationships" (ibid).

This essay thus develops a stimulating critique of the pretension to call each other "sisters" and proposes the more farsighted notion of "pluralist friendship". I feel deeply sympathetic with this line of thought in light of the issues mentioned above. In fact the work I am concerned with is aimed at building up a notion of friendship that is not limited to the circle of those we consider similar to ourselves but is rather nourished by moving in exactly the opposite direction. At stake is the awareness that it is precisely the other's own diversity, and not in spite of it, that constitutes her or his subjectivity. In other words, there is no need at all to legitimate the other as "similar to me".

The metaphor of sisterhood, on the other hand, confines solidarity to the dangerously narrow sphere of those who share common roots (expressed furthermore in the language of blood ties which is one of the traditions most imbued with the logics of war that our culture can offer). I believe that the other must be recognized as such, irreducibly different and distinct without the need for symbols to mediate the relationship, but precisely because other.

We are, then, neither "sisters" to women nor "sisters" to nature. Why do we need to grant value to nature by annexing it according to the codes of human culture? Cannot cats, mountains, rivers and stars be reconceptualized as elements endowed with their own meaning, without having to "humanize" them or subject

7 The feminist literature in this field is already quite vast; see especially Enloe, 1989, Liu, 1991, Saghal and Yuval Davis, 1992, Trinh, 1989, Yuval Davis and Anthias, 1989.

them to our mode of feeling? Would not a radical exercise in the conscience of limit and the awareness of partiality suggest greater caution in reckoning with our own subjective gaze, by refusing to extend the peculiar sensitivity of the human to other beings, living and not, as their inter-dependence with the rest of the world has to be moulded according to them and not to us?

We need at least to mention that complex maze through which, and not only metaphorically, the prime mediation of the relations between the sexes (and the elaboration of the sexes into gender) passes; I am referring to how, throughout history, women have been identified as mothers. Even though each of us is of woman born, the idealization of motherhood as a symbol has in fact functioned to subject real women to the patriarchal order. Although space does not permit a detailed analysis of the subject, I would remind us how, rather than women being obliged to recognize their natural destiny in bearing children, the principle of self-determination for every woman as regards motherhood, has for more than twenty years been the fulcrum of a radical transformation of gender identity in the context of a plurality of possible ways of self-fulfillment. One of the consequences of such thought is the attempt to remodel the universe of "care-taking" by attributing to "mothering" the task of relation making and reciprocal subjectivity building with the different-from-the-self, which does not necessarily coincide with the actual experience of child bearing (Cf. especially Chodorow 1978, Benjamin 1988, Ruddick 1989 for this line of thought).

In turning the traditional point of view upside down, a new capacity for relational autonomy both for the individual and for women as a gender is created, which can act in the world by delegitimizing, from the inside, that social and cultural pattern which still subordinates life and subsistence to production. In Maria Mies' lucid discussion (1986, ch VII), this is the cutting edge of "a feminist perspective of labour" which undermines the present relationship to the body and nature by granting value to those activities which produce "existence" rather than commodities. I believe that this proposal, rooted in the material nature of daily life and in the immediacy of the correspondencies between the unfolding of a subjectivity which is both particular and relational and the transformation of social relations, holds more promise and can be more effectively developed, than the "spiritual" values proposed by many ecofeminists.

Bibliography

Linda Alcoff, *Cultural Feminism Versus Post-structuralism: The Identity Crisis in Feminist Theory,* Signs 13 (1988)

Hannah Arendt, **Was Bleibt? Es Bleibt die Mutter Sprache,** in A.Reif (ed)., *Gesprache mit Hannah Arendt,* München: Piper, (1976).

Luisella Battaglia, *Donne e Natura. Considerazioni sull `ecofemminismo del Convegno Etica e Ambiente,* Genova (1990).

Jessica Benjamin, *The Bonds of Love,* New York: Pantheon (1988).

Judith Butler, *Gender Trouble: Feminism and the Subversion of Identity,* New York: Routledge, (1990).

Giovanna Calciati et al. ed., *Donne e Gerusalemme: Incontri tra Italiane, Palestinesi, Israel-iane,* Torino: Rosenberg & Selier (1989).

Nancy E Carawie, **The Challenge and Theory of Feminist Identity Politics: Working on Racism,** *Frontiers* 12 (1991), 109-129.

Nancy Chodorow, *The Reproduction of Mothering: Psychoanalysis and the Sociology of Gender* University of California Press (1978).

Simone de Beauvoir, *Le Deuxième Sexe,* Paris: Gallimard (1949).

Irene Diamond, **Ecofeminist Politics: The Promise of Common Ground** in Kramare & Spender, 371-378.

Elisabetta Donini, *La Nube e il Limite: Donne, Scienza, Percorsi nel Tempo,* Torino: Rosenberg Selier (1990).

Conversazioni con Evelyn Fox Keller, una Scienzata Anomala, Milano: Eluthera (1991).

Cynthia Enloe, *Bananas, Beaches and Bases: Making Feminist Sense of International Politics,* London: Pandora (1989).

Brian Easlea, *Fathering the Unthinkable: Masculinity, Scientists and the Nuclear Arms Race,* London: Pluto (1983).

Donna Haraway, **Situated Knowledges: The Science Question in Feminism as Site of Discourse on the Privilege of Discourse on the Privilege of Partial Perspective,** *Feminist Studies* 14 (1988), 575-599.

Simians, Cyborgs and Women: The Reinvention of Nature, London: Free Association Books (1991).

Sandra Harding, *The Science Question in Feminism,* Milton Keynes: Open University (1986).

Whose Science? Whose Knowledge? Thinking from Women's Lives, Milton Keynes: Open University (1991).

Nancy Hartsock, **The Feminist Standpoint: Developing the Ground for Specifically Feminist Historical Materialism,** in Sandra Harding, Merrill B Hintikka (eds.), *Discovering Reality: Feminist Perspectives on Epistemology, Metaphysics, Methodology and Philosophy of Science;* Dordrecht: Reidel (1983), 283-310.

bell hooks, *Yearning, Race, Gender and Cultural Politics,* Boston: South End (1990).

Inchiesta, **Pace e Guerra in Medio Oriente. Percorsi di Donne** 91-92 (1991) January–June.

Evelyn Fox Keller, *Reflections on Gender and Science,* New Haven: Yale University Press (1985).

A Feeling for the Organism: The Life and Work of Barbara McClintock, New York: W.H. Freeman (1983).

Ynestra King, **Toward an Ecological Feminism and a Feminist Ecology,** Joan Rothschild (ed.), *Machina ex Dea*: Feminist Perspectives on Technology, Pergamon (1983).

Healing the Wounds: Feminism, Ecology and the Nature/Culture Dualism, in Irene Diamond and Gloria Feman Orenstein (eds.), *Reweaving the World: The Emergence of Ecofeminism,* San Francisco: Sierra Club Books (1990), 106-121.

Cheris Kramarae and Dale Spender (eds.), *The Knowledge Explosion: Generations of Feminist Scholarship,* New York: Athene Series (1992).

Thomas S. Kuhn, *The Structure of Scientific Revolutions,* University of Chicago Press (1962).

Valerie Kuletz, **Eco-Feminist Philosophy: Interview with Barbara Holland Kunz,** *Capitalism Nature Socialism* 3 (1992), 63-78.

Grazia Leonardi (ed.), *Scienza, Potere, Coscienza del Limite,* Roma: Editori Riunite Riviste (1986).

Tessie P Liu, **Race and Gender in the Politics of Group Formation: A Comment on Notions of Multiculturalism,** *Frontiers* 12 (1991), 155-165.

Maria C. Lugones, (in collaboration with Pat Alak Rosezelle), **Sisterhood and Friendship as Feminist Models** in Kramarae and Spender, 406-412.

Mary Mellor, *Breaking the Boundaries: Towards a Feminist Green Socialism,* London: Virago (1992).

Carolyn Merchant, *The Death of Nature: Women, Ecology and the Scientific Revolution,* London: Wildwood (1979).

Maria Mies, *Patriarchy and Accumulation on a World Scale,* London: Zed Books (1986).

David Noble, *A World Without Women: The Christian Clerical Culture of Western Science,* New York: Alfred Knopf(1992).

Sherry B Ortner, **Is Female to Male as Nature is to Culture?** in M. Z. Rosaldo and L. Lamphere (eds.), *Woman,Culture and Society,* Stanford University Press (1974).

Judith Plant, *Healing the Wounds: The Promise of Ecofeminism,* London: Green Print (1989).

Sara Ruddick, *Maternal Thinking: Towards a Politics of Peace,* London: The Womens Press (1989).

Gita Sahgal and Nira Yuval Davies (eds.), *Refusing Holy Orders: Women and Fundamentalism in Britain,* London: Virago (1992).

Ariel Salleh et al, **Ecofemminismi ed Ecosocialismo: Una Discussione,** *Capitalismo Natura Socialismo* 2 (1991) 113-118.

Minh.Ha Trinh, *Woman, Native, Other,* Bloomington: Indiana University Press (1989).

Nira Yuval Davis and Floya Anthias (eds.), *Woman-Nation-State,* Houndmills: Macmillan (1989).

Zusammenfassung

Eine Geslechtsspecifizische-Kritik der Dichotomy zwischen Immanenz und Transzendenz ist benutzt um die Wiedersakralizierung der Natur auf der basis der öko-Feministischen Vorschlëgen zu diskutieren. Eine Analyse der Sozial und Historischen Charakteristiken der westlichen Wissenschaft enthüllt ein Fortbestehen zwischen Wissenschaft und Religion insofern dass beide von männlicher Tendenz zur Trennung und Aktion von draussen charakterisiert sind. Eine Feministische alternative verwurzelt in der Immanenz und Unsicherheit der konkreten abhängigen Beziehungen wird vorgeschlagen.

Sommaire

Une critique, fondée sur le genre, de la dichotomie entre l'immanence et la transcendance est le point de départ d'une discussion de la resacralisation de la nature qui est au coeur du projet écoféministe. Une analyse des caractéristiques sociales et historiques de la science occidentale révèle une continuité entre la science et la religion, dans la mesure où elles sont caracterisées à toutes les deux par la tendance masculine à la séparation et à l'action provenant de l'extérieur. Une alternative féministe est proposée, approche qui a ses racines dans l'immanence et la contingence d'une intersubjectivité concrète.

Elisabetta Donini teaches physics at the University of Turin. After several years of research into elementary particles she has turned her attention to the history and critique of science, concentrating, for some time now, on questions related to women and science and gender and science. Active in the women's movement, she pursues a "politics of diversity", intent on building multicultural relations across boundaries in times of conflict. She is also engaged in ecological issues and in a gender critique of development.

Celia Deane-Drummond

Response to Elisabetta Donini

Elisabetta Donini's discussion centres around the concept of 'ecofeminism', rather than science from the perspective of an ecofeminist. The first section of her paper is devoted to discovering the goal common to all eco-feminists: that is the building up of a new 'identity'. This is achieved either through the return to the goddess imagery linking female images to the earth, or through giving the earth a subjectivity, leading to a 'resacralization' of nature. The means through which these images are built up is through ritual and symbol. Elisabetta Donini rejects such means and prefers to start instead with the immediacy of relationships.

The question we wish to raise here is why the author is so resistant to the idea of symbol and ritual. Later on she uses specific examples of phrases such as 'sisterhood' as a term which does not seen to allow for the differences between women. However, we would argue that building up of a new identity must involve the use of new patterns of language. A rootedness in the immediacy of relations, which Donini argues is the basis for her position, has to find expression in new language, symbols and rituals. If we miss out this aspect of our existence we risk leaving 'religious' questions split off from 'secular' ones. Perhaps Donini's background in science makes any reference to more mystical, less 'concrete' aspects of reality seem more alien and detached from 'real' relationships. However, as we will discuss in more detail later, for many scientists the mystical is embedded in their own experience of relating to the 'world outside'.

In her article Donini raises the important point that there has been an ambiguity in the response by ecofeminists to the identity of women and nature. However, she does not spell out very clearly the possible confusion at this juncture. On the one hand we are asked to reject all identification of women with nature, the oppression of both by patriarchal systems amounts to a prison of 'immanence' from which we have to escape. On the other hand, the identification itself becomes the basis for an alternative culture. Donini seems to favour the second with nature and immanence, since any transcendence at all is alien and to be rejected.

As a consequence of the above view Donini rejects King's suggestion that we should work towards healing the split between rational and intuitive thought, and between science and faith. It seems to me that King's approach is to be preferred. If we retain the identification of women and the earth, but deny all spiritual worth or possibility of dialogue with 'science' we end up with a subjectivity 'rooted in the material nature of daily life'. This, ironically, still seems to me to come down on the side of 'science' as she explicitly denies 'spiritual' values a place in material relations. There is an inconsistency in the argument here:

1. On the one hand we find a radical rejection of the 'objectivity' of science, so that nature becomes more like a 'subject'.
2. On the other hand this same subjectivity is identified with the material, as opposed to the spiritual. The question which immediately springs to mind is: What kind of science is shaped by this apparently individual subjectivity, albeit whose identity comes from relationships?

Scientists have far more involvement in the 'objects' they investigate than is given credit for by the popular impressions of their work. Polanyi was one of the first to spell this out in his idea of 'personal knowledge'[1]. Again, Barbara McClintock, the geneticist who investigated maize chromosomes, believed that she became identified with these same chromosomes during the course of her research. More mystical experiences of those involved in the 'new physics' are more common, F. Capra has written several books to this effect[2]. The spiritual makes its presence felt in the most analytical of sciences, that of mathematics and physics. This is not a result of a split in the psyche of scientists, many of whom in the dawn of modern science were also theologians. Rather, it is a sensitivity to the numinous in the natural world, including human beings.

The idea of 'situated knowledge', has affinities with liberation theology. Both liberation theology and Donini reject capitalism and argue instead for a starting point in particular situations. The difference between them is that for liberation theology the traditions of the church are re-worked in the light of this new approach. An understanding of Christ emerges which is both concerned with the everyday and concrete, but looks to a future kingdom of God where injustices will no longer exist. The temptation to fall into despair or utopia is resisted by developing the concept of realistic hope.

The problem with Donini's paper is that is does not seem to give us an overall framework or basis for realistic hope. While in general we agree that vague notions such as 'sisterhood' are not all that helpful in allowing differences to emerge, we are not given any other language as a means to build a new community. The secular philosopher, Richard Rorty, argues that new directions in culture come from new languages. He believes that these emerge randomly in a culture and the most promising languages come from poets and novelists, rather than scientists[3]. While we would identify more closely with Habermas' view that

[1] M Polanyi, *Personal Knowledge*, Routledge, Kegan and Paul, New York 1958.
[2] F Capra, *The Turning Point*, Wildwood House, 1982.
[3] R. Rorty, *Contingency, Irony and Solidarity*, Cambridge University Press, 1989.

a philosophy of subjectivity needs to be replaced by a model of communicative dialogical action and rationality, both would agree with the importance of language in creating new patterns of thought[4]. Donini's suggestion of the material rootedness in relations does not take us very far in discerning how such a view challenges and directs the present social network.

Donini also makes the point that nature does not need to be 'humanized'. This is a fair point, though is not the introduction of the ideal of 'subjectivity' a form of humanization? It is not clear from this paper what value should be given to nature vis vis ourselves. What are the criteria which we draw on in order to come up with the idea of an 'ethic of responsibility'? The questions surrounding environmental ethics are hardly mentioned. We would agree that attempts to read into nature human attributes, including ideas such as whether animals have souls, do not take us very far. However, unless we have some framework for ethical decisions it is hard to see how an approach centred around material relations will help us decide in favour of one course of action rather than another. Should our relations to the rain forest have higher priority than relations to the poor of the land or the wealthy landowners? Does priority of relations simply rest on the contingency of our particular place of birth? Donini also raises the ideal of motherhood as that which is in need of transformation. She suggests that we include relationship-making and reciprocal subjectivity as a basis for the definition of motherhood. One wonders here if the term 'mother' is appropriate at all. The word 'feminism' might work instead, but then capacity for relationship-making is not confined to women. The idea that the rootedness of most women is in everyday life and relationships could also be a basis for a spirituality, rather than alien to any notion of the spiritual. The tradition of the early Celtic church, for example, drew heavily on the experience, but one which allows the full potential of the everyday to come alive[5].

The questions left to be explored include the following:

1. What kind of science can we move towards in the dialogue between women and men? We cannot move from the actual to the ideal overnight. Some sort of rapprochement creates a better climate for realistic change than total revolution. Such a change is to be achieved through a listening and openness to all points of view, including those of men.
2. Not all dualisms are threats to be neglected at all cost. The model of pluralism is in itself accepting of difference. The problem comes if a radical dualism prevents dialogue and mutual understanding and acceptance of difference.
3. 'Spiritual' issues cannot be ignored. Spiritual convictions motivate and inform our decisions. A greater sympathy and understanding of other religions

[4] R Bernstein, *The New Constellation*, Polity, 1991.

[5] See, for example, E de Waal, *World Made Whole: Rediscovering the Celtic Tradition*, Harper Collins 1991.

is called for: ranging from the immanence of Buddhism to the strong transcendence in Islam. Eco-feminism takes place in a multifaith as well as a multicultural context.

4. The spirituality of each faith can form the basis of a challenge to those practices in science which treat 'nature' as a resource, and split 'nature' off from ourselves.

Zusammenfassung

Der Idee der radikalen Immanenz, gegrundet auf materielle Verbindungen als Ausgangspunkt für Öko-Feminisimus, ist sehr schwierig, wenn sie geschrieben wird von 'Geistlichen' Werten. Das Letztere verhindert das Erste, um den Lauf in provinzielle und individualistische Subjektivitat zu geraten, in dem es einen breiteren Diskussionsraum schafft. Wenn Öko-Feminismus seinen wirklichen Beitrag haben soll, insoweit dass es zum Wechsel beiträgt, von einer den Humanen Bedürfnissen zugeschnitten Wissenschaft, zu einer Idealen Wissenschaft, welche dem Wert unserer eigenen Spezie gerecht wird, dann müssen wir mit einer Änderung in der Wissenschaft beginnen. Die ausdrückliche Herausforderung an die Wissenschaft von Öko-Feministen wird so lange ignoriert, so lange wir nicht im Dialog und in den interdisciplinaren Methoden aufeinander zugehen.

Sommaire

L' idée d'une immanence radicale, qui se fonde sur les relations matérielles, comme point de départ d' un éco-féminisme est problematique, si elle est divorcée de valeurs 'spirituelles'. Celles-ci empêchent celle-là de retomber dans un subjectivisme provincial et individualiste, en fournissant à la discussion un cadre plus large. Si l' éco-féminisme va vraiment être à même d'influencer l'orientation actuelle de la science en tant que discipline qui se voue entièrement aux intérêts humains pour la transformer en idéal qui tient compte de la valeur de toutes les espèces, y compris la nôtre, il faut commencer par nous rapprocher de la science. Le défi explicite que lance l' écoféminisme à la science ne sera relevé que si un dialogue est entamé dans le but de construire une méthodologie interdisciplinaire.

Celia Deane-Drummond gained a doctorate in plant physiology in 1980 and was lecturer/ researcher in plant nutrition for six years. She was awarded a BA in theology in 1989 and a PhD in theology in 1992. She is currently a consultant with The International Consultancy on Religion, Education and Culture (ICOREC).

Aruna Gnanadason

Response to Elisabetta Donini

Elisabetta Donini's article makes some important contributions to feminist discourse on ecology. What I find particularly important is her affirmation that "transcendence assumes precise connotations", which are obviously patriarchal, in a context of "the objectifying system of the new born scientific method" and the "entrepreneurial dynamic of modern capitalism", which were a direct consequence of the 1500-1600 industrial revolution in Europe. I cannot agree with her more when she asserts the need to grant value to those activities which "produce 'existence' rather than goods".

It is important to acknowledge the danger of calling each other "sisters" if we do not take into account the vast differences in our experiences as women *and* the contradictions in the world that have ensured that we are kept apart. "Pluralist friendship", however, is inadequate to express the need for women to transcend all "man-made" boundaries, in order to work together, as a conscious political decision, for a justice-filled world that lives in harmony with creation. Irreducible differences and distinct experiences do not need to come in the way of sisterhood and relationship, whether between us as women or between us and nature.

It is important that we carry forward the discourse regarding motherhood. Elisabetta acknowledges that she is unable in this article to analyze the statement she has made but I would refer to the way in which women in India see this debate. In Indian society, motherhood plays a key role and therefore has to be taken seriously by Indian feminist methodology. This becomes relevant when we place the creative principle at the heart of feminist consciousness. Denying themselves a life of their own, women have been engaged in creating and sustaining life for all. In Indian society by and large, a woman's selfhood depends on the life of the community. This creative nurturing urge rooted in giving birth to and protecting new life, is surrounded with ceremony and ritual in Indian homes, particularly in Hindu homes – an expression of the fertility associated with the earth and the gifts nature bestows on women.

Yet, Indian feminists do not ignore that it is this very creative principle and self-sacrificing life of women which is idealised, used and abused to restrict women's time, space and movement. It has also been the source of seeing women only in the childbearing role and putting tremendous burdens on women who are unable or do not want to bear children. As our Asian sisters describe it "there can be a danger of condoning the traditional self-effacing masochism of women, reinforced in the glorification of motherhood, keeping them in the depth of despair and resignation"[1].

The "idealization of motherhood as a symbol has in fact functioned to subject real women to the patriarchal order" is true but it is important to keep this debate open, especially because it is the basis of community life in many societies - where women's mothering role is important, even when they do not bear children biologically, themselves.

However, what is difficult for me to accept in Elisabetta's analysis is her rejection of "spiritual values" and symbols and rituals and her affirmation of the "material nature of daily life". Such sharp distinctions are not possible in societies where the struggles for survival are themselves seen as a spiritual necessity. In such contexts, symbols and rituals are part of the daily experience of life and livelihood.

For women of the South the concern for a ecofeminist view of the world is no academic exercise – it is about survival and is therefore a priority concern. Caring for creation is integral to their everyday lives.

> *Shakti (strength) comes to us from these forests and grasslands; we watch them grow, year in and year out through their internal shakti and we derive our strength from it. We watch our streams renew themselves and we drink their clear and sparkling water – that gives us shakti. We drink fresh milk, we eat ghee (melted butter) we eat food from our own fields – all this gives us not just nutrition of the body, but a moral strength, that we are our own masters, we control and produce our own wealth. That is why 'primitive', 'backward' women who do not buy their needs from the market but produce them themselves are leading Chipko. Our power is nature's power, our shakti comes from prakriti (nature). Our power against the contractor comes form these inner sources, and is strengthened by his trying to oppress and bully us with his false power of money and muscle. We have offered ourselves, even at the cost of our lives, for a peaceful protect to close this mine, to challenge and oppose the power that the government represents. Each attempt to violate us has strengthened our integrity. They stoned us on March 20 when they returned from the mine. They stoned out children and hit them with iron rods, but they could not destroy our shakti (Itwari Devi)*[2].

They could not destroy our *shakti*! ...this affirmation made by an unlettered tribal woman leader of the Chipko movement reflects the spiritual energy that has sustained Indian women in their years of struggle against patriarchy which has made systematic and organised attempts to silence women and their demands for a just and more human world. *Shakti* – the female power principle, was recognised in India thousands of years ago - and continues to energise women in the present phase of the women's movement. "In this form the women's movement represents, not merely an oppositional force fuelled by anger, a rather negative

[1] Sun Ai Lee Park and Mary John Mananzan, **Emerging Spirituality of Asian Women** in *With Passion and Compassion - Third World Women Doing Theology* Ed. Virginia Fabella and Mercy Amba Oduyoye, Orbis Books, NY, 1988, p.82.

[2] Itwari Devi, a village elder who led the Chipko movement against mining operations in the Doon Valley. Quoted by Vandana Shiva in *Staying Alive, Women, Ecology and Survival in India*, Kali for Women, New Delhi, 1988, pp. 208-209.

reaction to oppression, but the development of a distinctive female culture, a positive creative force inspiring men and women alike"[3].

The holistic vision of Indian women springs from their experience of being women in a world that has denied them a life of dignity and personhood. Millions of Indian women learn the hard and tedious way what it means to live and manage life with the minimum available. But as Itwari Devi expresses it, they learn to foster life-sustaining and life-enhancing ways to struggle against forces that make every effort to destroy the integrity of people and of all creation.

In India the destruction of the earth's resources is taking place with such intensity and rapidity that something urgent has to be done. Our forests are disappearing, (we lose 1.3 million hectares of forests every year); soil conditions are deteriorating, water and wind erode the land (56.6 percent of India's land has suffered), periodic floods and drought are causing serious damage every year, indiscriminate use of ground level water resources are causing serious shortages of water. Pollutants and chemical wastes as well as fertilizers and pesticides are eating into the core of our environment. In such a context the definition of words such as "ecofeminism" is not what is relevant but what is becoming increasingly evident is that we need to challenge the western patriarchal paradigm of development that has been at the root of the degradation of the earth. To do this we have to discover our energy in the spiritual bond between humanity and nature that had existed in our society and was in fact at the core of our cultures. We have lost it and it is women, particularly those "who work daily in the production of survival"[4] who know best and it is from their experience that we have to learn and draw our strength. The demand for an eco-feminist holistic view is rooted in this.

Thoughts on Indian cosmology have been reconstructed by feminists to emphasis the essential connectedness - that person and nature (purusha - prakriti) are a duality in unity and not a hierarchy. They were seen as:

> *inseparable complements of one another in nature, in woman, in man. Every form of creation bears the sign of this dialectical unity, of diversity within a unifying principle, and his dialectical harmony between male and female principles and between nature and man, becomes the basis of ecological thought and action in India. Since ontologically there is no dualism between men and nature and because nature as Prakriti sustains life, nature has been treated as integral and inviolable. Prakriti, far from being an esoteric abstraction, is an every day concept which organizes daily life. There is no separation here between the popular and élite imagery or between the sacred and secular traditions*[5].

However, what must be acknowledged and affirmed is that this essence was also distorted by some strains of Indian philosophy by patriarchal brahminical hinduism. The demand to return to our spiritual resources is therefore not a plea

[3] Joanna Liddle, Rama Joshi, *Daughters of Independence. Gender, Caste and Class in India* Kali for Women, Delhi, 1986, p.5.

[4] Vandana Shiva, op. cit., p.40.

[5] Vandana Shiva, op. cit., p.210.

for going back into a esoteric and distant past, or to harp on traditionalism and cultural relativism, but to draw strength from the role that nature plays in the daily lives of our people.

Vegetation and other gifts of nature play a key symbolic role in rituals and worship life, particularly in popular religious experiences of the people. The Goddess of small-pox, Mariamman, could be appeased only with leaves from a medicinal plant that is said to have antiseptic content. There is an ancient image of vegetation emerging from the body of the Goddess Devi-Mahatmyah where the Devi is said:

> *To nourish her needy people with vegetation produced from her own body. Her body is the earth, source of plant life and all that lives. As a vegetation goddess, a vital force concerned with growth of crops, the Goddess is known as Annapurna, Plenitude of Food, the nourishing sap of all being . . . The villagers among whom mother goddesses and fertility goddesses arose continue to centre their religious life on rituals intended to restore the force of the soil, and their earth deities are true vegetation goddesses in the ancient tradition. Since goddess-rituals handed down from a remote antiquity often centre on the springs of growth and nourishment, many plants are used in goddess worship*[6].

Forests have been central to Indian civilisation. Forests have been worshipped as Aranyani, the Goddess of the forest, the primary source of life and fertility. The diversity, harmony and self-sustaining nature of the forest formed the organisational principle guiding Indian civilisation. As a source of life, nature was venerated as sacred and human evolution was measured in terms of humanity's capacity to merge with her rhythms and patterns intellectually, emotionally and spiritually[7].

In such a context spirituality and the "material nature of life" cannot be separated and seen as opposing principles. A sacramental attitude to the earth and its resources is not an exotic past time - it is the source of people's lives, it is the only hope for a world which is increasingly dependent on objectivity, on scientific rationalism and the masculine preoccupation with the production of goods and profits. A sacramental, spiritual attitude is the only hope for a world which has denied itself the poetic, the lyrical, the intuitive.

---

[6] Ajit Mookerjee, *Kali, the Feminine Force*, London, Thames and Hudson Ltd, 1988, p.22.
[7] Vandana Shiva op. cit., pp.55 - 56.

Zusammenfassung

Es ist wichtig, das Wort "Schwester" in vollem Bewustsein der Differenzen zwischen Frauen zu gebrauchen. Sie stimmt mit Donini überein, was die kulturellen Werte einer mütterschaft angeht – so wichtig in India und doch in der Gefahr idealisiert zu werden und den Frauen weitere Bürden aufzuerlegen. Sie stimmt nicht überein mit der Ablehnung 'Geistlicher Werte', die sie als Teil täglicher Erfahrung und notwendig zum Überleben betrachtet. 'Shakti' oder das weibliche kraft-prinzip belebt Indische Frauen ununterbrochen im Kampf für die Integrität der Schöpfung. Indische Feministen haben die wichtige Verbindung zwischen Person und Natur als eine dualität in der Einheit reconstruiert, so dass sie eine Kosmologie widerschaffen, die für Höffnung in einer Welt sorgt, die beschäftigt ist mit dem Herstellen von Gütern und Dewin.

Sommaire

Il est important d'employer le mot 'soeur' en pleine conscience des différences qui existent entre les femmes. Elle accepte avec Donini la valeur culturelle de la maternité, qui a tant d'importance en Inde, et qui est pourtant en danger d'être idéalisée, ajoutant ainsi aux fardeaux des femmes. Elle n'est pas d'accord avec le refus de 'valeurs spirituelles' qu'elle considère comme faisant partie de l'expérience quotidienne et comme nécessaire à la survie. 'Shakti' ou le principe du pouvoir féminin continue à nourrir les femmes indiennes dans leur lutte pour préserver l' intégrité de la création. Les féministes indiennes ont reconstruit l'alliance essentielle de l'être et de la nature en tant que dualité unifiée, afin de recréer une cosmologie qui fournira de l'espoir dans un monde qui se préoccupe trop de la production de biens et de profits.

Aruna Gnanadason was educated in Bangalore, from where she holds an MA (English) and a BD. From 1982 she worked with the National Council of Churches in India mobilising a movement of Indian Church women. From May 1991 she has been on the staff of the World Council of Churches in Geneva as director of the sub-unit on women in Church and Society. Her latest book *Women and Violence* (WCC, 1993) reflects her commitment to justice for women and the integrity of creation.

Lene Sjørup

Response to Elisabetta Donini

Elisabetta Donini in her interesting article "Women and a Politics of Diversity" grapples with two important feminist issues:

1. How can the immanence - transcendence split be healed in the light of ecofeminism?
2. How can objectivist knowledge, which is seen as male "acting from the outside", be replaced by a more gender-aware epistemology, which embraces subjectivity and nature?

The attempts of mainly Plant (1989) and King (1983) at solving these two problems are criticized because:

1. An ecofeminism which tries to re-sacralize immanence stays within "the cultural matrix" from which the immanence - transcendence dualism springs;
2. An epistemology which attempts to bring together intuitive/spiritual and rational forms of knowledge will be "consubstantial with the same male-dominated genetic line".

Elisabetta Donini's arguments are thus parallel and they seem to be rooted in one main problem: how can a male-dominated culture be avoided and broken with? She herself points at a *historical* critique of male culture, including the immanence/transcendence dualism and objectivist knowledge. Her positive suggestions for a new feminist identity building and epistemology are :

1. "The immediacy of relations along the inexhaustible chain of material and cultural interdependencies", rather than ecofeminist's symbols and rituals.
2. A "contextualized knowledge" in which subjectivity is nourished in that critical/self critical process provided by continually shifting perspectives".

Elisabetta Donini stresses the importance of acknowledging racial and ethnic differences between women as well as the difference between women and nature, and she turns to mothering as a positive identification which, because it grants value to those activities "which produce 'existence' rather than goods" can be developed more effectively "than the 'spiritual' values proposed by many ecofeminists".

The editors have asked me to respond to Elisabetta Donini's article from my own viewpoint, which is that I, for a number of years, have been engaged in interviewing women about their religious experiences, and in that time have been inspired by the goddess movement.

In my project "Oneness", six North American and four Danish women were interviewed and these interviews were compared with archive material of 3,000 accounts of religious experiences (both women's and men's) at the Alister Hardy Research Centre in Oxford. This project showed that women's religious experiences in the North tend toward mysticism, ie an experience of oneness with the holy (James, 1958, p.292ff). Women's mystical experiences were triggered by nature, by the body (in sexuality and birth-giving), in social settings (friendships, political and religious groups, history), in aesthetical circumstances, in everyday circumstances, and in negative situations of fear and anxiety.

A phenomenology of mystical experiences shows that they are ineffable, give rise to a changed perspective of time, are filled with knowledge, and are passive. Epistemologically, they are placed in the area between the subjective and the objective; in short, they are paradoxical.

I think that the lesson which might be learned from mysticism has to do with the paradox that there neither is an identity with the holy nor an estrangement from it. Thus in the mystical experience transcendence and immanence are embraced simultaneously. This in fact is a major reason for the ineffability and the great noetic quality of mystical experiences: the commonly accepted law of non-contradiction is experienced as insufficient, and an alternative epistemology, rooted in nature, in the body, in the social, in aesthetical, everyday and negative situations is seen as possible.

Furthermore, my investigation shows that women and men both have mystical experiences. However, fewer men than women seem to have them; men's attitudes to these experiences differ from women's: (they tend to systematize, rationalise, define them much more than the women do), and men's mystical experiences seem to be triggered in different settings than women's (for example war).

I explain this through object-relations theory (Chodorow, 1978; Fox Keller, 1985) which on the one hand, might explain the tendency towards male objectivism in science (which I also find confirmed in the male study of mysticism) and acceptance on the other also might explain the greater female leaning towards mysticism and the acceptance of the alternative epistemology this gives rise to. Thus, men, because of the double dis-identification from the mother (a socio-cultural phenomenon), may tend to lean more towards objectivism, while women may have conserved a greater general capacity for symbiosis, a capacity which also furthers their ability to experience oneness with the holy. These tentative gender differences have implications, of course, for both theology and science.

What disturbs me in Elisabetta Donini's article is that it is not concerned with religious knowledge or theology. Therefore the immanence/transcendence problem is solved through an a-religious category "the immediacy of relations"; the theological problem of objectivist knowledge is solved through "contextualized knowledge" and the spiritual values of many ecofeminists are substituted by mothering because this produces existence and not goods. Elisabetta Donini, in other words, is opting so strongly for the immanent that transcendence, the other side of the paradoxical oneness, disappears. The spiritual paradox is not developed theologically into a questioning of objectivist epistemology, but rather into a socio-historical category, namely, contextualized knowledge.

What I find in the Goddess movement is a great joy through a particular spiritual praxis and a theological attempt at symbolizing this through the Goddess-symbol. This symbol is a metaphor just like Elisabetta Donini's concept of "motherhood" (McFague, 1982). However, it is a theological metaphor which is pointing at specifically religious experiences. I find this stimulating because it throws light upon how metaphors are used in patriarchal theology, as well. I therefore see it as:

1. A theological symbol which challenges traditional theology: (which mother would, for example, sacrifice her only-begotten son to still her wrath?).
2. A spiritual symbol which stretches my spiritual imagination (praying to a mother feels different from praying to a father).

However, in the end, I find it important to return to concrete spiritual experiences as the source for a new theology, as well as the basis for a dialogue with history. Religious experiences are embedded in history, culture, and social circumstances. Therefore, racial and ethnic differences must be acknowledged. However, new religious experiences also arise, and therefore there is hope that, little by little, we may change theology as a science.

Bibliography

Sallie McFague, *Metaphorical Theology: Models of God in Religious Language* Philadelphia: Fortress Press, 1982.

W. James, *The Varieties of Religious Experience* New York: Mentor Books, 1958.

Zusammenfassung

Das wichtigste Problem und die Lösung von Elisabetta Donini ist dargestellt. Im hinblick auf die Nachforschung in der religiösen Erfahrung der Frauen, und die Begeisterung in der Göttin-Bewegung, der Artikel von Elisabetta Donini wird kritisiert, weil ihre religiöse Erfahrung und Theologie zu Sozial-Historische Categoriën heruntergebracht werden.

Sommaire

Un aperçu est donné des principaux problèmes soulevés et des solutions proposées dans le travail d'Elisabetta Donini. La lumière de recherches sur les expériences religieuses des femmes et de l'inspiration que leur a donnée le mouvement de la Déesse, l'article d'Elisabetta Donini est accusé d'avoir reduit les expériences religieuses et la théologie à des catégories socio-historiques.

Lene Sjørup holds a PhD from the University of Copenhagen. Her dissertation *Oneness. A Theology of Women's Religious Experiences* is an investigation into women's religious experiences in the North, while her present project *Religious and Democracy: Poor Chilean Woman Speak Out* builds upon almost 300 interviews with marginalized women in Chile. She is a research fellow at the Centre for Development Research in Copenhagen.

Elisabetta Donini

A Final Response

Diversity in the Mirror: the Start of a Dialogue?

First of all I would like to thank my dialogue partners for their attentive reading of my text; they have carefully grasped my intentions before expressing their critical disagreement. These are good premises for a frank dialogue in which we remain both loyal to ourselves and to each other by listening carefully as well as stating our own point of view.This word of thanks is not a mere formality but alludes to one of the problems which seems, in light of this dialogue, the most fascinating and yet irresolvable. Reciprocal "com-prehensio" is not "reductio ad unum": what I find fascinating is that dialectical tension produced in the encounter between different subjectivities who, in order to recognize themselves as different, must still be open enough to understand the worldview which informs each other's discourse. What seems irresolvable, however, is precisely the paradoxical nature of such a relationship; the dynamic of diversity does not generate identity but rather re-proposes, from different and unexpected angles, a shifting variety of multiple meanings which are incommensurable[1].

A Crucial Asymmetry

This brings me to the point on which I have been most criticized: Lene Sjørup, Celia E Deane-Drummond and Aruna Gnanadason have all, although in slightly different ways, voiced their dissatisfaction with the perspective that I described as "the immediacy of relations along the inexhaustible chain of material and cultural interdependencies". They each observe that this "material rootedness in relations" is an ineffective "basis for realistic hope" (Deane-Drummond, p.71) or that "pluralist friendship...is inadequate to express the need for women to transcend all 'man-made' boundaries" (Gnanadason, p.75); or that opting for "contextualized knowledge" means being reduced to a "socio-historical category", and thus losing the spiritual dimension (Sjørup, p.80). I do not think further logical arguments in support of my "opting for the immanent" are to be found; rather I believe that precisely at this juncture the incommensurability between different standpoints which – despite the best of intentions - cannot be reconciled,(even

[1] Thomas S Kuhn (1962) introduced this term into the history and sociology of science and here I am using it in the same way, *viz* when compared with each other, different conceptions are generally not true or false but represent different viewpoints (or paradigms) each employing criteria which cannot simply be reduced one to the other and are therfore incommensurable

though they seek to be mutually comprehensible), plays a decisive role. I prefer to see not so much conflict between immanence and transcendence as a crucial asymmetry between our most profound existential identities: while I am radically outside the religious dimension, my dialogue partners are just as radically within it. This, I believe, is at the roots of the basic objection raised by Sjørup: "what disturbs me in Elisabetta Donini's article is that it is not concerned with religious knowledge or theology" (p.81). Likewise, Gnanadason states "what is difficult for me to accept in Elisabetta's analysis is her rejection of 'spiritual values' and symbols and rituals and her affirmation of the 'material nature of daily life'" (p.76). Right from the outset Deane-Drummond also states that she is eager to discuss why I am "so resistant to the idea of symbols and rituals", and thus lay myself open to the risk of "leaving 'religious' questions split off from 'secular' ones" (p.70). Honesty both towards myself and my dialogue partners obliges me to respond by making the meaning of my contribution even more explicit: the only framework in which I can perceive myself and my relationship to the world is a socio-historical one. This certainly includes the spiritual dimension, but only as one of the countless material and cultural forms into which human beings have organized their existence. I thus consider "religious" questions strictly "secular", products of the concrete and symbolic vicissitudes of history. In other words, the decisive question is not so much whether we lean towards immanence or transcendence but whether (or not) we grant them full autonomy before and beyond the men who, throughout the centuries have elaborated these concepts. (I use "men" in the sense of "males" and not "humanity" as the religious enterprise is completely characterized by gender imbalance). I am in full agreement with Deane-Drummond when she stresses "the importance of language in creating new patterns of thought" (p.72); but precisely for this reason: it is significant that in the replies to my article, the spiritual has been granted not only religious meaning but that this has been expressed in terms of positive religion, so that the ecofeminist proposal of the "resacralization of nature" has been re-proposed in terms of "faith" or a "sensitivity to the numinous in the natural world" (Deane-Drummond, pp.70, 71). The same idea pervades Gnanadason's response in which the term "creation" appears, from the title onwards, throughout. I do not find Sjørup's suggestion, that God the Father can be replaced by prayer to a mother as a "theological" or "spiritual symbol" (p.82) satisfactory, in that I am unable to imagine a presence which goes beyond the contingency and immanence of history and nature in which I am immersed.I regret if my lack of a religious perspective has offended my respondent's sensitivity and I would express a great deal of respect for their own standpoint (and much sympathetic solidarity when - as women - they express the need for liberation from patriarchal traditions). However, my aim is to understand why women and men have created and still create the spiritual dimension and not to measure myself against it, as if it were an autonomous reality, nor to see the world as divine "creation" whether the work of a God or of a Goddess.

Science and Faith: Transcendence and Alienation

In my article I tried to make clear why I believe that both religion and science in Western culture descend, on the male side, from a recourse to God the Father and how this has left its mark of transcendence on them. In light of the comments and criticisms I have received I shall clarify my position further. Celia Deane-Drummond wonders if my "background in science" stands behind my reluctance to accept "more mystical and less 'concrete' aspects of reality". She cites various examples from Barbara McClintock to Fritjof Capra to show that, on the contrary, "for many scientists the mystical is embedded in their own experiences of relating to the 'world outside'" (p.70). On the one hand, I must admit that if, many years ago, I opted to studied physics, it was precisely because I was seeking a rational and material relation to the things in the world far away from the biases and bonds of faith. On the other hand, however, I was then forced to alter my perspective drastically and, for some time now, I have been researching those biases and bonds which underlie the values science assumes to be true and thus actually orientate scientific production.

The various marriages between faith and science do not therefore surprise me, especially if we look at them in the light of their originating dynamics in the 17th century. As I have already mentioned, Galileo, Newton, Descartes and Leibnitz needed the Divine Mind to ground their research into the rational laws of nature. We need, however, to look more carefully at what meaning the mystical experiences of 20th century physics or the identification of the maize chromosome by Barbara McClintock, can have for us today. In any case, I think there is a big difference between McClintock's perspective, which Fox Keller has aptly called "a feeling for the organism", and the hypertechnological universe of quantum physics[2].

Deane-Drummond detects in such encounters between science and mysticism, "a sensitivity to the numinous in the natural world, including human beings"(p.71) and hopes that by stressing "spiritual values" ecofeminism can begin to effect a "rapprochement with science". I interpret such a project as a contnuation and confirmation of male- oriented thought and its obsession with a hierarchy which privileges the abstract over the concrete. In other words, it gives us one more reason to be suspicious of both science and mysticism. David

[2] Fox Keller has herself nore than once emphasized that McClintock was an extremely complex figure. In particular, she has recently made clear that "empathy was not McClintock's leading metaphor for herself. In fact, she rather romanticized a different metaphor which was that of a loss of self and she often evoked that as an ideal, a state where all sense of self disappears. . . a kind of Buddhist notion of loss of self". (For this and other relevant passages cf. Donini 1991, pp.154-159). This statement becomes relevant in light of the problem that Gnanadason raises, concerning the different meaning of "individual" or "the essential connectedness. . . a duality in unity and not in hierarchy" found in Western and Indian cultures respectively.

Noble's recent research becomes relevant at this point. According to Noble there is a continuity in the way science has been grafted onto relgion as a "world without women". Noble shows, through a detailed historical and sociological analysis of the changing reality both in the scientific community and the church, as well as of the way scientific production is organized, how science and religion are built on an extremely misogynist pattern. He thus establishes a connection between "transcendence" and "acting from the outside", rather similar to the line of reasoning which appeared in my article:

> *Despite its utilitarian rhetoric, and abundantly apparent consequences, science has carried forth what has been essentially a transcendent enterprise. For, in the eyes of its exclusively male inhabitants, the clerical culture always existed above and apart from society. It was a spiritual redoubt from within which the clergy could judge and guide the rest of humanity - as it were, from outside. In such a rarefied realm, masculinity readily came to be associated with separation and transcendence, manifested in the seemingly unambiguous authority of artifice and abstraction. The more "earthy" feminine, meanwhile, was disdained as disorder, dreaded as the embodiment of worldly corruption. As an extension of clerical culture, Western science inherited and per-petuated such associations which continue to mark the scientific mission and milieu. (Noble 1992, p. 281).*

To conclude on this topic, I shall now reply to Deane-Drummond's objection:

> *There is an inconsistency in the argument here. 1. On the one hand we find a radical rejection of the 'objectivity' of science, so that nature becomes more like a 'subject'. 2. On the other hand this same subjectivity is identified with the material as opposed to the spiritual (p.71).*

It is my opinion that criticizing the presumed objectivity of science does not mean projecting subjectivity onto nature. Probably I failed to express myself clearly enough at this point as Deane-Drummond (p.72) attributes me with a further contradiction: while on the one hand I affirm that "nature does not need to be humanized", on the other hand I maintain "the introduction of the idea of 'subjectivity'" which is in itself "a a form of humanization". The two issues need to be distinguished. The first concerns the process of knowing which does not occur when the observing subject gains control over an observed object, but when a relationship is established between two interdependent, interconnected and active terms. The second issue deals with the basis of the critique (which is not an exclusively feminist one) concerning the objectivity of science; and with the recognition that what scientists affirm of nature is not nature itself but a representation of nature. From this point of view, science - not nature - is granted subjectivity as a socially, historcally and culturally constructed discourse and not the necessary or exclusive bearer of phenomena.

Finally, I want to take up a very significant term which Deane-Drummond often uses, especially when she notes that I consider "any transcendence at all...alien and to be rejected" (p.70 - note the use of the word 'alien' in similar contexts on pp.70,72). I fully accept this characterization and this encourages me to be even more explicit. I am in fact aware that in my rejection of transcendence, my marxist formation is at work, but because of my feminist rereading this now seems to take on a new and different meaning: the metaphysical dimension appears alienated and alienating in so far as it claims to objectify subjectivity and to absolutize the contingent according to that exclusively male predilection for separation and acting from the outside.

Doubts about Mothering and the Feminine

I have dealt with Deane-Drummond's critique at some length because certain misunderstandings needed clarification. Once granted the basic asymmetry in our approaches, I read Sjørup's and Gnanadason's responses with great interest on account of the input each gave out of her personal experience. I will thus limit my comments to some marginal questions. Out of the references that Sjørup makes to her research on the differences between men and women's religious experience, I found her observation that "men's mystical experiences seem to be triggered in different settings than women's (for example in war)" (p.81) particularly helpful. War is one area in which we are beginning to see some of the most tragic aspects of the unequal distribution of power between the sexes, as the masculine is modelled more on obsession with death than on sensitivity towards life. It is worth mentioning that the creators of science were largely pervaded by the same mentality so that the thirst for knowledge and domination on the one hand and the race towards weapons of an increasingly destructive capacity, on the other hand, ultimately converged[4].

As for femininity, it is just as important to note that "women's mystical experiences were triggered by nature, by the body (in sexuality and birthgiving)...". It is imperative, in the ongoing feminist debate, that rootedness in the psychophysical experience of being woman's body is not identified exclusively with women's generative capacity. This is an aspect of patriarchal culture we need to get rid of; relational tension, the propensity to experience oneself in continuity with oneself rather than in isolation from the other, the ability to see events unfolding from within rather than projecting oneself from without, need to be related to the erotic dimensions of women's sexuality just as much as motherhood, pregnancy, parturition and caring for children. My dialogue partners have pointed out the ambiguity of my reference to "mothering" and I realize that my treatment of the topic was somewhat vague and inconclusive. Gnanadason, particularly, in her discussion of Indian feminist thought, indicates in mothering "the basis of community life in many societies - where women's mothering role is important" (p.76) and that mothering enables Indian women to articulate a holistic vision with its deep connexion to nature. At the same time, however, she points out that this can be "idealised, used and abused... seeing women only in a child-bearing role" (p.75). While we should also bear in mind from the cultural and symbolic perpec-

[4] A considerable amount of feminist reflexion follows these lines but a male critique also exists: cf Easlea (1983)

tive that feminists have reconstructed "the essential connectedness - that person and nature (purusha - prakriti) are a duality in unity and not a hierarchy", we should also recognize "that this essence was also distorted by some strains of Indian philosophy that had been influenced by patriarchal brahminical hinduism" (p.77).We thus come to another delicate issue: how much capacity for autonomy and self- determination exists in the various women's movements and in their cultures? Ynestra King has recently brought to our attention the critique of "the ethnocentricity of much White feminism" raised by

> *Women of color who draw on indigenous spiritual traditions and who argue that these White Western feminists are inventing and originating an earth-centered pro-woman spirituality while they are defending their indigenous spirituality against the imperialism of Western rationalism (King 1990, p.112).*

But, as we have just seen, no tradition is free from the mark left by male gender dominance. Together with King we should remember that in every context "women have a complexity of historical identities and therefore a complexity of loyalties" (ibid. p.113). I would also add that when identities and the awareness of our religious and ethnic roots are absolutized, they become static prisons and tend to produce nationalistic, ethnic, racial and religious intolerance, but when they are considered contingent, especially in the encounter with other subjectivities, they are open to transformation.

In responding to my critics, I realize that my emphasis on relations between women is a "weak" approach. However, I am still persuaded that working from within the women's movement is meaningful because, thanks to its historical characteristics, it is that collective political subject most able to erode, here and now, the injustices of our present world, injustices of North versus South, of gender and class, of our unbalanced relationship to nature. I sought to explain something of this conviction when I spoke of the complete reversal of perspective that can be achieved if we start from women's historical identity and on this basis, work to emphasize "those activities that produce 'existence' rather than 'goods'".

A Final Thanks

In the "vulgate" version of marxism on which, thanks to my mother, I was reared, there was a phrase which always used to strike me: "God is the help man gives to man". I used to like this phrase for two reasons: firstly, because it brought religion down to earth, showing it as a human product, removed from any transcendence, and secondly, because it underlined that solidarity is possible and individuals do not necessarily have to be divided and in conflict. Of course now I can no longer feel the same enthusiasm: the very word "man" strikes a negative chord straightaway as I can no longer accept that women are implicit (and indeed feminist thought has modified my relationship to marxism). However, while sincerely respecting those who find in the sacred a way to be linked with others in solidarity and interdependence I still find that little phrase a helpful synthesis as far as religious phenomena are concerned .

When, several months ago, Elizabeth Green invited me to write on ecofeminism and theology, I was a little perplexed, but I agreed to accept by Elizabeth's assuring me of the broad nature of the project which was to include a plurality of perspectives. Hindsight has perhaps revealed too great a difference between my standpoint and questions of a theological nature. However, I am still grateful to the editors for having set in motion this attempt at dialogue for at least it has forced me to measure myself against my own presuppositions, in order to better understand those intellectual and political choices I regard as meaningful and discover what margins of communication are possible when we respect diversity. I am also grateful to Elizabeth for having allowed me to express myself in my mother tongue - for as Hannah Arendt (1964) has taught us, there are no alternatives - and for having translated my writing with care and patience so that I feel at home even with the words she has lent me. Relations between women are also woven out of these acts of generosity.

Zusammenfassung

Im Aufblick auf die Einwände, die Unvergleichlische Art der verschiedenen Standpunkte ob religiös oder nicht wird hier diskutiert. Gewisse Themen (die Beziehung zwischen Wissenschaft und das Transcendenz, Objektivität und Subjektivität, feministische und traditionelle verständnissen der Weiblichkeit, die Wichtigkeit der Beziehungen zwischen Frauen), werden hier behändelt um einen dialog mit verschiedenartigen Meinungen offen zu halten.

Sommaire

À la lumière des objections soulevèes, la nature incommensurable de différents points de vue, qu'ils soient religieux ou non, est examinée. Afin de s'assurer que le dialogue avec la diversité reste ouvert, des questions spécifiques sont ensuite abordées (la relation entre la science et la transcendance, entre l'objectivité et la subjectivité, la féminité sous des perspectives féministes et traditionelles, l'importance des relations entre les femmes).

Harriëtte Blankers

Teresa of Avila: Experience of God

A full introduction of Teresa of Avila (1515-1582) would take a long enumeration of the many aspects of her life and personality. She was not only a mystic and spiritual leader, but also a writer, a reformer of the Carmelite order and foundress of sixteen reformed Carmelite convents. In her own lifetime the papal nuncio described her as a 'restless gadabout'. In the seventeenth century she was canonized by the Catholic Church. In 1970 she became officially a Doctor of the Church. Today she is one of the most popular saints of Spain, often referred to as 'la Santa simpática'.

From the many texts Teresa wrote, I have chosen a passage from her most famous work, 'Moradas del Castillo Interior' (The Interior Castle), written in 1577. Because I do not want to deprive Teresa of her own language, the passage is printed in the Spanish version[1]. My guide to this passage looks at the text as an articulation of a mystical process of the God-human encounter.

I have chosen this special text because it demonstrates Teresa's deep respect for creation. That is shown, first, on a profound level. Teresa sees God's presence in everything He created, a presence that primarily coincides with the 'being alive' of creation. Whoever is on his or her way towards God, according to Teresa, does not need to be averse to the world, for God also can be known through his very creatures themselves: *'en todas las que crió tan gran Dios, tan sabio, deve haver hartos secretos'*. This Teresa illustrates through using a comparison (two basins filled with water) to describe two experiences of God. Here she explicitly says that water is of more value to her than as merely a practical symbol for God's operations. This same idea of God's presence also concerns us humans: *'en nosotros mesmos están grandes secretos'*. Although sidestep to the water-comparison, it is the foundation of one of the two experiences of God. Moreover, there God's presence appears in all its dynamic possibilities: God as Himself starts to work in the human person. In relation to this, a second demonstration of Teresa's respect for creation is shown. According to her, even in a 'high degree' of mystical experience, all the aspects of our humanity still play a role.

Before this passage, Teresa explained the difference between two delightful

[1] Passage taken from: Santa Teresa de Jesús, Obras completas, transcripción, introducciones y notas de Efrén de la Madre de Dios y Otger Steggink, Madrid 1986(8), 499-501. Possible translations for a (necessary!) comparison with the Spanish text: Thérèse d'Avila, Oevres complètes, texte français par Marcelle Auclair, Bruges 1964; The complete works of St. Teresa de Jesus, translated and edited by E. Allison Peers, London 1946; Sämtliche Schriften der heiligen Theresia von Jesu, übersetzt und hrsg. von Aloysius Alkofer, München 1931-1941.

experiences of God, 'contento' (contentment; satisfaction) and 'gusto' (taste; enjoyment; pleasure). In both experiences we feel delight in our human nature. That is not what distinguishes them. In the text below, Teresa opens up once again the explanation of the difference, but on reading the passage one will notice that most emphasis lies in the explanation of the "gustos".

The "contento"-experience of God is (largely) made possible by human activity and efforts (*'nuestras diligencias'*). We acquire it in meditation, by working with our intellect and imagination. Moreover, the experience takes shape as such through these human faculties. In other words: we experience God in our human way, or we react to God in our human way. The cause of the experience then lies in the human, but the origin of the experience is also in our own human nature. To describe this origin, however, Teresa does not use the word *'nacimiento'*. She reserves that word in this text only for God. That is why it only functions in her explanation of the "gustos".

In that explanation the pronoun 'we' appears not only on one level. The only initiative to the "gusto-experience" is taken by God, the only activity that plays a part in the occurrence is God's operation, the only reason for it lies in God (Gods will): *'y ansí, como Su Majestad quiere, cuando es servido hacer alguna merced sobrenatural, produce'*. There is no effort on our side that is of any influence on this. Furthermore, the experience itself cannot come to us any more by way of our human faculties, for they are completely helpless with respect to what permeates them. I realize that this also changes the meaning of the term 'experience': from 'we experience God within the dimensions or proportions of our human experiencing' (contentos), into 'we experience God in the sense of God himself is happening within us, and that breaks straight through all the frameworks of experience we have' (gustos).

Teresa explains these two structures of mystical experience with a comparison of two basins that are filled with water. The central symbol is the living water, penetrating everything. Of equal symbolic importance, however, are the different locations of the two basins. When Teresa writes *'el otro está hecho en el mesmo nacimiento del agua'* she implicitly uses an opposition of a distance between the source and the basin (God-soul) with the "contentos", versus a nearness of the other basin being in the source itself with the "gustos". Implicitly, because with the "contentos" it does not suit her to mention a source. With the "contentos" she therefore stresses the movement of the water over a certain path and through conduits, while the explicit consequence of the nearness of the source and the basin with the "gustos" is an immediate event happening directly at the source.

With the "gustos" Teresa simultaneously speaks of water that comes from its origin itself (*'nacimiento'*) which is God, and of water that proceeds from the most interior part of ourselves. A bit further in the text, she uses the same term *'nacimiento'* also in connection with *'otra parte aún mas interior'* of ourselves (more interior to ourselves than the heart). By doing this, she seems to equate God with the most interior part of ourselves. In my opinion, Teresa here sees our deepest inner self as what is uncreated of the soul[2], as what is originating from God, as what is like God, as what is God. The most interior part of ourselves is the Other. From this perspective, the "gustos", as specific experiences of *delight*, are not anymore our joyful experiences of God, but God who starts to enjoy himself in us. As this is also the point where God and the human person touch each other, the delight that arises here is the event of the growing relation itself with the Other.

This delight we feel. At first, however, we feel it in that point in ourselves that is not a kind of (very deep) level of our humanity. We feel it in the indescribable point of contact between God and the human person (*'deve ser el centro del alma'*). Afterwards, according to Teresa, it also affects all layers and dimensions of our humanity in which we as creatures differ from God. The entire soul (person), the entire human nature, including the body (*'hasta llegar a el cuerpo'*) feels it. This means: the entire soul tastes the event of the growing relation with the Other. And it feels the same delight, not a derivative version of it. This effect must be a transforming effect. For we, in our entirety, become more sensitive for the divine, but God's acting also enables us to be more sensitive. This also means that the centre of the soul and 'the rest' more or less begin to cooperate. Therefore, with *'todo nuestro interior'* and *'toda el alma'*, Teresa says that the soul grows towards an interior unity.

In the last paragraph of the text this leads to a tension between speaking of real sense perception (*'mas el calor y humo oloroso penetra toda el alma, y aun veces...participa el cuerpo'*) and speaking of feeling or smelling *'para dárosla a entender*. I understand this as follows. In the normal anthropology of Teresa's time the senses were the means to perceive exterior stimuli. Now all the senses are united by the divine to become immediate receivers of this mystical experience. Nothing of the human person vanishes, and no special 'spiritual' sense is added to him or her, but our complete sense perception develops from functioning in a human way into an undivided sensitivity for the divine and into its immediate receiver. On the one hand Teresa's terminology is correct, but, simultaneously, it must be wide of the mark for an experience that goes far beyond any description. It is therefore inadequate sensory imagery for a sensual experience that is all-too-real.

2. *Hagamos cuenta, para entenderlo mejor, que vemos dos fuentes con dos pilas que se hinchen de agua. Que no me hallo cosa más a propósito para declarar algunas de espíritu que esto de agua; y es -como sé poco y el ingenio no ayuda y soy tan amiga de este elemento- que le he mirado con más advertencia que otras cosas, que en todas las que crió tan gran Dios, tan sabio, deve haver hartos secretos de que*

[2] In Teresa's sixteenth century antropology, the term 'soul' refers to the entire person. The 'higher part' of the soul consists of the three rational faculties ('voluntad', 'entendimiento', 'memoria'), in the 'lower part' of the soul she locates the sensible faculties, like the five senses. The body is related to the sensual.

nos podemos aprovechar, y ansí lo hacen los que lo entienden; aunque creo que en cada cosita que Dios crió hay más de lo que se entiende, aunque sea una hormiguita.

3. *Estos dos pilones se hinchen de agua de diferentes maneras; el uno viene de más lejos por muchos arcaduces y artificio; el otro está hecho en el mesmo nacimiento del agua y vase hinchendo sin nengún ruido; y si es el manantial caudaloso, como este de que hablamos, después de henchido este pilón procede un gran arroyo; ni es menester artificio ni se acaba el edificio de los arcaduces, sino siempre está procediendo agua de allí. Es la diferencia que la que viene por arcaduces es -a mi parecer- los contentos que tengo dicho que se sacan con la meditación, porque los traemos con los pensamientos ayudándonos de las criaturas en la meditación y cansando el entendimiento; y como viene, en fin, con nuestras diligencias, hace ruido cuando ha de haver algún hinchimiento de provechos que hace en el alma, como queda dicho.*

4. *Estotra fuente viene el agua de su mesmo nacimiento, que es Dios; y ansí, como Su Majestad quiere, cuando es servido hacer alguna merced sobrenatural, produce con grandísima paz y quietud y suavidad de lo muy interior de nosotros mesmos (yo no sé hacia dónde ni cómo, ni aquel contento y deleite se siente como los de acá en el corazón, digo en su principio, que después todo lo hinche), vase revertiendo este agua por todas las moradas y potencias hasta llegar a el cuerpo, que por eso dije que comienza de Dios y acaba en nosotros* [3]*; que cierto, coma verá quien lo huviere provado, todo el hombre esterior goza de este gusto y suavidad.*

5. *Estava yo ahora mirando escriviendo esto, que en el verso que dije: ≪Dilataste cor meun≫*[4]*, dice que se ensanchó el corazón, y no me parece que es cosa -como digo- que su nacimiento es del corazón, sino de otra parte aún mas interior, como una cosa profunda. Pienso que deve ser el centro del alma, como después he entendido y diré a la postre*[5]*; que cierto veo secretos en nosotros mesmos que me train espantada muchas veces; y ¡cuantás más deve haver!*

   ¡Oh, Señor mío y Dios mío, qué grandes son vuestras grandezas!, y andamos acá como unos pastorcillos bovos, que nos parece alcanzamos algo de Vos y deve ser tanto como nonada, pues en nosotros mesmos están grandes secretos que no entendemos. Digo tanto como nonada, para lo muy muy mucho que hay en Vos, que no porque no son muy grandes las grandezas que vemos, aun de lo que podemos alcanzar de vuestras obras.

6. *Tornando a el verso en lo que me puede aprovechar -a mi parecer- para aquí es en aquel ensanchamiento; que ansí parece que, como comienza a producir aquella agua celestial de este manantial que digo de lo profundo de nosotros, parece que se va dilatando y ensanchando todo nuestro interior y produciendo unos bienes que no se pueden decir, ni aun el alma sabe entender qué es lo que se le da allí. Entiende una fragancia -digamos ahora- como si en aquel hondón interior estuviese un brasero adonde se echasen olorosos perfumes; ni se ve la lumbre ni dónde está; mas el calor y humo oloroso penetra toda el alma, y aun hartas veces -como he dicho- participa el cuerpo.*

   Mirad, entendedme, que ni se siente calor ni se huele olor, que más delicada cosa es que estas cosas, sino para dároslo a entender. Y entiendan las personas que no han pasado por esto, que es verdad que pasa ansí y que se entiende y lo entiende el alma más claro que yo lo digo ahora. Que no es esto cosa que se puede antojar, porque por diligencias que hagamos no lo podemos adquirir, y en ello mesmo se ve no ser de nuestro metal, sino de aquel purísimo oro de la sabiduría divina. Aquí no están las potencias unidas -a mi parecer-, sino embevidas y mirando como espantadas qué es aquello. (4Moradas2)

[3] In 4Moradas1 Teresa used a model of two opposite movements to explain the difference between the "contentos" and the "gustos". Her description of the "gusto" movement was: *'Los gustos comienzan de Dios y siéntelos el natural'.*

[4] 'Dilatasti cor meum', Ps. 118,32 (Vulg.). For a more detailed explanation of the "gustos" Teresa used in 4Moradas1 'for you have enlarged my heart'.

[5] 7Moradas1-2.

Zusammenfassung

Theresia von Avila beschreibt im Zweiten Kapitel der "vierten Wohnung" aus "Die Innere Burg" zwei unterschiedliche, aber evenso erleuchtende Erfahrungen mit Gott, ("contento" = Zufriedenheit; "gusto" = Wonne). Der Artikel analysiert die Strukturen dieser Erfahrungen und erklärt die Metaphorik, mit der Theresia sie zum Ausdruck bringen will. Um Verständnis für die "gustos" zu bekommen, zeigt der Artikel die Wichtigkeit Theresia's Gottesvorstellung auf, welche den innersten Teil in uns selbst darstellt.

Sommaire

Thérèse d'Avila, au deuxième chapitre des 'quatrièmes demeures' du *Château interieur*, décrit deux expériences, bien distinctes mais également ravissantes, qu'elle nomme 'contento' (contentement) et 'gusto' (plaisir). Cet article analyse les structures de ces expériences et explicite les images utilisés par Thérèse pour les exprimer. Il démontre l'importance de l'image de Dieu – qui serait la partie la plus intime de nous-même – pour l'intelligibilité des 'gustos' (plaisirs).

Harriëtte Blankers studied theology in Tilburg and at the University of Nijmegen. She worked for two years in a centre for spirituality in Utrecht. Since 1992 she has been research assistant in the University of Nijmegen, preparing her dissertation on the subject of: *A Hermeneutical-Feminist Research into Corporeality in the Mystical Texts of Teresa of Avila.*

Katharina von Kellenbach

Frl. Rabbiner Regina Jonas (1902–1944): Lehrerin, Seelsorgerin, Predigerin

"Sind Sie nicht die erste Rabbinerin? "fragte Rabbiner Dr. F. Gutmann in seinem Glückwunschschreiben zwei Wochen nach Regina Jonas' Ordination am 1. Januar 1936, und fügte hinzu, "so werden Sie noch in die Geschichte des Judentums als Bahnbereiterin eingehen[1]. Trotz ihrer wichtigen Rolle als erste Rabbinerin blieb das Leben der Regina Jonas bislang im Dunkeln. Ihr Triumph, die jahrhunderte alte, männliche Vorherrschaft in der Synagoge gebrochen zu haben, wurde vom Holocaust zunichte gemacht. Nach ihrem Tod in Auschwitz wurde die Stimme dieser unbequemen, religiösen Frauenrechtlerin vergessen. Als in den siebziger Jahren im Zuge der zweiten Welle der Frauenbewegung die Zulassung von Frauen zum Rabbinat in den USA erneut diskutiert wurde, erwachte das Interesse an Rabbiner Jonas wieder[2].

Auf der Suche nach Informationen war man bislang auf die Erinnerung ehemaliger, männlicher Kollegen angewiesen gewesen. In deren Erinnerung wird Regina Jonas als eigenwillige und verbissene Einzelkämpferin, die nicht "ordentlich" ordiniert war, und nie als Gemeinderabbinerin arbeiten durfte, beschrieben. Dieses Bild der Regina Jonas kann nun, nachdem ihr Nachlaßim-Bundesarchiv Potsdam gefunden wurde, revidiert werden. Schon bei einer flüchtigen Schau des dort eingelagerten Materials stellt man fest, daß Jonas als Rabbinerin in der Öffentlichkeit erstaunlich bekannt und respektiert war und daß die Fülle der Korrespondenz das Portrait einer schrulligen Einzelgängerin nicht rechtfertigt.

Regina Jonas wurde am 3. August 1902 in Berlin geboren, erhielt 1923 das Reifezeugnis vom Oberlyzeum Weißensee und besuchte von Mai 1924 bis April 1930 die Hochschule für die Wissenschaft des Judentums in Berlin. Von dort wurde sie im Dezember 1930 mit einem Zeugnis als akademische Religionslehrerin entlassen. Ihr Talmudlehrer, Dr. Baneth, der ihre halachische (religionsgesetzliche) Arbeit zum Thema "Kann die Frau das rabbinische Amt bekleiden?" mit dem Prädikat "Gut" angenommen hatte, verstarb noch vor der mündlichen Prüfung. Sein Nachfolger wollte ihr die für das Rabbinatsdiplom notwendige, mündliche, talmudische Prüfing nicht mehr abnehmen. Aber Regina

1 Soweit nicht anders gekennzeichnet sind alle Zitate aus dem Jonas Nachlass zitiert: Bundesarchiv Potsdam, 75 Jg 1 Nr 15.

2 Sally Priesand, *Judaism and the New Woman*, New York: Behrman House. 1975 p.76. Roslyn Lacks, *Women and Judaism*, Garden City, Doubleday 1980 pp.193-195.

Jonas, die als Religionslehrerin sehr beliebt war, wollte sich nicht auf das Lehramt beschränken lassen. Sie wollte Rabbinerin werden. Leo Baeck stellte ihr eine Zusatzbescheinung über ihre erfolgreiche Teilnahme an seinem homiletischen Seminar, in dem sie sich als "gewändte Predigerin bewiesen hat", aus. Das Israelitische Familienblatt stellte am 4. Juni 1931 etwas mißbilligend fest, daß Jonas "schon in drei kleineren Gemeinden an Sabbathen die Predigerfunktion ausgeübt hat"[3]. Doch es sollte noch Jahre dauern bevor Jonas Anerkennung als predigende Rabbinerin zuteilwurde.

Regina Jonas gab Religionsunterricht an verschiedenen Schulen Berlins und forderte weiterhin Gleichstellung. Im Dezember 1935 willigte Max Dienemann, Rabbiner in Offenbach und Vorstand des Liberalen Rabbinerverbandes, ein, ihr die mündliche, halachische Prüfung abzunehmen und das Rabbinatsdiplom auszustellen. Vor der Einführung von Hochschulen für die Rabbinerausbildung im 19. Jahrhundert, war es üblich, daß einzelne rabbinische Gelehrte ihre Schüler als Rabbiner diplomierten. Auch heute noch machen einzelne bekannte Rabbiner von dieser Tradition Gebrauch. Die Reaktionen auf Dienemanns private S'micha (Ordination) waren sehr gemischt: zum einen erhielt Jonas Glückwünsche von ehemaligen Professoren (einschließlich Baeck) und Rabbinern aus Berlin, anderen Teilen Deutschlands und Israels sowie des Jüdischen Gemeindevorstand Berlins. Zum anderen durfte Jonas auch weiterhin nicht als Gemeinderabbinerin arbeiten, und wurde sogar von einigen aufgefordert, ihre S'micha zurückzugeben, da sie ungültig sei. Dienemann bestand zwar auf der Rechtmäßigkeit seines Rabbiner-diploms, gab ihr aber dennoch, fast ein Jahr später, den Rat, "keinerlei Anträge, sei es beim Rabbinat oder bei einzelnen Rabbinern zu stellen,... denn die Majorität ist gegen Sie". In dieser Zeit gestaltete Regina Jonas Oneg Shabbat (Feierstunde nach dem offiziellen Sabbatgottesdienst), predigte in Altersheimen und hielt Vorträge zu theologischen, biblischen und ethischen Themen beim Kulturbund, dem Jüdischen Frauenbund (JFB), diversen Logen, der Berliner Zionistischen Vereinigung (BZV) und der WIZO (Women's International Zionist Organization). Im August 1937 wurde sie offiziell vom Vorstand der Jüdischen Gemeinde zu Berlin als Religionslehrerin und zur "rabbinisch-seelsorgerischen Betreuung in den Sozialanstalten der Gemeinde" angestellt. Als Krankenhausseelsorgerin betreute sie Patienten in den städtischen Kliniken und übernahm rabbinische Funktionen in den Gottesdiensten des Altersheims und Krankenhauses in der Iranischen Straße, sowie anderen Altersheimen. Durch diese Predigten und Vorträge machte sie sich einen Namen in Berlin und es wurden gelegentlich Anträge an den Synagogenvorstand der Neuen Synagoge gerichtet, Jonas doch im regulären Sabbatgottesdienst predigen zu lassen. Je verzweifelter die Lage der jüdischen Gemeinden in Deutschland wurde, desto häufiger wurde

[3] Archiv der Stiftung Neue Synagoge Berlin, Centrum Judaicum.

Jonas als Aushilfsrabbinerin eingesetzt. Im September 1940 wurde Jonas die rabbinisch-seelsorgerische Betreuung der Gemeinde Woltersdorf übertragen, wobei es zweifelhaft ist, daß sie diese Stelle je antrat, da ihr Vorstellungsbrief wegen "unbekannter Adresse" zurückgesandt wurde. Außerdem wäre es wegen der extremen, gesetzlichen Bewegungseinschränkungen für sie fast unmöglich gewesen, öfter über die Stadtgrenze Berlins hinaus nach Woltersdorf zu fahren. 1940 wurde sie von der Reichsvereinigung der Juden auf eine dreimonatige Reise geschickt, um eine Reihe kleinerer Gemeinden in Stolpe, Braunschweig, Frankfurt (Oder), Gardelegen,Wolffenbüttel und Bremen "nach Auswanderung des Rabbiners" rabbinisch zu betreuen. Ob Jonas selbst versuchte, zu emigrieren und (aus finanziellen Gründen?) gescheitert war, oder ob sie sich entschied, weiterhin für die zurückgebliebenen Alten und Kranken zu sorgen, für deren Wohlfahrt sie manchmal Kontakte in die USA, nach Israel und China aufnahm, ist aus ihrem Nachlaß nicht ersichtlich.

Im Januar 1942 bat die Personalverwaltung der Berliner Jüdischen Gemeinde, nun genannt Kultusvereinigung, sie, ihr die Zeugnisse über ihre rabbinische Ausbildung zu übersenden. Dies muß wohl bedeuten, daß die Gemeinde angesichts der brennenden Krise und dem akuten Rabbinermangel nun doch bereit war, Regina Jonas' Zeugnisse anzuerkennen. Obwohl Rabbiner Jonas mittlerweile zur Zwangsarbeit in einer Berliner Kartonnagenfabrik eingezogen worden war, setzte sie ihre Arbeit als Seelsorgerin und Predigerin in den, soweit noch funktionierenden, sozialen Einrichtungen der Gemeinde fort. Zwei Wochen vor ihrer Deportation wurde sie offiziell von der Jüdischen Kultusvereinigung beauftragt, "ehrenamtlich", die Sabbatansprache in der Synagoge Schönhauser Allee zu halten.Diese Dokumente geben Zeugnis darüber, wie lange die Berliner jüdischen Institutionen im Chaos antisemitischer Gesetzgebung und brutaler Willkür noch funktionsfähig blieben, aber auch darüber, wie nahe dem Abgrund sie kommen mußten, bevor sie bereit waren, eine Frau offiziell als Rabbinerin zu akzeptieren. Am 3. November 1942 stellte sie gemeinsam mit ihrer Mutter, mit der sie in der gesamten Zeit zusammenlebte, ihre "Vermögenserklärung" aus. Ihr Besitz wurde zwei Tage später zu Gunsten des Deutsches Reiches eingezogen und später für 142 Reichsmark versteigert[4]. Am 6. November 1942 wurden sie nach Theresienstadt deportiert[5].

In Theresienstadt engagierte sich Rabbiner Jonas als Mitglied eines von Viktor Frankl organisierten Empfangskommitees, das Neuankömmlinge vom Bahnhof abholte und behutsam auf die grauenhaften Zustände vorbereitete. Da die Menschen von den Nazis mit Lügen über komfortable Altersheime im Osten getäuscht worden waren, war es für das Überleben vieler Menschen entscheidend, den Schock der ersten Stunden und Tage in dem hoffnungslos überfüllte,

4 Landesarchiv Berlin Rep. 92 Acc. 3924.

5 Yad Vashem, Transport I/75-I/89. Jonas war Nummer 9.

und von Krankheit und Hunger gezeichneten Lager abzufangen. Jonas predigte, um den erschöpften und entmutigten Leuten Perspektive und Hoffnung zu vermitteln, und um ihre Widerstandskräfte zu mobilisieren. Darüberhinaus setzte sie ihre Vortrags- und Predigttätigkeit neben der Zwangsarbeit fort und sprach über Themen wie die Frau in der Bibel, Talmud und jüdische Geschichte, jüdisches Brauchtum, Gebet, Sabbathfreude in der Not, und jüdische Pflichten in Theresienstadt. Eine Liste mit 23 Vortragsthemen liegt in den Archiven Terezins, darunter auch Stichpunkte einer Predigt über den Vers "Du sollst das Volk nicht verfluchen, denn es ist gesegnet" (4. Moses 22,12)[6].

Dieser Vers war für die Menschen, die in den Netzen der Endlösung gefangen waren, sicherlich von besonderer Brisanz. Jonas deutet Gottes Segen weniger als ein Versprechen, vielmehr ein Ruf in die Verantwortung:

> *"Unser jüdisches Volk ist von Gott gesandt worden als ein 'gesegnetes'. Von Gott gesegnet sein heißt, wohin man tritt, in jeder Lebenslage Segen, Güte, Treue spenden – Demut vor Gott, selbstlose, hingebungsvolle Liebe zu seinen Geschöpfen erhalten die Welt. Diese Grundpfeiler der Welt zu errichten war und ist Israels Aufgabe. – Mann und Frau, Frau und Mann haben diese Pflicht in gleicher jüdischer Treue übernommen."*

Jonas umgeht die Möglichkeit, daß Gott sein Segenversprechen in Theresienstadt gebrochen haben könnte, wie das spätere, "nach-Auschwitz" Theologen, getan haben, sondern bindet das Leiden ihrer Gemeinde in die theologische Mission Israels ein und vermittelt dadurch Perspektive. Sie vermeidet es, Theresienstadt als gottgewollt zu rechtfertigen, aber sie entläßt ihre Gemeinde auch nicht aus der Verantwortung. Hier, wie in Berlin, besteht sie auf der fundamentalen religiösen Gleichstellung von Frau und Mann. Rabbiner Regina Jonas überlebte fast zwei Jahre lang in Theresienstadt. Sie wurde am 12. Oktober 1944 nach Auschwitz deportiert, von wo sie nicht zurückkehrte.

---

[6] Pamatnik Terezin, Ustredni Kartoteka.

Summary

This article traces the career of Regina Jonas, (born 1902 in Berlin, died 1944 in Auschwitz) who became the first woman ordained as a Rabbi. Having completed her studies at the Hochschule für die Wissenschaft des Judentum in 1930, she was ordained by Rabbi Max Dieneman in 1935 and worked as a religion teacher and chaplain in Jewish hospitals and senior citizen homes in Berlin. Her responsibilities and duties grew as Jewish life became increasingly constricted by the Nazi state. She survived in Theresienstadt from November 1942 until her final deportation to Auschwitz on October 12th 1944.

Sommaire

Cet article esquisse la carrière de Regina Jonas (née à Berlin en 1902, morte à Auschwitz en 1944) qui devint la première femme ordonnée rabbin. Ayant achevé ses études au *Hochschule für die Wissenschaft des Judentum* en 1930, elle fut ordonnée par le rabbin Max Dieneman en 1935, et travailla comme enseignante de religion et chapelain dans les cliniques et maisons de retraite juives à Berlin. Ses responsabilités et devoirs s'élargissaient au fur et à mesure que la vie juive devenait de plus en plus contrainte par le régime nazi. Elle survécut à Theresienstadt à partir de novembre 1942 jusqu'au 12 octobre 1944, date de son ultime déportation à Auschwitz.

Katharina von Kellenbach (PhD) ist Theologin und an den Schnittpunkten von Antisemitismus und Sexismus interessiert. Ihre Dissertation über Antijudaismus in christlicher und postchristlicher feministischer Theologie wird demnächst bei Scholars Press als Buch veröffentlicht. Sie lehrt am St Mary's College, Maryland, USA.

Dagny Kaul

Ecofeminism in the Nordic Countries

Environmentalism and feminism partly coincide in nordic politics. The leader of the United Nations Commission on the Environment and Development; "Our Common Future", was Gro Harlem Brundtland, the Prime Minister of Norway. 40% of the ministers in her Government are women, and the President of Parliament is a woman. In an international perspective, the five Nordic countries are in the forefront when women's position in church and society is concerned. Each university in the Nordic countries has a Centre for Women's Research.

Ecological research has been strongly supported by the Nordic governments. In Norway each university has its own Research Centre for Environment and Development. Through the Norwegian Research Council the government explicitly supports women's research on environment and development.

What is meant by Ecofeminism?

Ecofeminism is here to be understood as a cultural expression of a fundamental, ontological principle which determines the global vital process: life's immanent ability to renew itself. This principle implies that life in all its forms can grow and renew itself only through an interplay of the vital process where the absorption of nutrients, procreation and human culture form a part of balanced whole.

This life-renewing principle is characterised as ecofeminist because of its critical and constructive function[1]. Ecofeminist research has established a connection between the scientifically based depreciation of nature and the discrimination against women. On the basis of preference given to the principle of life-renewal, ecofeminism intends to develop new understandings of nature and body in relation to freedom, to scientific and cultural creativity and to justice.

In Western cultures, natural sciences and technology have been employed to define the relationship to nature and to shape nature in a way that threatens the vital processes of the globe. In the field of women's research in the Nordic countries there is a widespread opinion that an ecofeminism which intends to counteract society's destruction of nature's vital processes, has to develop a theoretical basis for ecofeminist research. Ecofeminist theory is expected to serve

---

[1] Lotheringtron, A T: *Kvinner, utvikling og miljø: Utredning om et forskningsfelt*, FORUT-rapport SR0517, Tromsø Univ. 1991 p.44f.

feminist research in its attempts to turn science in an ecofeminist direction[2]. It is acknowledged that ecofeminist theory has to be developed on three, different levels which stay in interaction with each other.

1. Theories of science and knowledge that elaborate implications of the ecofeminist principle within different disciplines. Thus the necessary, interdisciplinary dialogue is made possible.
2. Fundamental, philosophical interpretations of the relationship between nature and human being/culture in a gender perspective will deepen the importance of ecofeminist research.
3. Ecofeminist theology interprets how the life process may be saved from ecological breakdown. In order to be relevant, ecofeminist theology needs to know the main lines of the theoretical reflection that is going on in science and feminist research.

Ecofeminist theory is as yet insufficiently developed. But there are elements of changes within Nordic, feminist research which reflect an ecofeminist commitment. In this report I focus on elements of change in areas where ecofeminism confronts masculine interpretations of nature; namely in the natural sciences, technology and in developmental and environmental research. It is a risky enterprise to cross the borders of one's own discipline. My intention, however, is to illustrate what is going on, and to highlight what problems - and hopes - are seen as central.

The Natural Sciences, Technology and Ecofeminism

Organisation

In Scandinavia much work has gone into the task of stimulating girl's interests in natural science. Particularly in Sweden this has had an impact all the way up to university level. Over a ten year period there have been books, seminars and conferences for students on "Gender, Technology and Science" at the Centre for Women's Research at the University of Lund and in Luleå[3]. In Sweden, scientific staff are appointed to work in this area. There is a tenured lectureship and one chair in "Gender and Science" in Luleå, as well as one time-limited chair (for guest-professors) at the university of Linköping. Women working in the field of natural sciences and technology have organised the largest supportive network in the Nordic countries.

Hilary Rose, a well known English theorist with theory of science as her speciality, claims that the lead the United States have in the development of feminist science, is visible to a lesser extent in the study of technology "where

[2] Troyer, Lena: **Forum i Lund - ett fritt rum für naturvetare,** Eds. Ullerstam, VBramming,Y.: *Festskrift til Ingrid Stjernquist,* Centre for Women's Research, Lund 1992; Munk-Madsen, E: *Kvinner, miljøog utvikling: Innsatsbehov påfeltet NAVF's sekretariat for kvinneforskning,* Oslo 1992 p.42ff. Koch, N.: **Linjen og cirkelen,** Artikler om køn og forskning, H Reitzels forlag, København 1990.

[3] C. Merchant held a Fullbright scholarship in Sweden in the spring of 1984 and stimulated this development.

European work is far more advanced and has possibly (especially work in Sweden and in Great Britain) influenced that in the United States"[4].

Theory

Ecofeminism challenges the understanding of nature which supports science and technology. Women with competence in science, engaged in ecofeminism, collaborate with women in social research and in the humanities on a central question: How can natural science be seen as an activity determined by culture, economics and politics, and at the same time as determined by the laws of nature which are the object of science? In order to develop links between ecofeminism and natural sciences, positivism, objectivity, and neutrality of values has to be challenged. Instead, the history of science, marxist and Kuhnian theories together with postmodernist constructivism have been starting points for feminist criticism of science and for the growth in feminist theory of knowledge[5].

Within feminist theory of natural sciences, biology formed a starting point. In this area it could clearly be shown how male metaphors and assessments influenced the results of research, for example, in the distinction of gender in cytology and primatology[6]. This led to an intensified criticism of natural sciences in general. Knowledge of this situation opened the perspective for development of ecofeminist, scientific discourses which would adopt other metaphors and other values.

Among others, Hilary Rose inspired Nordic scientists to employ theoretical based empirical research on feminist research within disciplines dealing with nature[7]. This approach to feminist research analyses theories and methods that actually are used, and finds presuppositions and values that often are more hidden. The question is: What conclusions can be drawn from the results of this research for the development of ecofeminist theory?

V. Shiva has initiated a research program in Norway for critical, feminist studies of biotechnology[8]. As part of this programme, a collaboration has been established between the Centre for Women's Research, Centre for Environment and Development and Centre for Technology and Culture in Oslo. As a result an anthology called "Questions concerning Biotechnology" is forthcoming. The intention is to challenge the new determinism where genes are treated as causes.

---

4 Rose, H.: **Femninistiska/genus-studier av naturveten-skapen. En översikt över forskningsfeltet"**, *i Genus, teknik ock naturvetenskap - en introduksjon till kvinnoforskning i naturvetenskap ock teknik*, Forskningsrådsnämnden, Stockholm 1992.

5 Gulbrandsen, E, HaugestadmA.K., Aas, G: **Forskning i forandring?** i *Nytt om kvinneforskning, NAVF*, Oslo 3/91 pp38-44. Troyer, L: 1992 p.35, Cronberg, T: *Experiments into the Future. A Summary of the Danish Social Experiements with Information Technology*. Lyngby 1991.

6 Benkert, S **Kvinnoforskningen utmanr naturwetenskapen**, i *Genus,teknik ock naturvetenskap, Forskningsrådsnänden*, Stockholm, 1992, pp.7-16.

7 This approach was demonstrated most interestingly in Haraway, D: Primate visions: Gender, Race and Nature in the Modern World of Science, New York, London, Routledge 1989.

8 The Indian, ecofeminist scientist Vandana Shiva has been guest-lecturer and has held a guest chair in Norway for several years. She was awarded the alternative Nobel prize, "The Right Livelihood Award", in Stockholm 1993.

The anthology will focus on alternative and more complex approaches in biology, where the organisms can be seen in within their natural and complex environment.

This project can be seen as representative because it shows how ecofeminist research seeks to initiate changes. The anthology focuses on the unpredictability and the danger of entering too far into the problems of genetics. The philosophical and ethical restrictions on research will be sought integrated within the discussion of biotechnology, and the research analysed within its social, economic and cultural context.

An example of radical criticism takes the ecological crisis as starting point, and stresses the ambiguity of research. To participate in modern society as a scientist means to contribute to the continuation of a scientific system that is an integrated part of a civilization which threatens life on Earth. Therefore, instead of examining the ecological crisis with the help of science and technology, the crisis is seen as a possibility to examine modern science and technology as parts of androcentric culture[9]. This approach is inspired by, among others, Sandra Harding, and sees the task of reconstructing ideas and concepts in connection with an engagement to change the social conditions for research. Feminist research is understood as searching for resources for movements of transformation.

When science is treated as gendered culture, the question arises: To what extent can natural science be adequately understood as culture? This problem cannot be solved within one single discipline, but requires a theoretical basis that reaches to the very depth of human knowledge and action.

Women, Environment and Development

The ecofeminist principle is found to be active in areas where one explicitly tries to integrate science, social studies and the humanities, as in environmental and development studies. A considerable problem in this area is the need to confront problems which are so extensive that they cannot be solved within a single discipline, and the scientists are reluctant to cross the borders of established disciplines.

The connection between development and environmental problems in women's situation was first found in the South, but turned out to be a very important perspective on relations in the North as well. I will use research carried out on **Same** people in the north of Scandinavia to represent this type of research.

In **Same** culture, men and women have different relations to nature. The **Same** women developed their culture through interaction with nature in their daily work. Beside taking care of children the old, the sick, **Same** women gathered grass, herbs, berries, wood. They prepared clothes and shoes from hides,

[9] Gulbrandsen. 1991 p.43.

milked the reindeer or cows, preserved and prepared the food. The relations to nature of both sexes were conditions for survival, and were part of a sustainable culture. This culture is characterised by a relative high equality of the sexes. The **Same** culture is the only herd culture in the world where women own their own animals.

Same women's research describes how mechanization and government control with the natural resources and the land of the **Same** culture led to an impoverished grazing land for the reindeers, and to a destruction of the combined farming and fishing culture in coastal areas. The **Same** Assembly now tries to get the control of the land back for the **Same** people.

During this development all control of natural resources came under male economic and political dominance. Women lost their importance for the sustenance of Samic life and culture, and their ecological knowledge was useless and in danger of disappearing. **Same** women's research seeks to counteract the **Same** women loss of identity and culture.

It introduces an important ecofeminist problem: what is the dynamic between the ecological and social crises? How is the **Same** women's relation to nature intertwined with the social, economic and political relation between the sexes? The **Same** people maintain that their own control of their land and indigenous natural resources is a presupposition for a modern sustainable **Same** culture. But could such a culture develop without some amount of equality between the sexes? Or could **Same** women continue their cultural traditions when the control of the basis for this culture is handed over to others? Ecofeminist research discloses the roots of the sexes's interaction with nature and culture - and with each other.

The ecofeminist principle is also expressed through other theories, like the sociological theory of "care-rationality" or "care-efficiency" which differs from the theory of technological efficiency. Care-efficiency is seen as a result of women's experience in health work and reproduction. It is assumed that women have a different relationship to nature from men because women also expand their care-efficiency to include the environment. Ecofeminism should thus be understood as thoughtful consideration for the environment.

Certain milieus within women's research resist the attempt to base ecofeminism on the theory of care-efficiency. It is claimed that by basing ecofeminism on care-efficiency, one ties women's environmental commitment to the everyday experience and ignores the scientifically based destruction of the environment.

For ecofeminist theory the research that deals with everyday life is of interest. In analysis of the household's consumption of energy and resources the natural sciences meet the humanities and social sciences. Everyday life develops around the close 'I-you' relations in and around the home, and especially represents a female reality. This kind of research is of a certain importance to the theories of ecofeminism because the ecological problem is analysed in relation to interpersonal I-you relations (the family), and the family is in interaction with the macro-level (the vital processes and the larger society) in addition to the micro-level (the personal ecological commitment and responsibility). The interaction between all these levels is crucial for the ecological balance.

Theology and Ecofeminism

There is no permanent position for feminist theology at and Nordic university. For 20 years lectures in feminist theology have been given, and some scholarships have been granted. Feminist theology has been included partially in the curriculum and subsequently been taught by male lecturers. Some 50% of the students of theology are women, but there are extremely few women in teaching positions. The Nordic countries all have Lutheran state-churches, and about 90% of the Norwegian population belongs to the national church. Lutheran theology has strongly influenced Nordic culture. Equality of the sexes is widely accepted as an ethical principle in church and theology; women priests and bishops are allowed because it is seen as a question "of order".

Theory

Many practical, ecofeminist activities are found in environmental movements, in medicine, agriculture and in politics. Practical feminism is often sustained by a mystical-religious understanding of nature and of nature's immanent, life-renewing power. In the **Same** people shamanistic traditions are kept alive. They convey a deep understanding of immanent forces in nature and a reverence toward nature that is missing in modern, science-based attitudes. Starhawk's movement and thought is interpreted and related to the Nordic situation by Jone Salomonsen[10]. Lene Sjørup has described mystical experiences of nature as an element in women's religiosity[11].

The question of nature actualized a tension in theology, Nordic theology included: how to interpret mystical experiences of the holy through nature in relation to the fact that humanity, created in the image of God, has started to destroy the life process of the globe? An ecofeminist theology which restricts the perspective to nature's relation to God, misses the estrangement between nature and humanity. This may be the reason why Nordic, ecofeminist thinking has concentrated on the interaction - and conflict - between the natural sciences and the social and cultural dimensions of life. Perhaps the Lutheran tradition is working "behind our backs"; Nordic ecofeminism gives the problem of estrangement and sin concrete expression in the relationship between nature and human culture.

Estrangement and sin as a theological issue is treated in Nordic theology by a trinitarian approach, rather than by a monistic, God-centred theology. If the

---

10 Salomonsen, J: *Da Gud var Kvinne,* Cappelens forlag, Oslo 1989.

11 Sjørup, L: *Enhed med Altet. Om kvinders religiøse erfaringer,* Gyldendal, København 1992, cfr. **Women's Lives, Women's Religiosity: Are Women's Religious Experiences Mystical Experiences?,** Studia Theologica 1/1994. See also, Lene Sjørup, **Response to Elisabetta Donini** in this volume.

actual possibility of science-based destruction of natural life processes is taken seriously, a differentiation between creation and salvation is proper. Thus the new element which ecofeminist thinking gives to Nordic theology, is a deeper understanding of the interconnections between nature and a gendered humanity in relation to God's creation and a *recreation of life* where estrangement may be overcome.

Zusammenfassung

In der diskussion der Öko-Feministischen Theorie hat nördlich-feministisches Gedankengut die Wichtigkeit der Tatsache betont dass Verbindungen zwischen Natur und Wissenschaft und Socio-Kulturellen Forschen gefunden werden sollen. Wissen gegrunden nür auf Naturwissenschaft beintrachtigt die natur so zu wechseln, dass sie zur Gefahr fürs Leben werden kann. Dieses ist ein direkter Konflikt mit dem Öko-Feministischen Prinzip: Die Erneuerung des ganzen Prozesses. Dieser Bericht beschreibt Versuche des nördlich-feministischen Gedanken gutes dass ihre Forschung in eine Öko-Feministische Richtung leitet. Manche feministische Theologen in den nördlichen Ländern sind mit einbegriffen in der Entwicklung einer Öko-Feministisch-Theoretischen basis mit neuen Forschungsauftragen in richtung sozialer Wechsel und Leben-sorientierung. Diese Arbeit hat eigentlich nür ihren Anfang erfahren.

Sommaire

Dans le discours de la théorie écoféministe, la pensée féministe nordique a souligné la nécessité de découvrir les liens entre les sciences naturelles et les recherches socio-culturelles. Le savoir fondé sur les sciences naturelles empiète sur la nature et rend possible de changer celle-ci d'une manière susceptible de menacer la vie. Ceci est en conflit direct avec le principe écoféministe, qui est le renouveau du processus vital de la terre. Ce compte-rendu décrit quelques tentatives, de la part de la pensée féministe nordique, de réorienter les recherches dans un sens écoféministe. Certains théologiens dans les pays nordiques participent au développement d'une théorie écoféministe qui appuierait de nouvelles approches aux recherches, tout en s'intéressant à l'évolution sociale, ainsi qu' à toute orientation vers la vie en tant que valeur éthique. Ce travail ne fait que commencer.

Dagny Kaul, a member of the founding group of ESWTR, has worked, since 1973, as assistant professor and research fellow, and is now freelance. She has lectured at Scandinavian universities, and she was the first guest-professor in feminist theology in Germany, University of Hamburg, winter 1983/84. Current research: Anthropological-ethical analysis of the women-child relationship; ecofeminist theory. Her list of publications includes 35 titles. Her thesis focusses on natural law and ideology in Tillich's theology.

ECOFEMINISM and THEOLOGY

1. Bibliographie – Bibliography – Bibliographie

Dutch

Van Asseldonk H, Boersma R, **Ecofeminisme en de overheersing van vrouw en natuur in de landbouw,** in: J. Beelen (red.), *Construeren,* Groningen, 1987.

Borsje J, **Vrouwenspiritualiteit,** in: *Religieuze bewegingen in Nederland,* 1987, nr. 14.

Bus W, **God als bondgenote, voortrekster, uitdaagster,** in: *Kerk en vrede,* jrg. 44, 1989, nr. 9, p. 19-20.

Cramer J, **Een feministische kijk op de ecologie: Utopie of werkelijkheid?** in: *Verslagbundel van de conferentie 'Feminisme en Filosofie',* Leusden, 1984, p. 52-63.

Van der Dool A, **De droom van Tine Halkes,** in: *Hervormd Nederland,* jrg. 45, 1989, nr. 44, p. 10-11.

Van Dijk-Hemmes F, **Want JHWH schept iets nieuws op aarde,** in: *Werkmap gerechtigheid, vrede en heelheid van de schepping,* Centrum voor educatie, Driebergen, 1988, p. 13-14.

De Groen E, **De vrouw als reddende engel van het milieu. Draaft het ecofeminisme niet een beetje door?** in: *Opzij,* jrg. 20, 1992, nr. 5, p. 88-91.

Grey M, *De verlossing van de droom. De christelijke traditie van de verlossing van de vrouw,* Kok, Kampen, 1992.

Halkes C.J.M, **Behoud alleen is niet voldoende,** in: *De Bazuin,* jrg. 70, 1987, nr. 49, p. 19-19.

- **Groeien door weerwerk,** in: *De Bazuin,* jrg. 70, 1987, nr. 48, p. 8-9.
- **Terug naar moeder aarde; Catharina Halkes over de schepping,** in: *Hervormd Nederland,* jrg. 44, 1988, juni nr. 24, p.24-25.
- **Verantwoordilijk voor de schepping,** in: *De Bazuin* jrg. 71, 1988, nr. 26, p.16-17
- *'...En alles zal worden herschapen'. Gedachten over de heelwording van de schepping in het spanningsveld tussen natuur en cultuur,* Baarn, 1989.
- **Verbond met heel de aarde,** in: *Ed Noort e.a.; Sleutelen aan het verbond,* Boxtel/Brugge, 1989, p. 149-169.
- **De verkrachting van Moeder Aarde - Ecologie en patriarchaat,** in: *Concilium,* jrg. 25, 1989, nr. 6; p. 80-87.

Van Heijst E.A, **Zuster Aarde,** in *Vrouwen doen het woord,* Amstelveen, 1987.

Janssen M, **Ekofeminisme: socio-biologie in een nieuw jasje of een nieuw perspectief op onderdrukkingsmechanismen,** Jaartal, plaats niet bekend.

Korte A-M, **Vrouwen, natuur en schepping in het licht van Hildegard von Bingen,** in: : *P Dijkstra: Zorg voor de Schepping,* Amersfoort, 1989, p. 74-81.

Sluis-Sluis L, **Vrouwen en natuur hand in hand,** in: : *De Bazuin,* jrg. 75, nr. 40,1992, p. 13-15.

Deutsch

Acklin B, **Sage und schreibe, was du siehst. Auf der Suche nach einer Theologie der Natur bei Hildegarde von Bingen,** in: *Schritte ins Offene,* 5/1991/s. 13-17.

Grisebach M.A, : *Eine Ethik für die Natur*, Zurich, 1991.

Die Grünen im Bundestag et al., Hg., Frauen gegen Gen - und Reproduktionstechnik. Dokumentation zum Kongress vom 19.-21.4.1985 in Bonn, Köln, 1986.

Grossmann S, **Schöpfer und Schöpfung in der feministischen Theologie**, in: : *Günter Altner Hg., Oekologische Theologie. Perspektiven zur Orienterung*, Stuttgart, 1989, S. 213-233.

Kitz V.M, Wodtke V, **'Frau Weisheit durchwaltet voll Güte das All' (Weish.8,1b). Zur Aktualität weisheitlicher Lebensgestaltung**, in: : *Verena Wodtke Hg., Auf den Spuren der Weisheit*, Freiburg i, Br., 1991, S.154-171.

List E, **Helden im Wissenschaftspiel. Geslechtsspezifische Implikationen der Wissenschaftskultur**, in *Beate Frakele et l., Hg., Über Frauenleben, Männerwelt und Wissenschaft*, Wien, 1987, S. 18-33.

Moltmann-Wendel E, : *Wenn Gott und Körper sich begegnen. Feministische Perspektiven zur Leiblichkeit*, Gütersloh, 1989.

Nowotny H, Hausen K, Hg., *Wie männlich ist Wissenschaft?*, Frankfurt a. M., 1986.

Oekumenische Frauenbewegung Zurich, **Feministisch-theologisch Thesen zu Gerechtigkeit, Frieden und Bewahrung der Schöpfung**, in: *Neue Wege*, 10/1988/S.291-293.

Praetorius I, **Der Frauen Verhältnis zur Schöpfung**, in: *Reformiertes Forum* 6/8/Februar 1991/S.9-11.

Praetorius I, Schottroff L, Schüngel-Straumann H, Art. **Schöpfung/Oekologie**, in: *Wörterbuch der Feministischen Theologie*, Gütersloh, 1991.

Roth C, Hg., Genzeit. *Die Industrialisierung von Pflanze, Tier und Mensch. Ermittlungen in der Schweiz*, Zurich, 3. erweiterte und nachgefürte Aufl. 1991.

Rübsamen R, **Patriarchat -der (un)heimliche Inhalt der Naturwissenschaft und Technik**, in: *Luise F. Pusch Hg., Feminismus - Inspektion der Herrenkultur. Ein Handbuch*, Frankfurt a.M. 1983, S.290-307.

Rüdiger L, Hg., : *Frauen Zukünfte, Ganzheitliche feministische Ansätze. Erfahrungen und Lebenskonzepte*, Weinheim, 1984.

Schottroff L, **Schöpfung in der Neuen Testament**, in: *Günter Altner Hg., Oekologische Theologie. Perspektiven zur Orienterung*, Stuttgart, 1989, S. 130-148.

Schüngel-Straumann H, **Macht euch die Erde untertan? Exegetische und katechetische Hinweise zum priesterschriftlichen Herrschaftsauftrag an den Menschen (Gen 1, 28)**, in: *Katechetische Blätter* 5/1976/S.319-332.

- *Die Frau am Anfang. Eva und die Folgen*, Freiburg, 1989.

Sölle D, : *Lieben und Arbeiten. Eine Theologie der Schöpfung*, Stuttgart, 1985.

Sölle D, Schotroff L, *Die Erde gehört Gott. Texte zur Bibelarbeit von Frauen*, Reinbek bei Hamburg, 1985.

Thürmer-Rohr C, *Vagabundinnen. Feministische Essays*, Berlin, 1987; ... **wir sind nicht Reisende ohne Gepäck. Gedanken zur Patriarchatskritik**, in: Luisi P.L, Hg., *Im Einvernehmen mit der Natur. Die Zukünft von Oekologie, Wirtschaft, Gesellschaft*, Stuttgart, München, Landsberg, 1991, S.217-287.

V.Werlhof C, Mies M, Bennholdt V, *Frauen, die letzte Kolonie*, Reinbek bei Hamburg, 1983.

Wider den Machbarkeitswahn. Frauen zur Gen-und Reproduktionstechnologie, in *Schritte ins Offene* 6/1986.

Zaug K, Praetorius I, **Verachtet und notwendig. Über das Putzen und ein erweitertes Oekologieverständnis**, in: : *Neue Wege* 1/1992/ S.5-8.

Übersetzungen

Daly M, : *Gyn/Oekologie. Eine Metaethik des radikalen Feminismus*, München, 1975.

Fox Keller E, *Liebe, Macht und Erkenntnis. Männliche oder weibliche Wissenschaft?*

D'Eaubonne F, *Feminismus oder Tod. Thesen zur Oekologiedebatte*, München, 1975.

Griffin S, *Frau und Natur*, Frankfurt a.M, 1987.

Halkes C.J.M, *Das Antlitz der Erde erneuern. Mensch, Kultur, Schöpfung*, Gütersloh, 1990.

Harding S, *Feministische Wissenschaftstheorie*, Berlin, 1989.

Hynes, H.P, *Als es Frühling war. Von Rachel Carson zur feministischen Oekologie*, Berlin, 1990.

Merchant C, *Der Tod der Natur. Oekologie, Frauen und neuzeitliche Naturwissenschaft*, München, 1987.

Shiva V, *Das Geslecht des Lebens. Frauen, Oekologie und Dritte Welt*, Berlin, 1989.

English

(For bibliography on related issues see theme articles and forum)

Cheney J, **Ecofeminism and Deep Ecology**, *Environmental Ethics* 9 (1987), 115-146.

Clifford A.M, **Feminist Perspectives on Science: Implications for an Ecological Theology of Creation**, *JFSR* 8 (1992) 65-90.

Diamond I and Orenstein G, (eds.), *Reweaving the World: The Emergence of Ecofeminism*, San Francisco: Sierra Club Books (1990).

Green E, **From Bondage to Hope: Women and Creation in the Process of Liberation**, *Theology in Green* 2 (1992).

Grey M, **Does Christianity Need the Goddess?** *Theology in Green* 6 (1993) 4-11.

- *Redeeming the Dream: Feminism, Redemption and Christian Tradition*, London: SPCK (1989).

Halkes C.J.M, *New Creation: Christian Feminism and the Renewal of the Earth*, London: SPCK (1991).

- **Violence to Mother Earth: Ecology and Patriarchy**, *Concilium* 25 (1989).

Haney E, **Towards a White Feminist Ecological Ethic**, *JFSR* 9 (1993) 75-93.

Jantzen G, *God's World, God's Body*, London: Darton, Longman and Todd (1984).

Kheel M, **Ecofeminism andDeep Ecology: Reflections on Identity and Difference**, in C S Robb and C Caseboll (eds)., *Covenant for a New Creation: Ethics, Religion and Public Policy*, Maryknoll: Orbis (1991).

Lardner Carmody D, *Feminism and Christianity*, Nashville: Abingdon (1982) 126-161.

McFague S, *The Body of God: An Ecological Theology*, London: SCM (1993).

- *Models of God: Theology for an Ecological, Nuclear Age*, London: SCM (1987).

Plant J, ed., *Healing the Wounds: The Promise of Ecofeminism, Santa Cruz: New Society (1989).*

Primavesi A, *From Apocalypse to Genesis: Ecology, Feminism and Christianity*, Tunbridge Wells: Burns and Oates (1191).

- **Gaia and God**, in U.King ed., *Liberating Women: New Theological Directions*, Bristol (1991), 94-98.

Raphael M, **Doing Green Justice to God: Immanentism in Contemporary Feminist Spirituality**, *Theology in Green* 5 (1993) 34-42.

Robb C, **Principles for a Woman-Friendly Economy**, *JFSR* 9 (1993), 147-160.

Ruether R R, *Gaia and God: An Ecofeminist Theology of Earth Healing*: New York: Harper Collins (1992).

- *Liberation Theology: Human Hope Confronts Christian History and American Power*: New York: Paulist (1972).
- *New Woman, New Earth: Sexist Ideologies and Human Liberation,* New York: Seabury (1975).
- *Sexism and God-Talk: Towards a Feminist Theology,* London: SCM (1983).
- *To Change the World: Christology and Cultural Criticism, London: SCM (1981).*

Shiva V, *Staying Alive: Women, Ecology and Survival in India,* London: Zed (1988).

Sölle, *To Work and To Love: A Theology of Creation,* Philadelphia: Fortress (1984).

Thistlethwaite S. B, **God and Her Survival in a Nuclear Age,** *JFSR* 4 (1988) 73-88.

- *Sex, Race and God*: Christian Feminism in Black and White, London: Geoffrey Chapman (1990).

2. Rezensionen – Book Reviews – Critique des Livres

Sally McFague
The Body of God: An Ecological Theology, London, SCM, 1993

This is the most ambitious of Sallie McFague's books and indicates how far a theologian seriously committed to the world's problems can relinquish an earlier, more limiting position. On her own admission McFague was an "Erstwhile Barthian" and for years resistant to a nature spirituality (p. 208), yet now she has developed a full-blown ecological theology, exhorting us to "hold fast to the huckleberries"(!) – as metaphor for the concreteness, homeliness and sheer materiality of the embodiment of God.

"The Body of God" is spell-binding in its comprehensive sweep through Christian theology – (the doctrines of God/ salvation/ Christology/ Sin/ pneumatology/ eschatology are all thoroughly discussed) – in the concern to show that Christian doctrines can make sense against the background of postmodern science, and in its conviction – which I share – that if people think differently about themselves and the world, they will be empowered to act differently towards it.

McFague's starting point is the ecological crisis, for which human beings are almost totally responsible: "We are dealing with a wily, crafty enemy – ourselves" (p.3). Her chosen key word is "embodiment", within an organic model of science, subsequently explored as an organic model for theology. (She is not the first to do this – and refers to Grace Jantzen's 'God's World – God's Body', though only 'en passant' to Anne Primavesi's 'From Apocalypse to Genesis"). Her organicism differs from Jantzen's in preserving a metaphoric quality. We can never describe the face of God: it is as if we are always observing from behind. So the huckleberries, giant redwoods and galaxies of stars are all images of Divine transcendence/immanence and not to be confused with it. And yet the world can still be regarded as the suffering body of God: God's Body will suffer the consequences of environmental devastation with the poor and oppressed of the world.

In such a courageous attempt to re-conceptualise the major doctrines ecologically, three major points could be highlighted. First, ecological, organic theology always comes unstuck on the question of the agency of God: how is this to be imaged except in an interventionist way? McFague makes a valiant attempt to combine the organic model (the world as Body of God), with the agential model, through her notion of the Spirit of God as the Breath of Life through the whole of Creation, empowering rather than directing creation. This has great significance for prayer and spirituality and enables personal language about God in terms other than male or female persons, which has always been one of the sticking points. Secondly, an ecological Christology is developed, wherein nature (= the new poor) is seen as oppressed by unjust power structures, (the deconstructive moment), as subject for the healing praxis of Christic community, (the reconstructive moment), and as participant in the Messianic banquet, (the prospective moment). This is a far more effective and coherent way of interpreting the organic quality of the ministry of Jesus then to struggle to show that he talked about lilies of the field and mustard seeds etc! Thirdly, a very helpful concept of ecological sin is developed, on the basis of taking "space" and "place" seriously. Salvation is the direction of creation and creation is the place of salvation (p. 180 ff). Space is what puts us on the same level as all living things and highlights the relationship between ecological and justice issues. "We are ruining the space" (p. 101) sums this up. Hence sin is the refusal to accept our place and space: we can live this lie with regard to other human beings , with regard to animals and with regard to nature.

In a book which is so rich in insights, (and in bibliography – the references are a goldmine for works in contemporary science and ecological theology and spirituality!) inevitable questions still remain. The first is the question on which the book rests: namely the relationship between metaphor and the concreteness of materiality – can one have it both ways ? Is the world the body of God or simply 'seen' as such? If all seeing is in fact the Wittgensteinian "seeing as", have we lost the shock of realisation that if, for example, the fishes and birds die off, God dies – and therefore the horrifying embodiment of the suffering of God? Secondly, it is not clear whether, of the world as imaged as "Body of God", whether we can make sense of the Body of Christ, and 'cosmic body of Christ': – are there just too many bodies?

Finally, McFague is explicit about the inevitability of suffering: this is a "given", both because of the randomness of natural selection, chance, wastage and death, as well as because, "the radical inclusiveness that is at the heart of Christian faith, especially inclusion of the oppressed, is not compatible with evolution, even cultural evolution" (p.173). A response of solidarity is called for –

first, resistance to oppression, and secondly, a passive solidarity in suffering – that of God and of the oppressed. But surely, there is a transformative dimension which is missing here, an ethic of transformation of culture which is part of the Christian task? And secondly, the response of "passive suffering" is not the witness of many liberation communities, for example the 'mothers of the missing ones' of Argentina, to give one example.

These questions are indicators of the depth and richness which this book offers: but its success will be measured by its own aims - that at the eleventh hour human beings will develop a renewed sacramentalism in which nature has intrinsic merit, and structures of caring which inspire a new ethic.
Mary Grey, Southampton, UK

Rosemary Radford Ruether, Anne Primavesi
A l'École de Théologie[1]

Dans la prise de conscience accrue, durant ces vingt dernières années, de l'urgence qu'il y a à trouver des solutions aux graves problèmes d'environnement qui menacent notre planète, il s'est trouvé des voix pour dénoncer la responsabilité chrétienne dans cet état de choses. La "maîtrise de la création", telle qu'elle était énoncée dans la Genèse (Gn 1,28), était peut-être à l'origine des abus et dévastations constatés aujourd'hui. Cette hypothèse, conjuguée à la gravité de la situation, a convaincu des chrétiens et des chrétiennes de la nécessité de repenser une théologie de la création. Il me paraît qu'un des éléments moteurs dans cette recherche théologique est actuellement le mouvement féministe.

J'ai choisi de présenter la pensée et les œuvres de deux femmes théologiennes, qui ont fait de la recherche écologique le centre de leurs travaux récents. L'une est américaine, Rosemary Radford Ruether; l'autre est irlandaise vivant au Royaume Uni, Anne Primavesi. Toutes deux sont catholiques romaines, mais l'appartenance à l'une ou l'autre Église Chrétienne n'était pas un critère dans ma sélection.

Approches féministes

Il faut commencer par préciser ce que l'on entend par l'écoféminisme. Selon R. Radford Ruether, celui-ci est né de la rencontre du mouvement écologique radical (ce que l'on a appelé l'écologie profonde) et du féminisme. Dès la fin des années 1960, l'écologie s'est précisée comme une étude socio-économique et biologique de l'usage que fait l'humain de la nature, en provoquant la pollution du sol, de l'air et de l'eau, et la destruction du système naturel végétal et animal, menaçant ainsi la base vivante dont la communauté humaine elle-même dépend. L'écologie profonde fait un pas de plus: elle examine les schémas symboliques, psychologiques et éthiques, des relations destructives des humains avec la nature;

[1] A longer version of this article appeared in *Lumen Vitae*, March 1993, No. 1, pp.51-65, and is printed here with permission of the Editor.

elle se demande surtout comment les remplacer par une culture d'affirmation de la vie. Le féminisme est également un mouvement complexe qui compte de nombreuses strates; on peut le définir comme un mouvement, dans les sociétés démocratiques libérales, luttant pour obtenir la pleine participation des femmes aux droits politiques et l'accès économique à l'emploi. Il peut encore se définir, de façon plus radicale et dans une tradition socialiste libératrice, comme la transformation d'un système socio-économique patriarcal, dans lequel la domination mâle sur les femmes est le fondement de toutes les hiérarchies socio-économico-culturelles. Le féminisme peut aussi être vu en termes de culture et de conscience, établissant le schéma des interrelations symboliques, psychologiques et éthiques, de domination des femmes, avec la monopolisation par les mâles des ressources et du contrôle des pouvoirs. Ce troisième niveau de l'analyse féministe est en relation étroite avec l'écologie profonde; certains diraient même que le féminisme est l'expression première de l'écologie profonde.

Rosemary Radford Ruether

On peut aujourd'hui la considérer comme une pionnière des recherches en éco-feminisme. Sans employer le mot, elle dévoile et dénonce déjà, dans un livre publié en 1975[2], la collusion existant entre la domination exercée sur les femmes et la domination et l'exploitation de la nature; c'est la thèse qu'elle ne cesse de défendre, avec toutes les implications qui en découlent.

Quelle maîtrise, et pour qui?

Bien sûr, en tant que théologienne chrétienne, elle admet qu'une responsabilité de cet état de choses doit être attribuée au caractère judéochrétien de notre civilisation occidentale et à la mauvaise interprétation des textes initiaux de la Genèse. Il est certain que Gn 1, 28, parlant de la maîtrise à exercer sur la terre et de la domination sur les animaux, a été interprété par la suite dans les perspectives chrétiennes et séculières d'une société pour laquelle "domination" se comprend dans le contexte de la dualité entre corps et esprit, entre société et nature, et non plus dans la perspective des religions anciennes de la nature, dont l'influence est encore très présente dans les vues de la nature exprimées dans l'A.T. Contrairement au christianisme, la religion hébraïque (plus spécialement dans la période d'avant l'exil) n'est pas une religion d'alienation, qui voit la nature comme inférieure ou mauvaise. La religion hébraïque est une religion de renouveau socio-naturel; société et nature cœxistent dans une seule communauté, créée sous la souveraineté de Dieu. La rupture de l'alliance avec ce Dieu produit la ruine du contrat social et aussi la ruine de l'alliance avec la nature. Le retour à la fidélité à Dieu apporte la restauration de la justice sociale dans les relations

[2] Rosemary Radford Ruether, *New Woman, New Earth: Sexist Ideoligies and Human Liberation*, San Francisco, Harper and Row, 1975, 221 pages

humaines, comme la douceur et la clémence dans les relations de la société avec la nature.

Un dualisme aliénant?

L'auteur relève que, avec l'influence de la philosophie classique grecque, la relation de l'esprit au corps devient une relation de répression, de subordination et de maîtrise. L'existence matérielle est ontologiquement inférieure à l'esprit; elle est aussi la racine du mal moral. Qui plus est, ce langage de dualisme hiérarchique est identifié à la hiérarchie sociale: la supériorité hiérarchique de l'esprit sur le corps s'exprime dans la domination du masculin sur le féminin, des hommes libres sur les esclaves, des Grecs sur les "barbares".

A ses débuts, le christianisme a, d'une certaine façon, fusionné des éléments du judaïsme messianique et du dualisme platonicien. En dépit des efforts des Pères de l'Église pour arriver à concilier le Dieu de la création et le Dieu de la rédemption eschatologique, une aliénation cosmique et un dualisme spirituel ont prévalu dans la spiritualité chrétienne classique. Ceci ne sera pas sans conséquences, on s'en doute, sur la position des Églises chrétiennes vis-à-vis d'un engagement dans le combat écologique actuel.

Dans un autre ouvrage de 1981[3], l'auteur revient sur la thèse du lien indéniable qui existe entre crise écologique et domination sociale; elle souligne longuement que, si Gn 1,28 a enjoint à "l'homme" de dominer la terre, ce n'est jamais l'humanité entière qui a exercé cette "maîtrise", mais seulement une minorité: les "mâles" de la classe dirigeante. Elle étudie ensuite les essais de réponses qu'ont tenté de faire le libéralisme de progrès, le marxisme révolutionnaire et le romanticisme "rousseauiste". Dans chacune de ces tentatives il ya des éléments positifs: les libertés du libéralisme, la justice économique de la tradition socialiste, le retour à la nature du romanticisme. Mais ces éléments ne permettent pas d'être assemblés pour donner une vision cohérente du monde, encore moins d'être transcrits en un guide d'action efficace.

La vision nouvelle d'un monde d'eco-justice exige d'abord la fin du rêve occidental, c'est-à-dire le rêve d'un monde dans lequel la croissance est indéfinie, avec l'accroissemennt constant des richesses qui en résulte. Il faut remplacer cette vue par une "acceptation" de la finitude, la nôtre et celle du monde, et des limitations - non certes dans le sens d'une "société statique", qui fixerait simplement les situations actuelles de pauvreté et d'injustice, mais dans une conversion qui redécouvrirait la finitude de la terre dans un équilibre des éléments à harmoniser, afin de promouvoir la vie de tous les membres de la communauté.

La fin de toute hiérarchisation?

Conversion signifie aussi interrelation de toutes les composantes de la création,

[3] Rosemary Radford Ruether, *To Change the World*, New York, Crossroad Ed, 1981, 85 pages

afin qu'aucune part ne puisse dorénavant être florissante, alors que d'autres parts sont blessées ou détruites. Dans un système d'interdépendance, aucun élément de la communauté n'est intrinsèquement "supérieur" ni "inférieur" à un autre. La vision hiérarchique de la "maîtrise de la nature" par une domination du sommet vers la base est donc une illusion. Dominer la nature ou des humains d'une façon qui détruit leur bien-être n'accroît pas la maîtrise que nous avons sur eux.

La vision non hiérarchisée du monde remet en question beaucoup d'affirmations de la théologie occidentale. La pensée hébraïque a repris aux religions anciennes de la nature le concept d'un renouveau cyclique de la nature et de la société, mais elle en a déplacé le centre vers l'histoire plutôt que vers les saisons. La lutte pour rétablir la justice dans la société et l'harmonie avec la nature deviennent, pour les Hébreux, un projet historique. Les désastres naturels ne sont plus perçus comme le fait de pouvoirs naturels capricieux: ils reflètent les injustices sociales.

Leur modèle de rédemption messianique, basée sur le Jubilé, est peut-être un modèle à reconsidérer aujourd'hui (voir Lv 25, 8-12): le Jubilé nous apprend qu'il y a certains éléments fondamentaux qui rendent la vie sur la terre comme Dieu l'a voulue, c'est-à-dire où chacun possède sa propre vigne et son figuier et où personne n'est l'esclave d'un autre; le sol et les animaux ne sont pas surmenés. Mais la nature pécheresse de l'homme tend à créer une échappatoire à cette situation voulue par Dieu: la terre de certains est expropriée par d'autres; des personnes sont vendues comme esclaves et la nature est épuisée. Périodiquement, il doit se produire une conversion radicale. Les dettes injustes accumulées sur une longue période doivent être liquidées; ceux qui ont été vendus comme esclaves doivent être libérés; les terres expropriées doivent être rendues et la nature et les animaux mis au repos. Ainsi, l'humanité et la nature retrouvent leur juste équilibre. On ne peut s'empêcher d'être frappé par la résonance actuelle d'une telle vision. Le Royaume qu'annonçait Jésus s'inscrit dans cette perspective, puisqu'il est libération pour les captifs, rémission des dettes et pain quotidien pour tous.

Le dernier livre de Rosemary Radford Ruether vient de sortir de presse[4]; dans cet œuvre l'auteur passe en revue l'héritage de notre culture chrétienne occidentale, pour mettre en lumière de nouveaux modèles de "guérison" des blessures infligées à notre environnement. La "guérison écologique" est un processus théologique, psychique et spirituel, écrit-elle.

Après avoir rappelé trois récits de création dans trois traditions religieuses (babylonienne, hébraïque, grecque), l'auteur se demande si la science a une nouvelle version à nous proposer; elle passe en revue les progrès réalisés dans la compréhension scientifique du monde et de ses origines. Par exemple, la thèse de James Lovelock, *Gaia*, donne une nouvelle vision de la terre, en tant qu'organisme

[4] Rosemary Radford Ruether, *Gaia and God: an Ecofeminist Theology on Earth Healing*, San Francisco, Harper Collins, 1992, 310 pages

vivant fait d'un réseau complexe d'interdépendances et de bio-rétroactions. Une éthique humaine devrait être plus sensible à cet aspect d'interdépendance naturelle; elle devrait enjoindre aux humains d'imaginer et d'éprouver les souffrances des autres, pour trouver les moyens par lesquels l'interrelation devient coopérative et génératrice de vie mutuelle, pour les deux parties de la relation.

Si nous devons retrouver un "mythe planétaire" pour construire une nouvelle éthique et une nouvelle spiritualité, de même qu'une nouvelle compréhension scientifique de l'univers à travers la vision cosmique de la physique astrale et atomique, il est nécessaire d'effacer la cassure entre "fait" et "valeur", théorie et pratique, privé et social, cassure si présente dans la pensée occidentale. La pensée mécaniciste est réductrice: elle limite les interrelations complexes et vivantes de la nature à ses seuls composants et elle est plus préoccupée des composants non vivants que du tout dynamique. Encore, elle se fonde sur des normes et une expérience uniquement masculines.

Nous avons besoin de scientifiques-poètes, conclut l'auteur, pour conter le cosmos et l'histoire de la terre d'une façon qui nous appelle à l'émerveillement, au respect de la vie, à une vision de l'humanité vivant en communauté harmonieuse avec tous les frères et sœurs existants.

Anne Primavesi

Cette théologienne indépendante a collaboré avec le scientifique James Lovelock; elle a publié récemment un livre qui fera date dans l'histoire de l'écoféminisme: *From Apocalypse to Genesis* [5]. Elle y propose de replacer le paradigme chrétien traditionnel par un paradigme écologique, en faisant une présentation détaillée de l'un et l'autre des paradigmes.

Qu'est-ce qu'un paradigme?

Pour clarifier ce terme, elle en propose une définition: <<Un paradigme est un agrément commun sur la conduite, dans une communauté donnée, acquis à travers les schémas relationnels en usage dans cette communauté>>. Dans le déroulement de leur existence, plusieurs paradigmes peuvent coexister pendant un certain temps. On pourrait résumer leur durée en quatre phrases:

- d'abord un stade initial, dans lequel des personnes s'intéressent à des façons de penser différentes de celles qui ont cours et commencent à les étudier;
- ensuite un stade de premiers développements théoriques et pratiques, où les chercheurs et chercheuses essaient d'établir de nouveaux paradigmes et de convaincre de la valeur de ceux-ci;
- troisièmement un stade de maturation, au cours duquel un ou plusieurs paradigmes deviennent dominants, tandis que les autres tendent à disparaître;

[5] Anne Primavesi, *From Apocalypse to Genesis: Ecology, Feminism and Christianity*, Tunbridge Wells, Burns and Oates, 1991, 324 pages De la même, en collaboration avec Jennifer Henderson, *Our God had no Favourites: a Liberation Theology of the Eucharist*,Tunbridge Wells, Burns and Oates, 1989, 105 pages

- finalement un stade de "post-maturation", dans lequel chercheurs et chercheuses commencent à ressentir une certaine frustration devant l'inconstance des résultats expérimentaux et devant l'incapacité du nouveau paradigme de répondre aux questions qu'ils auraient voulu résoudre. Ainsi, la recherche de nouveaux paradigmes recommence dans un processus quasi-perpétuel.

Anne Primavesi situe son propre livre dans le deuxième stade: c'est un essai pour tracer un itinéraire de dépassement du paradigme hiérarchique de la tradition chrétienne, avec son remplacement par un paradigme écologique.

Mises en question: la faute?

A la lumière de la thèse *Gaia*, elle remet en cause, dans une relecture des textes de la Genèse, les notions du péché originel, de la rédemption et du salut. L'histoire d''Eve, elle ne la lit pas comme l'histoire d'une "faute" de la race humaine, mais plutôt comme l'histoire d'un passage à la maturité, après l'expérience de l'Éden. La notion du Dieu, Esprit de vie qui soutient la Création, n'est pas compatible avec celle d'un Dieu trônant sur la doctrine de la chute et de la rédemption, qui apparaît comme Celui qui décrète que la mort (et non la vie) sera transmise à travers la fertilité de l'espèce humaine, végétale ou animale. Ce Dieu qui aurait jugé les corps humains comme capables seulement d'apporter le péché n'est apparemment concerné que par le seul fait d'être obéi ou non. Appeler leur action "péché" est une impossibilité logique: pour qu'une action puisse être qualifiée de "blâmable" ou mauvaise, elle doit provenir d'un choix et d'une volonté délibérés. Mais s'ils n'avaient pas la connaissance du bien et du mal, comment pouvaient-ils choisir entre les deux? Le moyen de faire le choix correct était aussi l'objet de leur choix. Dans le récit de la Genèse, l'action d'Adam et d''Eve n'est jamais préjugée coupable ou blâmable. La doctrine, au contraire, insiste sur ce qu'ils auraient dû faire et n'ont pas fait; ce qui leur arrive après est alors considéré comme une punition. La condamnation à l'exil, l'effort, la souffrance et la mort, la "domination" de l'homme sur la terre et sur la femme sont vus comme les résultants d'une cause évidente par elle-même.

On peut relire à ce sujet Julienne de Norwich et le récit qu'elle fait d'une de ses visions (*Showings*): c'est l'histoire du Maître qui envoie son serviteur "faire des courses"; or celui-ci tombe dans un trou profond dont il n'arrive plus à sortir. Julienne décrit minutieusement les sept souffrances endurées par ce serviteur, dont la principale est la solitude, en étant privé de la présence de son Maître. Julienne veut nous faire comprendre qu'une fois hors de l'Éden, Adam et 'Eve étaient privés de la présence de Dieu; il n'était plus possible, pour eux, "de marcher avec Dieu dans la fraîcher du soir, ni quand l'aube se levait ...". Ce qui est remarquable, dans cette vision, c'est qu'elle n'attribue aucune responsabilité au Maître quant à la chute du serviteur, même si c'est pour exécuter ses ordres que le serviteur s'est dépêché de se mettre en route, pas plus qu'elle ne blâme en aucune façon le serviteur pour sa chute. Cependant le revers de cette vision poétique, c'est qu'elle fait de l'Éden le seul lieu où la présence de Dieu est affirmée. Elle rejoint ainsi, en conclusion, la doctrine traditionnelle, profondément ancrée dans la conscience chrétienne. En dehors du jardin, se trouve un lien "de labeur et de souffrance", maudit par Dieu à cause d'Adam. Et cette dévaluation de la nature, en dehors du lieu édénique, ne fut pas sans effet sur l'avenir écologique de la planète.

Une vision trop étroite de la Trinité?

L'auteur met aussi en question une interprétation trop rigide du dogme de la Trinité: Père et Fils en relation l'un avec l'autre, d'où jaillit l'Esprit. Cette relation obscurcit d'une certaine manière la relation directe de l'Esprit avec le monde créé, comme sa présence au monde avant même la Création (Gn 1,1) avec la constance de cette présence tout au long des Écritures (ainsi 1 R 19, 11-14). Cette dévaluation du rôle de l'Esprit a conduit à une Église christocentrique, dans laquelle l'Esprit devient la propriété exclusive des "successeurs des Apôtres"; les figures à connotation féminine, comme la Sagesse, sont dès lors assimilées à celle du Christ. Dans cette logique, les femmes n'ont pas d'accès direct à l'Esprit, et l'Esprit n'est pas infusé dans la nature créée...

Redécouvrir le rôle de l'Esprit dans l'histoire du monde à partir d'une nouvelle lecture de la Genèse[6] nous donne un modèle "écologique" de la Trinité, comme source de vie pour toute création et re-création. La relation entre l'Esprit de Dieu et tout ce qui vit et respire est ainsi mieux reconnue dans son plein droit, comme la "force intérieure" de toute la création, et non pas limitée par un système de pensée dogmatiquement défini. Et Jésus n'a pas fait autre chose, dans son existence humaine, que de reconnaître la présence de l'Esprit, indépendamment de lui ou du Père; c'est une attitude qu'il faut apprendre à suivre. Le pouvoir de l'Esprit-qui-est-en-nous est comme le vent qui souffle où il veut; il est discernable seulement par ses effets. Il a forcé un berger nommé Amos à abandonner ses moutons, pour devenir un prophète en Israël; por Ezéchiel, il a transformé des ossements desséchés en une grande foule, la maison d'Isral; il a activé les entrailles de Sarah, Hannah, Elisabeth et Marie. Il a conduit Jésus au désert pour prier, et il a assuré sa subsistance. Dans le Livre de l'Apocalypse enfin, il appelle les assoiffés à se désaltérer à la source de vie.

Un paradigme écologique

Le paradigme écologique propose l'auteur, en opposition au paradigme traditionnel, se réfère à l'hypothèse *Gaia* des scientifiques, de James Lovelock en particulier qui fut le premier à l'exposer en parlant de la planète Terre comme "constituant une entité" à elle seule, "capable de manipuler" l'atmosphère terrestre suivant

[6] cf M P Korsak, *At the Start: Genesis Made New, A Translation of the Hebrew Text*, European Association for the Promotion of Poetry, (Coutereelstraat 76, B-3000 Leuven), 1992, 210 pages

les besoins généraux, et "dotée de facultés et de pouvoirs qui dépassent de loin ceux de ses constituants". La représentation graphique de ce paradigme est alors la sphère, ce qui impliquerait le changement de toutes les notions de valeur, de poids et de pouvoir, puisque:

- ce paradigme ne dresse pas de séparation entre les niveaux d'existence, mais accorde une valeur à toute existence, par le seul fait d'exister, et non à cause de relations imputées avec Dieu ou le genre humain;
- il ne perçoit pas la diversité comme une menace envers l'orde, comme une exception à la règle des espèces. Au contraire, la diversité est reconnue comme une sauvegarde et une garantie du rebondissement de la vie: elle célèbre un Dieu qui se réjouit de la diversité;
- il n'approuve pas l'usage du "pouvoir" d'une catégorie d'êtres sur une autre; il dévoile au contraire le mystère du pourvoir-à-l'intérieur de *Gaia* et du pouvoir-avec-*Gaia*. Il respecte ce pouvoir, qui se manifeste dans l'aptitude à produire et à soutenir la vie, dans le mystère de la fertilité de la terre et des créatures;
- il exige une nouvelle éthique; on ne peut plus, dorénavant, prendre la norme morale kantienne comme norme de la conduite humaine: "faire aux autres ce que l'on aimerait qu'il nous soit fait". Il faut plutôt traiter les autres comme ils souhaitent être traités. Le point de référence n'est donc plus soi-même et ses propres désirs, mais les autres - ce qui signifie qu'il faut accorder une totale attention à ceux qui ne sont pas comme nous et leur reconnaître une valeur tels qu'ils sont.
- il nous force à une attitude d'humilité écologique, en relativisant le statut des êtres humains; en même temps, il nous ouvre au mystère impénétrable de la création, qui est plus que tout ce que nous pouvons décrire ou comprendre;
- il encourage à une attitude positive à l'égard de la mort, qui n'est plus perçue comme un châtiment du péché, ni comme un drame devant être à tout prix retardé. Elle fait partie au contraire d'un cycle naturel: chaque créature vivante est soutenue par la mort d'autres êtres vivants; - il exige une nouvelle approche de la solution des problèmes: chaque phénomène doit être étudié en relation avec son éco-système; il encourage donc un sens communautaire, en refusant les séparations.

Ce changement de paradigme proposé par A. Primavesi doit réussir pour que les relations humaines avec la planète soient "guéries" et pour que le christianisme garde une pertinence dans l'avenir. Dans les facteurs qui poussent au changement de paradigme, l'auteur voit cette prise de conscience des "usagers" d'un paradigme dépassé comme un élément important. Comme ce sont plus spécialement ceux et celles qui se sentent marginalisés ou exclus par un paradigme qui ressentent en premier ses anomalies et ses injustices, il est clair que les mouvements de femmes jouent un rôle important et les théologies féministes

sont déjà à l'œuvre dans ce sens.
Denise Peeters, Brussels, Belgium

Evelyn Fox Keller
Reflections on Gender and Science, Yale University Press, New Haven & London 1985

Sandra Harding
The Science Question in Feminism, Open University Press, Milton Keynes 1986

These two books have been significant in opening up the feminist discussion of science. Their authors seek to identify in what manner; science may said to be sexist or androcentric and to suggest ways in which this might be counteracted. Neither wishes to discourage or deny science the necessity of systematic androcentricity science as we now know is geared to the needs and interests of one subgroup of society. Both Keller and Harding have published more recent considerations of their ideas[1,2], which were unfortunately not available for this review. However, their earlier books are still of interest, especially to those who are new to the discussion.

Keller is a mathematical biophysicist who came to question the way in which the nature of science is bound up with that of masculinity. Her book consists of a collection of essays which chronicle the development of her analysis of that relationship. Her stated intention is to offer a critique of science and philosophy of science which takes account of the fact that 'Boyle's Law is not wrong' while recognising that 'the anonymity of the picture that [scientists] produce is revealed as itself a kind of signature'. She argues that the subject/object distinction presupposed by modern science is the product of a stage of psychological development which lays excessive emphasis on separation and independence and which fails to recognise that autonomy is the product of both relatedness and delineation. This leads to a situation in which dominance and control, the hallmarks of modern science, become paramount.

Keller suggests that the assumption that nature is knowable and objectifiable must be relinquished. Quantum mechanics has shown us that this position is untenable: subject and object are 'inevitably, however subtly, entwined.' Scientists should be wary of imposing causal relations on more complicated systems, for in doing so they 'risk imposing on nature the very stories we like to hear.' Order should be sought rather than laws. While recognising 'the androcentric bias in prevailing definitions of science' she calls for a healthy science 'that allows for the productive survival of diverse conceptions of mind and nature, and of correspondingly diverse strategies.' She does not wish to reject science but to reclaim it as a human project.

1 Evelyn Fox Keller, *Secrets of Life, Secrets of Death*, Routledge, New York & London 1992
2 Sandra Harding, *Whose Science, Whose Knowledge?* Cornell University Press 1992

Although Keller recognises that claims to hegemony are political rather than scientific, she concentrates on the scientific as personal. Harding's central concern is the connection between the scientific and the social. From her philosophical background she offers an analysis of the various feminist critiques of science, and points out that even the more 'unthreatening' approaches - those which criticise the scientific community as predominantly male and those which contend that masculine bias is evident in the definition of scientific problems and the approach to research – in fact call for a radical reassessment of the relationship between science and society. She criticises Keller, among others, for an inadequate analysis of this relationship. Harding understands science to be value neutral in the sense that it takes on the social attitudes of the world in which it exists. The values and interests which determine science's choice of and approach to problems reappear in the universe which it depicts. In this way, science's claim to be 'value free' is a form of self- legitimation of the biases within its value system. Objectivity can only be increased through an raising awareness of these biases.

Both Harding and Keller criticise the historiography of the natural sciences for having neglected social and gender analysis. Harding suggests that there are similarities between the ideals held by members of the new science movement in Puritan England and those of modern feminists. She calls for an awareness of the ease with which such ideals are lost to prevailing sexist and racist norms. Keller demonstrates that assumptions about the proper relationships between genders influenced definitions of knowledge and attitudes towards nature. However, their discussion misses the crucial role played by mathematics in the development of modern natural sciences and scientific methodology.

The particular certainty of mathematical proof is remarked upon by authors as various as Plato, Roger Bacon and Thomas Aquinas. When confidence in theology's authority began to be shaken its replacement was sought in mathematical certainty. The adoption of mathematics as the measure of objectivity was crucial to Enlightenment thinking, and attempts were made to apply the rigour of mathematical proof in all fields. The fields of investigation which responded best to this approach came to be regarded as the most important, and thus science became what Harding calls a 'totalising system' in which highest priority is assigned to the problems which it is best equipped to answer. Questions about the legitimacy of this mathematical standard have been raised by many twentieth century thinkers, and Harding and Keller continue that tradition. But the adoption of the mathematical standard is not without gender implications. It has its roots at least in part in a Platonic ideal of knowing which Keller shows to be based on particular assumptions about gender relations. Further investigation needs to be done into the move from theological to mathematical authority and the relationship of that shift to the definition of gender.

A theologian may ask what implications these critiques of natural science have for theological questions. Theology too has been dogged by the requirement to be objective and the necessity of finding a scientific approach. Therefore, the questions raised by Keller and Harding about the historical, psychological and social origins of claims to objectivity provide a useful stimulus to discussions of feminist epistemology and can illuminate feminist critiques of traditional theology. Further, Harding offers valuable insights into the way in which the subject-object dichotomy of the prevailing norm defines both its own field of investigation and the world-view of the 'other'. She attributes the 'curious coincidence' between the feminist and African world views to this dichotomy. This insight is of considerable importance in the quest to define a common basis for different liberation theologies.

Charlotte Methuen, University of Edinburgh, Scotland

Asphodel Long
In a Chariot drawn by Lions: the Search for the Female in Deity. Exploding the great myth that God is male, London, The Women's Press, 1992. ISBN 0 7043 4295 2. UK 8.99

For fifteen years, Asphodel Long has run discussions in classes and workshops on the subject of the female aspects of deity. She has observed that, rationally speaking, everybody knows that God is gender free. Yet, when it is suggested that God can be addressed as"Queen","Lady", or"Mother", people react emotionally. Men get angry and women weep.

In her book, Asphodel tries to answer the question: why ? She takes the reader on a journey to meet divine female figures of the ancient world. The figure of wisdom is found in the Bible. Outstanding passages describing Wisdom are found in the **Book of Proverbs** and the **Book of the Wisdom of Solomon**. In Hebrew, she is called Hochma, in Greek, Sophia. Wisdom is seen to do everything that God does. Referring to her, the Bible uses the pronoun"She". We are instroduced to other Hebrew Goddesses, Asherah, the consort of Jahweh, and the Queen of Heaven. Although the latter were rejected in the name of monontheism, signs of their cult have not been completely eradicated from biblical texts. We also meet Hellenistic goddesses. Prayers and poems, dedicated to the mother of the gods, show how much these deities hold in common with the biblical figure of wisdom.

So far one has the impression that the writer enjoys acting as guide. But then comes a turning point: in the New Testament, the ancient figure of wisdom is seen to be projected onto Jesus. The female is assimilated by the male and the female aspect of the deity disappears. A cry of pain is heard as the writer, a woman of Jewish background, depicts the damage inflicted by Christianity on Jews and women alike. Quotations illustrate the misogyny of the Fathers of the Church, and in case the reader should assume this belongs to the long-forgotten past, a link is made with certain clerical voices today. The journey does not stop

here. One finds oneself turning the pages eagerly to see where the path leads next...Its conclusions are practical: they concern both womens' self-images and the relations between the sexes. Asphodel Long is a long-experienced journalist. She writes simply, directly, almost as though she is holding a conversation. Considering her scholarly approach, and the serious religious matter she is dealing with, her style of writing is refreshing. This is a challenging book that will disturb some and be welcomed by others. The reader will be changed before the book is finally put down.
Mary Phil Korsak, Brussels, Belgium.

Clementina Mazzucco
E fui fatta maschio: La donna nel Cristianesimo primitivo (secoli I-III).Firenze, Casa Editrice Le Lettere, 1989.

Kerstin Aspegren, éd. Ren Kieffer
The Male Woman. A Feminine Ideal in the Early Church. (Uppsala Women's Studies. A. Women in Religion 4). Stockholm, Almquist & Wicksell International, 1990.

Adriana Valerio
Cristianesimo al Femminile. Donne protagoniste nella storia delle Chiese. (La Dracma 1). Napoli, M. D'Auria Editore, 1990.

Adriana Valerio
Domenica da Paradiso. Profezia e politica in una mistica del Rinascimento. Spoleto, Centro italiano di studi sull'alto medioevo, 1992.

(Volume I of the Year Book presented this review in an incomplete form: we now print it in full with apologies to Professor Kari Børresen, eds.)

Depuis 1970 environ, les "Women's Studies" en sciences religieuses se sont situé es l'avant-garde des disciplines humanistes, en utilisant le caractère sexué de tout être humain, à la fois biologiquement programmé et culturellement déployé, comme principale catégorie analytique[1]. Quatres ouvrages nouveaux ont paru, qui se complètent pour clarifier l'interaction entre discours patristiqe concernant les femmes et discours matristique sur Dieu, de l'ancienne Eglise jusqu'a à la Renaissance.

Avant le sixième siècle, de textes écrits par des femmes n'ont survécu qu'en nombre très limité. Il est significatif qu'il nous reste environ cent lettres adressées à des femmes par Jean Chrysostome, Jérôme et Augustin, tandis qu'aucune lettre de leurs correspondantes n'a été jugé digne d'être conservée. Parmi les sources latines, nous possédons le journal écrit en prison par Perpetua et inséré dans sa

[1] Kari Elisabeth Børresen, Kari Vogt: *Women's Studies of the Christian and Islamic Traditions. Ancient, Medieval and Renaissance Foremothers.* Dordrecht, Kluwer Academic Publishers, 1993

Passio, la paraphrase biblique du **Cento** virgilien écrit par Proba et le récit du pèlerinage d'Egeria. A partir du haut Moyen Age, le nombre de textes provenant de femmes et conservé augmente sensiblement.

Clementina Mazzucco présente un compte-rendu précis et bien documenté des sources principales concernant les femmes dans le christianisme primitif. Etant donné que ce matérial provient quasi exclusivement de textes écrits par des hommes, il est extrêmement difficile de reconstruire l'expérience vécue des chrétiennes au cours des trois premiers siècles. Mettant l'accent sur le journal de Perpetua, Mazzucco interprète le thème de devenir mâle au sens d'une transformation en virilité christomorphe. Néanmoins, elle n'approfondit pas le caractère constitutif de cette virilità exemplaire dans l'anthropologie chrétienne classique.

La motivation christocentrique de la promotion des femmes à l'humanité mâle est moins explorée dans l'ouvrage posthume de Kerstin Aspegren, édité par René Kieffer. Le sous-titre est plutôt déroutant, parce qu'il ne s'agit nullement d'un idéa; féminin, mais d'un idéal de déféminisation proposé aux femmes et même internalisé par elles. En devenant mâles par l'incorporation au Christ dans l'ordre rédempteur, les femmes peuvent acquérir une pleine humanité théomorphe malgré leur féminité, subalterne selon l'ordre créateur. Néanmoins, Aspegren offre une vue d'ensemble utile sur l'androcentrisme antique, exemplifié par Platon, Aristote, le Stoïcisme et Philon. Un appendice sur Méthode d'Olympe, rédigé par Ragnar Holte, souligne la virginité christomorphe louée par le discours de Thècle. Ce théme de devenir mâle par assimilation au Christ Sauveur, incarné dans la parfaite humanité du sexe masculin, est ici explicite.

Dans la perspective d'un tel encratisme mitigé, qui définit la virginité comme vertu de force virile, une étude récente sur Philon est éclairante[2]. Elle montre comment toute autonomie humaine est a priori réservée à Adam et à ses fils. Ainsi, le nous théomorphe est représenté par le premier homme, tandis qu'Eve représente l'aisthésis: "as the lower, sense-centred part of Everyman, and as the person Everywoman" (p.109). En effet, un concept d'autonomie féminine est impensable dans ce judaïsme hellénistique, matrice du christianisme.

Dans l'Eglise primitive, la rédemption des femmes s'actualise donc par leur accession à l'humanité masculine parfaite, en s'assimilant au Christ. A l'âge patristique, ce motif de devenir mâle fait place à la définition de l'image de Dieu comme privilège asexuel, c'est-à-dire attribuable aux femmes dès la création en dépit de leur sexe non-théomorphe. Cette notion est élaborée par Augustin, qui précise que les femmes aussi possèdent une ratio superior où réside l'image Dei. D'autre part, il souligne que cette prérogative spirituelle n'abolit pas la subordination dans l'ordre de la création, imposeé aux femmes par leur féminité qui est dérivé. Il est essentiel de noter que ces deux concepts successifs présupposent également l'incompatibilité fondamentale du divin et du féminin. La nouvelle

[2] Dorothy Sly: *Philo's Perception of Women. Brown Judaic Studies 209*, Atlanta, GA, Scholars Press, 1990.

définition holistique de l'image, comprenant tout être humain en tant que masculin ou féminin, est une inculturation post-patriarcale devenue normative seulement au vingtième siècle[3].

De même que la doctrine classique s'est construite par l'inculturation grécoromaine des Pères de l'Eglise, la matristique s'est épanouie au Moyen Age, avec Hildegard von Bingen, Hadewijch, les moniales d'Helfta et Julian of Norwich. Il est significatif que ces Mères de l'Eglise sont toutes de l'Europe du Nord, sans doute en raison du statut supérieur des femmes dans les pays plus longtemps préservées du christianisme méditerranéen. Il faut remarquer que la plupart des mulieres sanctae de l'Italie du quatorzième siècle sont illettrées, dictant leurs œ uvres aux clercs. En Europe du Sud, les femmes écrivains n'apparaissent que dans la Renaissance.

L'étude proprement matristique d'Adriana Valerio est donc centrée sur le Moyen Age et le Rinascimento, avec Héloïse, Guglielma da Milano, Domenica Narducci et Vittoria Colonna. Valerio souligne un faut paradoxal de l'histoire des chrétiennes: l'androcentrisme traditionnel semble être accepté par les femmes elles-mêmes. En effet, l'axiome de la subordination féminine établie par l'ordre créateur ne se trouve contesté dans aucun écrit matristique conservé. D'autre part, toutes ces Mères de l'Englise invoquent leur équivalence dans l'ordre du salut pour franchir, au maximum de ce qui est possible dans l'existence terrestre, les limites imposées par leur *feminei sexus natura devilis.*

Valerio analyse ce que j'appellerais le féminisme déféminisant des femmes martyrs et prophètes du second siècle, où Blandina et Perpetua s'incorporent à la passion du Christ Sauveur, cependant que Maximilla et Priscilla servant d'instruments à l'Esprit-Saint. Au Moyen Age, un exemple exceptionnel de pouvoir institutionnalisé des femmes est fourni par le monastère double à Goleto (fondé ca. 1135), où les moines sont soumis à la juridiction de l' abbesse. A partir du sixième et jusqu'au treizième siècle, la culture monastique féminine, que la création des universités reservées aux hommes fera disparaître, fleurit en France (Caesaria d'Arles, Radegundis de Poitiers, Héloïse), en Angleterre (Hilda of Whitby), et en Allemagne (Hrotsvith von Gandersheim, Herrad von Landsberg, Hildegard von Bingen, Gertrud von Helfta).

Avec justesse, Valerio insiste sur l'originalité de la pensée théologique d'Héloïse (morte en 1163/4). Cette docte amante, mariée à contre-coeur pour devenit par la suite une excellente abbesse, reste tourmentée par l'antinomie de ses positions à l'égard de deux principes fondamentaux de la doctrine traditionnelle. Héloïse approuve la scission postulée entre amour pour Dieu et amour sexuel, mais elle récuse le conflit corrélatif incessamment dénoncé par son examant et mari Abélard, entre activité sexuelle et amour du conjoint. Persistant

[3] ed. Kari Elisabeth Børresen, *Image of God and Gender Models in Judaeo-Christian Tradition*, Oslo, Solum Forlag, 1991.

dans la valorisation positive de leur expérience amoureuse, Héloïse énonce son éthique d'intention. Il est significatif que les historiens androcentriques aient affirmé qu'elle est ici influencée par son maître Abélard. Il serait beaucoup plus probable que la causalité de cette *etica di responsabilità* soit en sens inverse, Abélard ayant écrit son Scito teipsum, où il préconise la volonté intentionnelle comme déterminant la moralité d'un acte, après la confrontation existentielle avec Héloïse.

Au cours du Moyen Age se produit une transformation importante de la christologie en sens féministe. Le Christ incarné et crucifié est ici décrit comme gynécomorphe, précisement en raison de sa kenosis salvifique. Il en résulte que les femmes peuvent devenir christomorphes sans masculinisation androcentrique, ni déféminisation spiritualiste, mais s'assimiler au Christ par et dans leur propre *genderedness* [4]. Subordination, corporéité et maternité souffrante symbolisent désormais la nature humaine du Christ. Il est à remarquer que cette nouvelle inculturation doctrinale ne supprime pas la connexion classique entre Dieu andromorphe et le mâle théomorphe, constitutive de la typologie du nouvel Adam. L'incompatibilité traditionnelle entre le divin et le féminin persiste, dans la mesure où la divinité du Christ reste liée à l'image de l'homme et où Dieu est normalement décrit par des métaphores masculines, comme roi, guerrier, juge et surtout Père. Anticipée par la christologie sapientielle de Hildegard von Bingen[5], Julian of Norwich (morte après 1416) est devancière de *l'aggiornamento* post-patriarcal du discours sur Dieu. Afin d'exprimer verbalement la totalité du dalut, Julian insiste sur la maternité créatrice et rédemptrice de Dieu, révélée par la seconde Personne de la Trinité. Parce que "oure moder Cryst" (Christ notre mère) est "oure Moder God alle wysdom" (notre Mère Dieu la sagesse), Julian élargit la métaphorique féminine du niveau humain au niveau de la divinité une et trine.

Cette synthèse aussi harmonieuse que sophistiquée de l'érudite recluse reste malheureusement exceptionnelle au Moyen Age, où l'Englise institutionnelle s'efforce âprement de contrôler le féminisme religieux. Avec raison, Valerio parle du "conflitto permanente' drammatico, che attraversa la storia della chiesa", mettant l'accent sur l'espace plus ou moins réel laissé aux femmes en marge de la grande Église. Néanmoins, Valerio précise que les femmes ne sont pas prépondérantes dans ce groupes très variés, mais écartés ou exterminés comme hérétiques. Un exemple très frappant du *disagio femminile,* causé par l'androcentrisme théologique traditionnel, est la doctrine attribuée à Guglielma da Milano, morte (1281) en "odeur de sainteté" et ensevelie dans le monastère cistercien de Chiaravalle. Une généalogie hagiographique fascinante est établie par

[4] Caroline Walker Bynum: *Holy Feast and Holy Fast: The Religious Significance of Food to Medieval Women,* Berkeley, CA, University of California Press, 1987.

[5] Barbara Newman, *Sister of Wisdom: St. Hildegard's Theology of the Feminine,* Berkeley, CA, University of California Press, 1987.

le fait (vérifié à Prague en 1988 par mon collègue Ladislav Reznicek) que cette Guglielma la Boema, venue comme veuve à Milan, était fille (Blazena Vilemina) du roi Premysl I Ottakar et sa seconde femme Constance de Hongrie. Elle était donc soeur ainée de saint Agnès de Prague et cousine de sainte Elisabeth von Thüringen! Selon les Actes du procès tenu en 1300, ses disciples Maifreda da Pirovano, qui était cousine du *vicario imperiale* Matteo Visconti, et Andrea Saramita ont affirmé que Guglielma serait une incarnation de l'Esprit-Saint, qui devrait revenir en gloire pour établir une nouvelle Eglise sous le pontificat de Maifreda, afin de réaliser le salut de tous, y compris Juifs, Musulmans et païens. Les protagonistes moururent sur le bûcher, brûlés en compagnie des restes exhumés de Guglielma. Analysant cette aventure malmené dans le contexte de la *mistica femminile,* Valerio clarifie son sens à la fois existentiel et doctrinal, en tant que nouvelle incarnation du divin dans le sexe féminin.

Parmi les exemples apparemment réussis de féminisme charismatique, signalons Birgitta de Suède (morte en 1373). Invoquée comme témoin de la légitimité du pontife romain contre le rival d'Avignon, Birgitta fut canonisée dès 1391 par Boniface IX, mais sans référence à son message gynécocentrique.

Valerio présente une nouvelle étude sur les textes dictés par Domenica Narducci (1473-1553), en grande partie inédits. Cette madre spirituale d'origine paysanne et illettrée, nommée Domenica da paradiso, fut d'abord liée au cercle de Girolamo Savonarola et plus tard accusée d'hérésie. Se disculpant avec succès, Domenica réussit en 1515 à fonder un couvent de Dominicaines à Florence, approuvé par Léon X (Giovanni de'Medici). Avec une efficacitée tant adminstrative que mystique, cette prieure exerça une grande influence, à la fois spirituelle et politique, entre autres sur Caterina Cybo. Domenica a laissé cinq œuvres majeures, une centaine de lettres, une trentaine de compte-rendus des visions, et plusieurs sermons, dont vingt sont littéralement transcrits. Valerio souligne l'interprétation de I Cor. 14,34 donnée par Domenica dans un sermon tenu devant ses soeurs et confesseurs en 1507, où elle s'efforce de justifier sa propre activité de prédicateur. L'argument principal correspond au motif souvent invoqué par la matristique du Moyen Age: Dieu utilise la faiblesse féminine comme instrument pour confondre l'orgueil masculin. La nuit après son sermon, Paul lui-même instruit Domenica dans un rêve, précisant qu'il n'a nullement voulu s'opposer à l'inspiration du Saint-Esprit, qui peut aussi opérer par les femmes. Comme les hommes, elles sont creature del Signore. Passons sous silence la comparaison finale avec d'autres créatures, comme les *bestie* et *idioti,* qui peuvent aussi servir comme instruments pour l'action divine! Il est significatif que l'annotation de ce texte faite par son biographe (1637/40) cherche à rendre Domenica inoffensive en interprétant la prohibition paulinienne comme visant seulement la prédication publique.

Introduite en 1630, la cause de canonisation de Domenica Narducci n'aboutit pas en dépit de plusieurs tentatives. En effet, les nonnes enérgiques sont difficilement canonisables. Hildegard von Bingen se trouve encore au point mort en dépit de trois procès, mais son culte est permis en Allemagne depuis 1940. La causa de Caritas Pirckheimer (1467-1532), introduite en 1932 et reprise en 1961, est actuellement suspendue par la disparition des Actes en 1969!

Sous Paul IV (1555-59), l'Inquisition romaine a rassemblé un dossier contre l'archévêque de Canterbury Reginald Pole, cardinal de la *Riforma cattolica* et donc suspect d'hérésie. Par ordre de Mary Tudor ce *gentleman* a évité de retourner à Rome, ce qui lui valut de mourir de cause naturelle (1558). Son dossier, encore conservé sub secreto, contient aussi des matériaux concernant sa collaboratrice Vittoria Colonna, qui eut la chance de mourir dès 1547. Un autre cardinal réformateur, Gasparo Contarini, mourut opportunément en 1542. Son collègue Giovanni Morone fut libéré du Castel Sant'Angelo par Pie IV, après deux ans de prison (1557-59), pour présider en 1563 à la conclusion du concile de Trente.

Valerio présente une analyse solidement documentée de la pensée théologique de Vittoria, exprimée surtout dans sa vaste correspondance, *Carteggio*, et ses méditations sur l'Ecriture sainte. Avec Giulia Gonzaga, Caterina Cybo, Renée de France et Marguerite de Navarre, Vittoria participe au ressourcement biblique des femmes aristocrates. Cet *evangelismo* inspire une foi centrée sur le Christ "nudo e pouro", qui s'efforce par conséquent de réformer l'Eglise en tant qu'instrument christique du salut. Fortement liée à Pole, Contarini et Morone, Vittoria partage leurs efforts pour surmonter la rupture de la chrétienté, provoquée par l'excommunication de Martin Luther en 1520. Il est donc significatif que *l'Epistula de iustificatione,* écrite par Contarini pour le colloque inter-confessionnel de Ratisbonne en 1541, soit transmise à Vittoria.

Il est important de noter que toute exégèse matristique semble être inconsciente de l'androcentrisme foncier des textes bibliques, un fait qui constitue le problème principal pour la théologie féministe actuelle. Néanmoins, Valerio se réfère à l'interprétation du titre traditionnel donné à Marie Madeleine, *apostola apostolorum,* avancée par Vittoria dans une lettre à Costanza d'Avalos. Il est à noter que Jean 20, 11-18 est ici paraphrasé de manière féministe, c'est-à-dire en sens inverse de l'exégèse traditionnelle. Vittoria précise que Marie Madeleine n'est pas seulement qualifiée d'apôtre en tant que première annonciatrice de la résurrection du Christ. Elle souligne que le Christ a choisi Marie Madeleine comme témoin primaire précisement afin de confirmer sa vocation apostolique: "per certificarla ch era sua apostola".

Valerio termine son ouvrage en présentant une femme active au vingtième siècle, l'historienne Marianne Weber (1870-1954). Luthérienne et femme de Max Weber, elle est la seule figure de cette série matristique qui dans ses écrits valorise le mariage en tant qu'union à la fois charnelle et spirituelle. En effet, l'autonomie féminine partiellement anticipée par l'éthique d'Héloïse ne se trouve réalisable que dans notre civilisation post-patriarcale, déjà entrevue par Marianne Weber. Avec perspicacité, elle critique le contrôle clérical exercé sur les femmes catholiques.

Il est à constater que malgré le riche héritage des Mères de la grande Eglise, le catholicisme tant orthodoxe que romain persiste encore aujourd'hui à exclure les femmes du domaine culturel. Récemment définies comme théomorphes aussi en tant que femmes, elles sont néanmoins considérées incapables d'agir comme prêtres *in persona Christi*. Il faut donc s'inspirer de nos Mères de l'Englise dans l'effort actuel de Réforme catholique, pour que les institutions ecclésiastiques cessent de s'ériger en obstacle entre les femmes et Dieu!
Kari Børresen, Oslo.

3. Rezensionen Dissertationen – Reviews of Doctoral Dissertations – Revues des Thèses Doctorales

Ina Praetorius
Anthropologie und Frauenbild in der deutschsprachigen protestantischen Ethik seit 1949, Gütersloher Verlagshaus Gerd Mohn 1993, 264 S

Mit diesem kritisch-analytischen Werk ist der Autorin ein starker Schachzug gelungen. Endlich eine ins Detail gehende Analyse eines fundamental wichtigen Bereichs protestantisch theologischer Reflexion aus einem Zeitraum, in der die Proklamation der Gleichheit der Geschlechte sowohl auf der Tagesordnung steht, als auch verfassungsrechtlicher Grundsatz ist. Diese an logischer Präzision ausgerichtete Arbeit wurde als Dissertation an der Theologischen Fakultät Heidelberg angenommen. Die Autorin unterzieht die Wahl des Gegenstandes einer eingehenden und auch selbstkritischen Begründung. Von der im Gefolge der dialektischen Theologie bloßpraktischen Disziplin am Rande der Theologie hat sich die Ethik zur Steigerungsform von Theologie entwickelt, ohne jedoch ihren vorrangingen dogmatischen Bezugsrahmen einzubüßen. An der Nahtstelle zwischen theologischer Reflexion einerseits und weiblicher und männlicher Lebenswirklichkeit andererseits wird der Bezug zur dogmatisch-systematischen Theologie über die allgemein anthropologischen Aussagen hergestellt. Dadurch wirft die Kritik der Ethik ein entsprechendes Licht auf das Ganze protestantischer deutschsprachiger Theologie seit 1949, zumal die analysierten Texte sich selbst als Theologie im Vollsinn verstehen.

Die Autorin untersucht ihr Objekt auf den von feministischen Wissenschaftlerinnen im gesamten abendländischen Wissenschaftsdiskurs aufgefundenen Androzentrismus aus Vorurteilsstruktur, der einer allgemeinen und von den Ethikern selbst anerkannten Vernunftorientierung im Wissenschaftsdiskurs zuwiderläuft und immer wieder zu Inkonsistenzen innerhalb der sporadischen Aussagen zur Weiblichkeit und zu Widersprüchen zwischen diesen Aussagen und den quasi geschlechtsneutralen anthropologischen Aussagen in systematischen

Diskursen führt. Die Gattung Lehrbuch mit dem Aufbauschema Grundlegung/ Anwendung verspricht Vollständigkeit im Sinne eines klassischen Verständnisses der Disziplin, als auch Repräsentativität in bezug auf deren Gegenstand. Die Zielgruppe dieser Gattung sind Multiplicatorinnen, die eine enstprechende Funktion im gesellschaftlichen Bereich ausüben werden bzw. ausüben werden.

Die Beschränkung auf den Zeitraum seit 1949 hängt eng mit ihrem ausführlich dargestellten Erkenntnisinteresse zusammen. Die immer wieder anzutreffende Auffassung von dem in freiheitlich-demokratischen Rechtsstaaten gelösten Geschlechterproblem könnte durch die ideologierkritische Neubesinnung der Nachkriegszeit ihr Recht einfordern, soweit die erfolgte Erschütterung ebenfalls die Geschlechter-ideologie erfaßt hätte.

Insofern geht die Autorin also der Frage nach, ob sich im protestantisch-ethischen Diskurs deutscher Sprache seit 1949 auch noch androzentrische Strukturen nachweisen lassen.

Diese Strukturen sind durch den jahrhundertelangen systematischen Ausschlußweiblicher Subjekte aus dem etablierten Wissenschaftsbetrieb entstanden und haben zu Verzerrung in der Realitätswahrnehmung geführt, die schon dem wissenschaftstheoretisch immanenten Anspruch auf Neutralität und Objektivität widersprechen. Ein auf der einen Seite schon vorausgesetztes Herrschaftsverhältnis zwischen männlichen und weiblichen Subjekten ist damit neu vergegenwärtigt und untermauert auf der anderen Seite sogar künftige Herrschaftsstrukturen zwischen den Geschlechtern...In zwei ausführlichen reflektierten methodischen Schritten geht Praetorius zielstrebig vor, zunächst eine ausführliche, textimmanente Kritik der Lehrbücher, die das Verhältnis zwischen geschlechtsneutralen Zentralasussagen und peripheren Weiblichkeitsentwürfen überprüft.

Dann konfrontiert Praetorius die anthropologischen und weiblichkeitstheoretischen Aussagen der Lehrbücher in einem 2. Schritt texttranszendierender Kritik mit den Realitäten weiblichen Lebenszusammenhanges in hochindustrialisierten Gesellschaften, also mit dejenigen historischen Ausformung weiblicher Existenz, die das soziale Umfeld der ethischen Texte bildet. Um dem Zweck als Maßstab zu dienen, erstellt sie ein durch empirische Forschung belegtes, nachvollziehbares und kohärentes Orientierungsmodell weiblichen Lebenszusammenhanges, das sich am Konzept des Subjekts Frau orientiert und damit den dem "schönen Geschlecht" durch jahrhundertelange androzentrische Wissenschaftskultur zugewiesen Objektstatus überwindet. Aufgrund der neueren feministischen Diskussion um die Wahrheit des Subjekts Frau läßt die Autorin die Definition dieses Subjekts offen.

Praetorius konstituiert das Orientierungsmodell "weiblicher Lebenszusammenhang in der modernen Industriegesellschaft"anhand historisch-ökonomischer und ideengeschichtlicher Determinanten. Jede Frau wird mit dem Anspruch der Orientierung auf Familienarbeit hin konfrontiert, so daßnicht die linear aufsteigende Karriere, sondern verschiedene, konfliktreiche Formen von biographischen Kompromissen zwischen unbezahlter Familienarbeit und Erwerbstätigkeit der Norm entsprechen. Sogenannte Doppelbelastung, beruflicher Wiedereinstieg und Lohnungleichheit konstituieren weibliches Leben, sowie der Anspruch an die Frauen, die der Familienorientierung nicht ganz widerstehen, eine komplexe Aufgabe erfüllen zu müssen, zu der sie weder ausgebildet sind, noch irgendeine Wissenschaft dieses Aufgabenfeld der Theoriebildung für würdig erachten. Selbstentwickelte Strategien dienen als Lösung. Die soziale Isolierung der Hausarbeiterin wird durch die Idee der unantastbaren Privatsphäre verstärkt. Allgegenwärtige Erfahrung von Diskriminierung, wie misogyner Humor, Verdinglichung der Frau in den Medien, Pornographie, sexistische Belästigung am Arbeitsplatz und berufliche Diskriminierung sowie Bedrohung durch direkt Gewalt verlangen nach Bewältigung. Eine verwirrende Fülle von Deutungsangeboten für weibliche Existenz, die Frage nach Praktiken zur Regulierung der Fruchtbarkeit und die sich verändernde rechtliche Stellung von Frauen in der BRD gehören zu den Existenzbedingungen von Frauen, die theologisch ethischer Theoriebildung zu unterziehen wären, um dem Anspruch zu genügen, die Existenz von BRD-Frauen seit 1949 zu reflektieren.

Paul Althaus, Helmut Thielicke, Wolfgang Trillhaas, Wolfgang Schweitzer und Trutz Rendtorff sind die Männer der Theologie, deren Lehrbücher zur Ethik die Autorin analysiert hat. Alle folgen im Aufbau dem Schema Grundlegung/ Anwendung. Die ausführliche analytische Arbeit der textimmanenten Kritik der Ethiker umfaßt zirka ein Drittel des Praetorius-Textes. Präzise arbeitet sie den Weiblichkeitsentwurf des jeweiligen Autors heraus und setzt ihn in Beziehung zu ethischen Aussagen aus den Anwendungskapiteln wie Berufsethik, politische Ethik der Kunst bzw. zu ethischen Aussagen über "den Menschen", in denen Frauen aber nicht explizit thematisiert werden, dann zur allgemeinen Anthropologie des Grundlagenteils. Die Lektüre dieses traurigen Kapitels protestantischer Theologie geriet mir fast ausnahmslos zum befreienden Lachen über diese Vorführung theologisch-ethischen Gruselkabinetts. Nur gut, daßdie theologisch-ethische Theoriebildung, die unser Bild beherrscht, den realen Existenzformen vieler Frauen gar nicht mehr gerecht wird. So hart ist das Urteil. Daß die Frau in Trillhaas 'Kapitel zur politischen Ethik' nicht anders Erwähnung findet als als Gebärende und einkaufende Hausfrau (Trillhaas benutzt diese Erwähnung als Beispiele für vorpolitische Lebensvorgänge), ist nicht weiter verwunderlich, besteht für Trillhaas der Wert einer Partei doch im wesentlichen darin, daß sie "...Männer hat, denen wirklich etwas einfällt." Ein Beispiel aus tausend und einer Nacht theologischer Männerethik.

Allen fünf Ethiken gemeinsam ist die durchgängige androzentrische Struktur, d.h., das Paradigma des Menschen und alles Menschlichen schlechthin ist eben "der erwachsene Mann". Alle Lehrbücher weisen unreflektierte Identifizierung der Konzepte Mann und Mensch auf, indem z.B. Fragen des aktiven Militärdienstes als Fragen des Menschen breit ausgeführt werden, während die Behandlung des "naturnahen Berufs" der Hausfrau in der Arbeitsethik keine Berücksichtigung findet. Die theologische Anthropologie schließt Frauen aus, denn deren behauptete Geschlechtsnatur, die auf Liebe, Unterordnung und Mütterlichkeit gerichtet ist, ist ein Bild des sich durch Hybris und Selbstbezogenheit versün-digenden Menschen nicht eingeschlossen.

Ina Praetorius forgert logisch, daßsich bei den Ethikern so das theologische Paradoxon von der geringeren Sündhaftigkeit der Frauen gegenüber den Männern herausbildet. Ob unseren Ethikern diese Implikation und ihre eigen geschlechtsbedingte Standortgebundenheit, die weiter greift als die von ihnen schon zugestandene Zeitgebundenheit, bewußt war? Ihre Geschlechts-, Klassen- und Kulturgebundenheit steht eben ihrem Anspruch, "die Lebensführung des Menschen" zu reflektieren, entgegen.

Es ist jedoch eine historische Entwicklung in Bezug auf die Weiblichkeitstheorie zu verzeichnen. Von der ausgeführten Geschlechterontologie bei Althaus und Thielicke wird über den onthologischen Ausschlußder Frau aus dem Zentrum des Menschlichen bei Trillhaas, Schweitzer und Rendtorff der faktische weibliche Lebenszusammenhang vergessen, obwohl man die Gleichheit der Geschlechter coram Deo und im sozialen Bereich postuliert. Auch die theologische Anthropologie bleibt am männlichen Sozialcharakter orientiert.

Aufgefundene grammatische Ungereimtheiten wie die "Gleichheit alle Staatsbürger" und die "Wehrpflicht aller Bürger" deuten auf die typisch patriarchale Methode der Unsichtbarmachung der Frauen, die sich aber stets die Rückzugsmöglichkeit auf die behauptete Inklusivität des generischen Maskulinums offenhält.

Da, wo Ina Praetorius die herausgearbeiteten Faktoren weiblichen Lebenszusammenhanges in der modernen Industriegesellschaft mit der jeweiligen theologischen Ethik konfrontiert, bleibt das Ergebnis ähnlich. Konflikte des weiblichen Lebenszusammenhanges werden nicht thematisiert und Widersprüche gar nicht erst bearbeitet.

Inwieweit die protestantische Ethik der achtziger Jahre diese Defizite und ihre eigene androzentrische Vorurteilsstruktur aufgearbeitet hat, ist Thema des essayistischen und vorletzten Kapitels, bevor die Autorin im letzten Kapitel ihre Sicht der künftigen Aufgabe protstantisch-theologischer Ethik vorstellt. Nachdem die beinahe geschlossen wirkende deutschsprachige Diskursgemeinschaft theologischer Ethik in den achtziger Jahren die harmonistische Vorstellung von der Ergänzung der Geschlechter und die These von der Vergangenheit des Patriarchats weiter zelebriert hat, weicht sie bei wachsender Ratlosigkeit bis auf wenige isolierte Beiträge vor der Auseinandersetzung mit dem androzentrischen Vorurteil aus. Das Eingeständnis dieses Vorurteils hätte eine tiefgreifende Neuori-

entierung zur Folge, die zunächst eine reale Zulassung von Frauen als gleichberechtigte Geschlechtspartnerinnen im wissenschaftlichen Diskurs im Sinne objektiver Wahrheitsfindung nach sich zöge. Vorraussetzung dazu wäre die Anerkennung der von Ina Praetorius nachgewiesenen androzentrischen Parteilichkeit des ethischen Diskurses. Mit inklusiven, nicht androzentrischen, anthropologischen Modellen, die sich entweder an Egalität, Ergänzung oder Differenz zwischen den Geschlechtern orientiern, läßt sich die theologische Aufgabe dann skizzenhaft neu formulieren: aufbauend auf das befreiende Erbe der Bibel und die Gottesebenbildlichkeit von Frau und Mann wird die Dekonstruktion androzentrischer Theologie weiter betrieben, bis hin zu einer Rekonstruktion christlicher Ethik, die inklusive ihrer Androzentrismuskritik mehr ist als nur oberflächlich renovierte Theologie. Möge gesammelter Scharfsinn gelernter Theologinnen zusammen mit Einsicht und Machtverzicht auf männlicher Seite dem Durchbruch einer befreienden christlichen Botschaft dienen. Diesem Wunsch der Autorin kann ich mich zur Halbzeit der oekumenischen Dekade "Solidarität der Kirchen mit den Frauen" nur wärmstens anschließen, wo doch die Theologie dieser aufbrechenden Kirche dienen sollte.
Ulrike Timmerberg-Schutt

Maaike de Haardt

Dichter bij de dood. Feministisch-theologische aanzetten tot een theologie van de dood, Zoetermeer, (boekencentrum), 1993.

In the introduction to her study, "Nearer to death. Feminist-theological attempts towards a Theology of Death", Maaike de Haardt writes that she wants to stress the importance of a reflection upon death as a 'central existential' as well as a central theological issue for feminist theology. At the same time she wants to underscore the relevance of a feminist theological reflection upon death in the light of questions and problems with which death confronts both individuals and society as a whole. In my opinion De Haardt succeeds in her intention. Her thorough analysis of feminist theological visions of death, which, as she writes, are not easily discovered, because feminist theologians mostly do not speak extensively or explicitly about death, shows that death is indeed a central question. A central issue that has many connections with other important theological themes such as christology and God image. At the same time she demonstrates how the concrete death of real people challenges (feminist) theological views on death, and repeatedly invites further reflection. In the first chapter of her study De Haardt discusses the classical Christian theological reflection on death and shows how this reflection is related to the christologically-founded expectation of the resurrection from the dead, which forms the grounds for rejecting the theory of natural death. Death is not seen as natural, but as the result of, or the judgement of God on, sin. De Haardt points to the fact that in this highly metaphorical meaning of death, the mortal body appears to be the ultimate symbol of negativity and of God-forsakenness. In the second chapter, this negative qualification of death within classical theology appears to be one of the major points of criticism in feminist theological visions of death. De Haardt classifies two ways of discussing death within feminist theology. In the first one death is discussed within the context of 'coping with death', in which death is seen as the end of life. Here De Haardt considers the work of Perkins, Washbourn and Ochs. In the second one death is discussed as a metaphor. 'Death' as a negatively qualifying metaphor stands here against 'life'as a positively qualifying metaphor. De Haardt shows how in the work of Ruether and Daly the concept 'death' is used in this way. 'Death' functions as a concept to qualify and to criticise the state of the world, or of a specific society, or the situation of a particular group. De Haardt argues that in both ways of discussing death, the theory of natural death, as the natural ending of life, is affirmed. Death is seen as a natural part of life. In the third chapter, the feminist theological discourse on death is subjected to a more detailed analysis. This is done by means of a number of feminist views on christology and soteriology. Given the fact that in Christology death has a very concrete place, at least in the reflection on the suffering and death of Jesus, De Haardt expects that along these lines a light can be thrown on the more general meaning of suffering and death. In this chapter she discusses the work of Kassel, Heyward, Grey and Brock, and shows how all these "(implicit) theologies of death "work out very worthwhile insights, but also that in each view questions can be raised. In the last chapter she collects the problems and tries to come to terms with them. Two important issues are discussed further. The first one concerns the question of God. This question of God concentrates on the issue 'immanence-transcendence' in relation to 'finitude-infinitude'. The second problem in the last chapter, in which De Haardt tries to develop a 'theology of finitude', is connected to the question as to how the death of real people could be integrated in the theological reflection upon death. Concerning the death of real people, De Haardt makes a plea for an incarnational theology, in which the mortal body and death have a central place. The affirmation of the presence of God to the mortal body also forms the grounds for rejecting all the many forms of the denial of death and finitude, as well as of the many forms of suffering and death to which this denial leads. By her study De Haardt shows with much clarity that the reflection upon death is in many respects of central importance for (feminist) theological models. By discussing the vision of death of so many influential feminist theologians, she provides other feminist theologians with very worthwhile foundational work. This foundation invites further contemplation and reflection upon this fascinating theme.

Christa Anbeek, Vrije Universiteit, Amsterdam.

Rapport Sur La Conférence Commission Écologie at Bio-Éthique du Forum à Rome:

"Le Printemps Silencieux, Trente and Apres"

C'est ce thème que la Commission Écologie et Bio-Éthique du Forum avait choisi pour la Conférence qu'elle avait convoquée, du 14 au 20 Avril, 1993, á Santa Severa (Rome). Quarante-trois femmes, en provenance de 19 pays différents, se sont donc retrouvées au Centre Evangélique Baptiste de cette petite ville en bordure de la mer. C'est la chronique "au jour le jour" de cette rencontre qui est rapportée ici.

Jeudi 15 avril: "L'Arbre de la Sagesse"

Avez-vous déjà essayé de vous identifier, de vous "sentir" un arbre, vos deux pieds fermement ancrés au sol, vos bras comme des ramures balanant leurs feuilles au souffle du vent? C'est l'experience à laquelle on fut invitées, au cours de la méditation matinale, et qui s'est révélée une merveilleuse á "mise en condition" pour écouter Anne Primavesi parler de l'Arbre de la vie, á "c'est la Sagesse pour ce qui la saisissent, et bienheurex ceux qui la tiennent", (Prov 3,18). En suivant ce fil rouge de l'Esprit de la Sagesse et de'Arbre de la vie, Anne entraîna l'auditoire dans une méditation d'abord à travers la légende du héros irlandais Fionn Mac Cumhaill et du sage Finegas. Pour nous, dit Anne, la Sagesse se trouve dans le royaume de nostre existence quotidienne, dans notre attitude vis-à-vis de notre environnement et de la place que nous y tenons. Rendant ensuite hommage à la femme "Sage" que fut Rachel Carson, Anne rappella l'oeuvre de cette biologiste, pionnière de ce qui est aujourd'hui l'écologie, pour laquelle elle mena une courageuse et tenace croisade tout au long de sa vie et dans ses différents ouvrages.

Anne nous invite à découvrir, au cours du travail de cette Conférence, les liens entre science et religion, écologie et Sagesse. Les groupes de travail mettaiant en cause les relations "pathologiques" avec la Terre qui sont celles du monde occidental. La vision proposée par Anne, est elle capable de renverser le mythe du standard de vie du monde occidental, si vivace et tellement attirant pour les autres mondes? Réponse d'Anne: "Le péché originel, n'est-ce pas le refus de donner un home à la Sagesse? C'est le refus du monde occidental de dire: 'J'ai assez!'" L'après-midi de ce premier jour fut consacrée à differents groupes de réflexions (Femmes et Bioéthique, Spiritualité des Femmes, Les Quatre Eléments,

Les Conférences de Miami et Rio). L'avant-soirée réunit des ateliers créatifs, à propos d'études bibliques, danses et chants.

Vendredi 16 avril: "L'Arbre qui pousse"

La journée s'ouvre par une méditation sur la plages, face au Centre. Chacune est en charge de récolter un objet, quelque chose évoquant la Nature, et aussi quelquechose provenant de l'intervention "humaine" dans la nature. Au moment où les chants et les prières débutent, l'intervention humaines se mainfeste par l'arrivée sur la plages d'un gros camion-pelleteuse symbolisant bien les nuisances humaines de notre civilisation!

C'est Elizabeth Green née en Angleterre mais résident en Italie qui était en charge de la conférence du jour. Professeur de théologie féministe, elle a exposé "la croissance de l'Arbres" et les branches anciennes et nouvelles de l'écofeminisme. Elle compare les recherches et travaux des theologiennes éco-féministes à l'oeuvre des alchimistes du Moyen-Age: au lieu de manipuler des métaux et des vapeurs chimiques, ce sont les concepts, les symboles et métaphores de la tradition chrétienne avec lesquelles se débattent les théologiennes écoféministes d'aujourd'hui. Vice-Présidente de l'association-soeur du Forum, l'AFERT, Elizabeth donne ici en primeur l'exposé qui parait dans ce numéro de l'Annuaire (pp. 48-58). Cette étude et analyse laisse l'auditoire avec bon nombre de questions: Quelles ressources la tradition chrétienne offre-t-elle à la théologie écoféministe? Femme et Nature: quelles sont les différences qui existent entre femmes, mais aussi dans la nature? Comment écouter ces différences? Pouvons-nous et devons-nous les intégrer dans notre travail?

Le soir, amies de Biélorussie, en charge de "l'Action Humanitaire pour les Enfants de Tchernobyl" ont apporté des témoignages bouleversants de l'action qu'elles mènent depuis des années. Les préoccupations d'Irina et de Ludmilla resteront profondément présentes au coeur des participantes, et se concrétiseront sans doute en soutien efficace au retour de chacune dans son pays.

Dimanche 18 avril: "L'Arbre de la Vie"

"Christ est réssuscité! Il est vraiment réssuscité". C'est par cette salutation propre au rite Orthodoxe que s'est ouverte la journée de ce Dimanche, jour áde la Pâ que orthodoxe. L'allégresse pascale est exprimée et signifiée, tout au long de la "Célebration d'ouverture de la journée", ponctuée par des danses méditatives, des chants et un accompagnement de flte.

On a écouté ensuite Grace M. Jantzen, canadienne, Maître de Conférence au Kings College de Londres. C'est revêtue de la déjà célèbre "Robe de la Paix" du Forum qu'à partir de son expérience de membre de la Commission Royale

Canadienne des Technologies de Reproduction, Grace a partagé les leçons des travaux, des recherches, des découvertes, des doutes et des incertitudes de la Commission.

Avec une grande clarté, Grace nous a guidées dans le dédale des questions d'ingénièrie génétique qui ont pour l'humanité l'importance capitales qu'avaient les questions atomiques dans les dernières décennies. Elle conclut en disant: Où est la théologie, dans tout cela? Certainement pas dans un Dieu "qui est là -haut", qui "révèle la Verité" mais dans Celui qu'on rencontre dans les luttes concrètes et quotidiennes: "J'étais affamé, nu, enchaîné..."

Beaucoup de questions ont surgi parmi les groupes de réflexion, et Grace s'est efforcée d'y répondre. On est attuellement dans une phase très nébuleuse, quant'à un règlement éthique, au plan national ou international. Il n'est pas facile de faire coincider les "valeurs" des scientifiques avec celles des citoyens et citoyennes. Mais Grace pense qu'il y a des scientifiques qui cherchent le contact avec "le gens", qui demandent leurs avis et essaient d'en tenir compte.

De nouveaux groupes de travail se réunirent dans l'après-midi (Bioéthique, Le "printemps silencieux persistant", "L'Agenda 21 des Femmes", L'interprètation de la Genèse). La soirée réunit les participantes autour des amies de Tchéque et de Slovaquie, qui toutes deux firent part des actions entreprises par leurs associations et des enfants, de la ville et de l'éducation à l'écologie urbaine.

Lundi 19 avril: "L'Arbre dépouillé"

Après "l'ouverture de la journée" Adriana Cavina, Pasteure et Psychologue, va entraîner les participantes à la recherche des racines écologiques de leur "moi". Citant l'écrivaine américaine, Adrienne Rich, Adriana constate que "pour la première fois dans l'histoire, nous avons la possibilité d'évaluer le 'royaume des Pères' et d'en prendre la mesure"! Dans une perspective psycho-analytique et féministe, Adriana tente de cerner le "moi" et les femmes, et tout le débat autour de la "fémininité". Le "moi nucleaire", produit de la patriarchie, peut ê tre utilement remplacé par "le moi écologique", celui qui met l'accent sur la relation, non seulement avec les autres ê tres humains, mais aussi avec tout ce qui nous entoure. En suivant la pensée de Rich, Adriana affirme: Nous les femmes, qui sommes et avons toujours été celles que savent tisser, je suis sûre, que nous avons le pouvoir et la force de tisser notre toile d'intégralité (wholeness) pour le monde entier.

Au cours de la séance plénière, des décisions ont été prises en conclusion à la Conférence. Les participantes ont été d'accord pour recommander au Forum Oecuménique des Femmes Chrétiennes d'Europe, au nom de la Commission "Ecologie et Bioéthique" de:

1. soutenir et communiquer à toutes les branches du Forum le document Position Paper on Prenatal Diagnosis rédigé par un groupes des femmes suisses, avec les commentaires de la Conférence sur ce document.
2. soutenir et communiquer également à toutes les branches du Forum l'Agenda 21 des femmes, rédigé à la Conférences des Femmes pour une Planète Saines, Miami, novembre 1991.
3. sur les questions atomiques, soutenir les recommandations de l'atelier "Printemps silencieux persistant" qui s'est réuni dans le cadre de cette Conférence.

Ce qui compte, pour l'avenir du Forum et de sa Commission, c'est la volonté des participantes de ne pas faire de cette Conférence un aboutissement, mais au contraire un nouveau départ, pour la réalisation, chacune dans son domaine spécifique, des impulsions et inspirations reçues en commun à Santa Severa. Restent aussi présentes les grandes interpellations de la Conférence:

- Qu'en est-il du suivi de la Conférence de Rio? Au plan international, au plan national, au plan local?
- Que font nos Églises, que faisons-nous pour rencontrer les angoisses écologiques des femmes et des hommes aujourd'hui?
- La course aux nouvelles technologies de reproduction, a-t-elle vraiment pour objectif prioritaire le mieux-être de toutes les femmes et couples désirant des enfants?

Denise Peeters, Brussels, Belgium.

Association Européenne Des Femmes Pour La Recherche Théologique Rapport Sur La 5ième Conférence Bi-Annuelle à Louvain:

"Les Femmes Face Aux Traditions Réligieuses en Europe"

"L'Association européenne des femmes pour la recherche théologique" (AFERT) a réuni à l'Université de Louvain les 16-20 août, 1993 environ 140 femmes - membres en invitées - autour du thème: "Proclamons notre identité. Les femmes face aux traditions réligieuses en Europe." Il s'agissait de la 5'eme Conférence internationale de l'orgnaisation - conférence qui a lieu tous les deux ans dans différents pays européens. C'est le comité belge de l'AFERT qui a, cette fois-ci, précisé le thème et a choisi les intervenantes.

Pas D'identité Authentique Sans Libération des Images Reçues

L'idée clé qui est sortie des quatre jours d'échanges et de travaux, fut celle de la libération du sujet féminin. On a compris que l'établissement d'une authentique identité pour une femme ne se fait sans libération des images, des représentations supposées normatives dans la société où elle se trouve. Il fallait donc évoquer les principaux où cet objectif devient urgent; libération du système dualiste de las pensée phallocentrique occidental, libération du sujet féminin des représentations traditionelles, qui l'empêchent de s'ouvrir à de nouvelles possibilités d'existence, libération des systèmes oppressifs qui réduisent l'identité de la personne humaine à des catégories de race, sexe, couleur, nationalité....

Le critère théologique à l'oeuvre dans les différents lieux de travail de la conférence fut, bien entendu, celui qui assure la cohérence entre la praxis et l'idéal selon lequel la dignité de la personne humaine relève de sa création à l'image de Dieu. Cette intuition fondamentale fut présente comme un leit-motif dans les différentes conférences, ateliers et rencontres.

Grands exposés de la Conférence

Le rythme de la conférence fut ponctué chaque jour par de grands exposés destinés à approfondir le thème. Trois femmes européennes ont accepté la tâche difficile de répérer les changements à apporter dans la compréhension actuelle du sujet connaissant: Rosi Braidotti, philosophe italienne, actuellement professeur à l'Université de 'Utrecht, Annelies van Heijst, théologien hollandaise, et Ellen van Wolde, également hollandaise, professeur en exegèse du Premier Testament. Rosi Braidotti a adopté la métaphore du nomade pour illustrer son idée qu'il faut déplacer le discours sur la différence sexuelle. A ses yeux, l'image du voyageur évoque bien la nécessité pour chaque femme de se désinstaller, de traverser les multiples couches naturelles, historiques, philosophiques, etc. qui caractérisent la manière occidentale de définir les différences sexuelles. Ce "voyage" s'avère indispensable si, à la fin de son parcours, elle veut être à même de nommer clairement son identité propre. C'est là, tout un programme, que Rosi Braidotti appelle un "projet politique nomade" du fait qu'il s'agit d'une stratégie de libération du système dualiste en Occident dont lest enjeux sont nécessairement politiques.

Annelies van Heijst a intitulé son exposé: "Le 'Nous' dans le 'Moi': solidarité, le corps fragile, et Dieu". Selon la conférencière, le problème aujourd'hui n'est plus de définir nos relations interpersonnelles à partir de simples échanges extérieurs, contractuels, mais de les intérioriser. En cela, il s'agit de reconnaître que le "je" des autres constitue une dimension authentique du "moi" qui est le "nous". C'est un véritable projet qui s'engage à partir de cette reconnaissance, car la découverte d'une altérité en soi-même qui est, en fait, celle de l'autre, demande la création de nouveaux types de relations. Mais c'est un projet qui n'est pas sans risque pour nos égoismes traditionnels. en admettant que la différence en moi n'est pas indépendante de la différence de l'autre, je deviens vulnérable sur le plan du corps qui se trouve au centre de nouvelles solidarités.

Ellen van Wolde a abordé son thème sous le titre: "Mme Job et les filles des hommes: guide pour le sujet-lecteur". Son souci est de rendre compte du processus qui caracteri sée toute lecture d'un texte: un seul texte est ouvert à de nombreuses interprétations, sans qu'aucune soit considérée comme la "bonne". En même temps, il n'y a pas de de totale liberté en matière exegétique: le texte et le lecteur sont les produits culturels enracinés dans un réseau complexe de relations qui limitent mais ne déterminent pas l'interprétation.

Ce fait est à garder à l'esprit surtout en lisant les textes bibliques qui parlent du rapport homme-femme: "Les filles des hommes" (Gen.6,1-4) et la femme de Job (Jb. 2,9; Jb. 2,3) ne sont pas des figures enfermées dans une seule (et négative!) interprétation. La rencontre entre texte et lecteur est transformatrice non seulement pour le sujet humain vivant mais aussi pour les catégories et concepts qui font vivre le texte. Le rappel de ce principe libère non seulement le lecteur mais La Bible elle-même: impossible alors de prendre la lecture reçue, souvent misogyne, comme la seule et unique possible.

L'Apport D'autres Sensibilités et Cultures

La Conférence n'a pas voulu restreindre son réflexion aux seules dimensions du continent européen, mais a accueilli des "Voix différentes": Sanjukta Gupta Gombrich, indienne hindoue, Diana Hayes, théologienne des Etats-Unis et Fatima A.Ibrahim, soudanaise, ont élargi la réflexion de la Conférence pour inclure d'autres sensibilités et expériences culturelles. L'exposé de Sanjukta Gupta avait comme titre: "Sarasvati Vac: La parole sacrée et la déesse suprême cosmique". Au bout d'une complexe évolution, la figure de la déesse, Sarasvati Vac, se trouve associé à l'oeuvre du Créateur (Prajapati) comme Parole, ou principe cosmique, actif. Elle renvoie alors au pouvoir divin dans la femme qui est sa fécondité. Les repercussions de ce pouvoir dans la religion hindou sont ambivalentes, car il engendre, chez l'homme, une attitude mélangée de peur et de respect. Concrètement, cela se traduit par l'identification de la femme à la double fonction d'épouse et de mère - fonction qui, par sa nature, se prête le mieux à la surveillance économique et sociale de l'homme.

Diana Hayes, théologienne catholique de la faculté de théologie à Georgetown University à Washington, D.C., a tracé une rare itinéraire pour une femme noire américaine. On peut mesurer le degré de son succès à partir de l'une des thèses majeures de son exposé, à savoir la triple oppression de la femme noire: race, sexe, et infériorité culturelle par rapport aux femmes blanches. Cette dernière oppression affecte ses relations mêmes avec les féministes qui ont aliené leures soeurs noires par le fait qu'elles n'ont pas su intégrer les aspirations de ces dernières dans leur properes programmes de libération. C'est dans cette infériorisation de la femme noire qu'il faut situer la création du "Womanist" mouvement chez les noires, dont une partie de l'originalité réside dans sa prise au sérieux de la catégorie propre de l'oppression qui est celle de la "victime". Finalement, la soudanaise, Fatima A. Ibrahim, a donné des éclairages importantes sur la femme en Islam. En tant que présidente de "l'Union des femmes soudanaises", et victime elle-même des diverses formes d'oppression, elle fut particulièrement bien placée pour rendre compte de la lutte des femmes islamiques. Pour Fatima Ibrahim, leur libération passe la fausseté de certaines idées reçues au nom desquelles les femmes sont opprimées. Selon elle, l'Islam est, non pas une théocratie, mais une démocratie qui est contre la polygamie et pour la paix.

Une Déclaration de l'AFERT

Suite à une réflexion sur l'Ex-Jougoslavie et le "péché structurel" à la racine des terribles événements qui frappent les peuples impliqués, l'AFERT a fait une déclaration publique exprimant sa solidarité avec toutes les victimes de cette querre. Tout spécialement, la déclaration a évoqué les atrocités perpétrées sur les femmes et les enfants, car le "violence et la mutilation sont devenus des méthodes spécifiques de domination militaire dans ce conflit".

D'autres informations Impossible, bien sûr, de rendre compte de toute la richesses des différents ateliers et des rencontres personnelles pendant la Conférence. Cet apport reste le secret de chaque participante, même si les nombreux échos et commentaires ne laissent aucun doute, pour le Comité belge d'organisation, que ses différentes activités furent loin d'être les moins significatives.

Deux visiteurs à la Conférence doivent être signalés: Mgr. Vangheluwe, évèque de Bruges et l'Abbé J.Delobel, doyen de la Faculté de théologie de l'Université catholique de Louvain. Ce dernier a fait connaître aux participantes la nomination d'Annelies van Heijst à une chaire de "Womens' Studies" en théologie dans cette même université. Finalement l'AFERT a élu sa nouvelle présidente, Ursula King, professeur à l'Université de Bristol (l'Angleterre). On a annoncé également la prochaine conférence de l'Association qui se tiendra en 1995 en Scandinavie (La Suéde), sur la théologie dans le contexte Nord/Sud. (Textes de Conférence, à l'AFERT, c/o Denise Peeters, Ave Jules César, 16 -bte 9, 1150 Bruxelles).

Donna Singles, Lyons, France.

EUROPEAN SOCIETY OF WOMEN IN THEOLOGICAL RESEARCH

EUROPÄISCHE GESELLSCHAFT FÜR THEOLOGISCHE FORSCHUNG VON FRAUEN

L'ASSOCIATION EUROPÉENNE DES FEMMES POUR LA RECHERCHE THÉOLOGIQUE

President - Präsidentin - Président:
Professor Ursula King, University of Bristol, Great Britain

Vice-President - Vizepräsidentin - Vice-Président:
Professor Lone Fatum, University of Copenhagen, Denmark

Secretary - Sekretärin - Secrétaire:
Monika Jakobs, Saarbrücken, Germany

Vice-Secretary:
Magda Misset -van de Weg, The Netherlands

Treasurer - Schatzmeisterin - Trésorière:
Irene Löffler-Mayer, Friedberg, Germany

Vice-Treasurer:
Maaike de Haardt, Tilburg, The Netherlands

Revisor - Revisorin - Reviseur:
Regula Ströbel, Fribourg, Switzerland

Contact for Bulletin of the ESWTR:
Magda Misset van de Weg, The Netherlands"